DAUNTLESS

DAUNTLESS

PAUL HILLIARD
IN WWII AND A
TRANSFORMED AMERICA

ROB CITINO
WITH KEN STICKNEY AND LORI OCHSNER

LOUISIANA LEGACIES SERIES

an imprint of the
UNIVERSITY OF LOUISIANA AT LAFAYETTE PRESS

Louisiana Legacies Series is an imprint of the
University of Louisiana at Lafayette Press

ISBN 13 (paper): 978-1-959569-02-2

http://ulpress.org
University of Louisiana at Lafayette Press
P.O. Box 43558
Lafayette, LA 70504-3558

Printed in the United States

Library of Congress Cataloging-in-Publication Data

Names: Citino, Robert Michael, 1958- author. | Stickney, Ken, author. |
    Ochsner, Lori, author.
Title: Dauntless : Paul Hilliard in WWII and a transformed America / Rob
    Citino, with Ken Stickney and Lori Ochsner.
Description: Lafayette, LA : University of Louisiana at Lafayette Press,
    2023. | Includes bibliographical references.
Identifiers: LCCN 2023013749 | ISBN 9781959569022 (paperback)
Subjects: LCSH: Hilliard, Paul (Clayton Paul) | World War,
    1939-1945--Veterans--United States--Biography. | Energy industry
    executives--United States--Biography. | Lobbyists--United
    States--Biography. | Philanthropists--United States--Biography. |
    Petroleum industry and trade--Louisiana--History. | United
    States--History--20th century.
Classification: LCC E748.H574 C58 2023 | DDC 973.9092
    [B]--dc23/eng/20230414
LC record available at https://lccn.loc.gov/2023013749

*For
Madlyn
and
Kathryn*

TABLE OF CONTENTS

WRITING PAUL HILLIARD

Anyone who considers writing a biography had better be ready to justify it. After all, there is a towering mountain of such books sitting around, and any would-be biographer needs to explain why they're adding another rock to the pile.

In general, a worthwhile biography must check three boxes. First, and fundamentally, the life in question must be interesting enough for a reader to open the book, start reading, and feel the urge to continue. That's probably the easiest hurdle, however, given the endless variety of human personality and experience. Every human life has the potential to be interesting, even in its most mundane or quotidian details, and you don't have to conquer the world to be worth a biography. As Plutarch reminds us in his *Life of Alexander*, "a chance remark or joke may reveal far more of a man's character than the mere feat of winning battles in which thousands fall, or of marshaling great armies, or laying siege to cities."[1] Everybody has a story.

Second, the book needs to go beyond a mere shopping list of events, the discrete facts and moments of an individual life. It has to be more than a "he did this, then he did that" chronicle: it must also speak to history, conveying some sense of the context and historical times in which the subject lived, and the relationship of the person to the era. Call it the "life and times" approach to biography.

Finally, and this is probably the toughest standard of all, a good biography must aspire to speak to our own times as well as to the past. The reader should come away from the book with a greater insight, not only into the subject's life and times, but also into their own current condition and the state of today's world. We might refer to this as the "relevancy test."

Now, getting a perfect grade in one of those three areas is a tall order under any circumstances, and requiring a biography to check all three boxes might well disqualify a large percentage of the currently published works. Fortunately, as we consider the life of our subject, Clayton Paul Hilliard, we find a nearly ideal candidate for a full-dress biography. Indeed, if there were such a thing, he might have been recommended by Biography Central Casting.

Just consider our list. An "interesting life"? Mr. Hilliard has lived one, *con brio*. He has been many things in the course of his ninety-eight years: a Wisconsin farm boy, a Marine aviator in World War II, a successful entrepreneur and oilman, a political lobbyist for his industry, a philanthropist and a generous patron of culture and the arts. And, at a time of his life when most men are well and fully retired, he's become more active than ever in the museum world. Based on longevity alone, he's seen it all, from Pearl Harbor to the pandemic, with all stops in between. He's also thought long and hard about everything he's seen, done, and been through, and he has been blessed with the gift of gab and the wit to talk about them in a consistently interesting way. Speaking with Paul is like taking a long, fascinating global journey through the past century with an incomparably witty tour guide You never know what you'll learn or what new insight you will glean.

So far, so good, but what of the book's relationship to the history of its times? Here, too, we hit pay dirt. While Paul was born poor, a farm kid on a dead-end track in Wisconsin, he came of age as a young man in the greatest military conflict of all time, the global struggle against the Axis known as World War II. He volunteered for the US Marine Corps before he was old enough to do so (and had to have his mother sign a letter of permission), trained as a radioman and gunner, and flew dozens of missions in the South Pacific in the famed Douglas SBD "Dauntless" dive-bomber.

Let's ponder that last one for a moment. You needed a certain mental toughness to be part of the two-man Dauntless crew. Imagine hurtling down from an altitude of 12,000 feet or so in a nearly vertical dive, pulling up at about 1,500 feet, practically the last second before splattering yourself into the ground or water. You deliver a bomb straight into the enemy's lap, as it were, shaking off the "Gs" you just pulled as you turn and scoot away. The thought is enough to get the heart racing and the blood pumping. Now imagine doing all those things while facing *backward*. The pilot flew the plane, rode hard into the dive, and delivered the bomb. Paul manned the radio and worked the machine gun in case they got tailed by Japanese aircraft. Oh, and one more small detail: if you're firing those twin .30-caliber machine guns, be sure not to shoot off your own tail. If you can wrap your head around that experience, then you can understand Paul's service in the Pacific. It's a truism that all young people think they're going to live forever, but surely there had to have been moments of doubt in Paul's mind from time to time. Flying into action in a Dauntless was enough to shock even the most happy-go-lucky teenage American boy into manhood.[2]

Going beyond the hair-raising nature of the duty, World War II was also the key catalyst, an agent of change, in Paul's life. The war changed America forever, unleashing its enormous potential as an industrial and military giant. Our often-fractious country pulled together for a common purpose. America's free and open society, with its dynamic and entrepreneurial character, proved vastly more efficient at prosecuting modern, machine age war than our fascist enemies (or even our communist ally, the Soviet Union).[3] We emerged from World War II as the world's greatest superpower. The war transformed America so profoundly that it represents something like a second founding of the Republic.

Just as it changed America forever, the war also changed Paul. It made him aware of the vastness of the country, of its nearly limitless potential, of the ties that bound the United States to the rest of the world, whether Americans wanted them to or not. He became aware—and this idea possesses him to this day—of the personal and political benefits of living in a free society. Just as the war liberated captive nations from German and Japanese occupation, it liberated him as well, freeing him from the narrow contours of his boyhood and aiming him toward something broader and greater—limitless, really. For both Paul and for the country, new horizons beckoned in the postwar world.

Paul's later career, likewise, is inconceivable without World War II. Like millions of veterans, he went to college on the GI Bill, a nearly impossible prospect for someone of his social class. He received a law degree, but the practice of law was not to hold him. Like so many millions of

Americans, he became more geographically mobile, trading in freezing
Wisconsin winters for sweltering Louisiana summers.

Now ensconced in the South, he was one of many who entered
the burgeoning field of energy exploration and production. The new
American superpower had a nearly unquenchable thirst for oil, and
while the big producers tend to dominate our imaginations, the smaller,
independent producer played, and continues to play, a key role in slak-
ing that thirst. Paul's career—first as a small cog in the gigantic oil firm
of H. L. Hunt, then as an entrepreneur, independent producer, and
founder of Badger Oil, and finally as industry spokesman and lobbyist—put him at the center of the nation's political economy in the postwar era. From his spot in the Louisiana oil patch, he came to appreciate
the complexities of free market capitalism, he learned what government
can and cannot do, and he came to perceive the pitfalls of even the most
well-meaning legislation when it tries to micromanage an industry that
has to compete on the global market. These were all the same problems
facing the country at large after World War II, and indeed, the country
still confronts them today.

Finally, let us address the question of present-day relevance. What
does Paul Hilliard's life have to tell us about our own times? Here, we
need to focus on Paul's later years, after he handed over the day-to-day
operations of Badger Oil to two of his most capable lieutenants, Dave
Etienne and Art Price. Like so many veterans of the World War II generation, Paul decided to give back, and to do so in abundance. He founded
the Badger Excellence in Education Foundation to support educational
initiatives and schools in his adopted state of Louisiana. He donated millions of dollars to finance an art museum at the University of Louisiana at
Lafayette (today the Hilliard Art Museum), and then many millions more
to help support one of America's most influential institutions of learning
and public memory, the National WWII Museum in New Orleans. He
eventually wound up in a leadership role in the latter, serving as chairman
of the museum's Board of Trustees from 2018 to 2020.

That last connection is critical, especially since it links the past and
present of Paul's life into a cohesive whole. Once again, as with so many
veterans in his generational cohort, Paul didn't talk a lot about World War
II when he returned home. Virtually every able-bodied male had taken

part in the war in some capacity, and so bragging about one's exploits simply wasn't done. Moreover, in those years, Paul was too busy studying and improving himself, founding a business, and supporting a family to think much about his wartime service. Only decades later, in the reflective nature of his later years, did he realize how important the war had been: to him, to the country, to the entire world. "Once I began to realize that I had been privileged to play a minor role in an enormous event," he says many years later, "I became, and still am, an assiduous student of World War II." The war showed the country in an almost ideal light, he believes: strong leadership at the top, a committed and united citizenry, and, everywhere, a willingness to sacrifice personal interests for the greater and communal good.

In Paul's view, that story is not being passed on to present-day Americans, at least not with the energy and profundity it deserves. Youth, he thinks, is the key. Young Americans grow up today immersed in a very different narrative about their country than the one that nurtured Paul, the one that led him to the cockpit of that Dauntless dive-bomber so long ago. Today's national narrative highlights disunity and strife, emphasizes past wrongs that have gone uncorrected for too long, and shows American power usually serving greedy or nefarious purposes. Paul recognizes the intricacies of history and the importance of historical debate, and he is always up for a good argument with friends and foes alike. Still, he makes no bones of the fact that, in his view, the "bad America" thesis is one-sided and tendentious at best, and a deliberate falsification of history at worst.

In the end, the heart of Paul Hilliard's legacy may well lie in the work he has done with the National WWII Museum. As one of the relatively small number of wartime veterans still around, he has decided to donate his resources and his time to the museum so generously because it preserves and presents America's wartime saga, and it does so in a vivid, immersive, and interactive way—methods that are designed precisely to appeal to younger visitors. He remembers his own youth, including his service in the South Pacific. "We were mostly teenagers," he says, "and much of our leisure was spent thinking about food, talking about food, or complaining about food."

Young people hunger for more than food, however. They desire belonging, a purpose, some signpost to their future. "World War II," Hilliard tells them, "is the story of America at its best." Even in our fractured day, when America seems to agree on so little, he believes that this is an idea that we can all share, and one that can provide younger Americans in particular with a measure of hope for the future of the country, and for their own.[4] And the American experiment is about nothing so much as it is about hope. Indeed, America is the "land of hope," as historian Wilfred M. McClay tells us in his 2019 book of that title:

> Nothing about America better defines its distinctive character than the ubiquity of hope, a sense that the way things are initially given to us cannot be the final word about them, that we can never settle for that. Even those who are bitterly critical of America, and find it hopes to be delusions, cannot deny the enduring energy of those hopes and are not immune to their pull.[5]

These are words that Paul Hilliard has lived by and continues to live by. Hope—in the future, in his country, in his fellow Americans—has shaped the biography, not only of a successful man, but of a good one.

A full and fascinating life that is still going strong, a story that not only links up directly with the most dramatic historical action of the twentieth century, but also offers food for thought to all of us as we forge ahead at top speed into the uncertain twenty-first, and, above all, a distinctly American life: meet Paul Hilliard.

Welcome to *Dauntless*.

PART I
THE FARM

CHILDHOOD AND EARLY LIFE

"A Real Barn Burner"

We live in the age of so-called "chaos theory," which warns us that even the tiniest events can have serious repercussions. A butterfly can flutter its wings in Beijing and eventually a hurricane may hit New York. Without indulging in too much nonlinear math or fine philosophical discourse, let us concede the point. Little things can be critical to the subsequent course of history. What might seem like a minor event at the time can change a life and can have ripple effects the world over.

Armed with those thoughts, let us go back in time, to July 1936. We are on a poor farm in rural northern Wisconsin, in the obscure region known as Spring Creek, in Buffalo County. The locals actually call the place "Sand Burr Coulee," but that's only because the omnipresent sand burrs, weeds with sharp, painful spines, sometimes seem to be the principal crop. Whatever we call it, the weather is scorching, and it hasn't rained in ages—indeed, we are in the middle of a great drought, a part of a wider national event known then and now as "the Dust Bowl"—and a curious four-year old boy is playing with matches.[1]

To this day no one knows how little Wally Hilliard got hold of them. His older brother, Clayton Paul Hilliard, known universally as "Paul," is now in his late nineties and still recalls how fascinated his little brother was by the box of wooden matches the family kept in their farmhouse. It wasn't much of a treasure: a box of some one hundred long, thin matchsticks, but it held a strong allure to the young boy. The Hilliards were

1

forever pulling the box away from Wally's grip, getting there in the nick of time, we might say. But on that hot July day, they came too late. As Paul walked toward the family barn, he saw Wally fiddling with something—a match. Paul was only eleven, but he decided to take charge. Big brothers are like that. As he was walking toward the barn, however, the match in Wally's hand suddenly ignited. Frightened by the sudden flame, Wally did the sensible thing: he dropped it.

And that was that. The blaze caught dry hay at Wally's bare feet and from there spread quickly to the rest of the stacks in the barn. Years later, Paul still remembers the suddenness of the event: "It was like lightning!" he recalls. "The fire spread in seconds": "It hit that dry hay on the ground. It took just a couple of seconds to take the fire to the haymow. Flames shot up some fifteen to twenty feet. My brother Bill was up in the haymow and he jumped. In a flash, that thing was a ball of flames."[2]

Several states, including Wisconsin, had been battling a severe drought for years, threatening crops and livelihoods. It was so dry that Paul and his brothers joked that in Sand Burr Coulee, "the fire hydrants chased the dogs."

Facing an emergency, the Hilliards sprang into action as best they could. Oldest brother Bill, then thirteen, had been working in the barn. He managed to jump to safety. All three boys ran to the house to alert Mom and Dad. Paul remembers his mother rushing to call their small-town fire department. Armed with a single water pump, the family needed help, badly. The fire truck was a good ten miles away, however, and even before it arrived, it was clear that the barn was a total loss.

Losing a home is never a good thing, but it's worse when you're poor. The five Hilliards were barely scraping out a living as it was, and as the eighteen tons of hay stored in the barn went up in flames, they had lost the feed to keep the livestock alive over another bitter winter in Wisconsin. As William and Gladys stared at the roaring blaze, watching the local fire department struggle to put it out, they knew they were staring at a tragedy. They had always worked hard: Father William suffered from health problems—a condition known as bronchiectasis, easily treatable with antibiotics today—and lacked the necessary strength for farming. He toiled as a watch repairman. Mother Gladys, "Gladiola," they called her, was the farmer, and it was a life she loved. Paul would later remember that she had names for just about every chicken, turkey, or cow on the place. "She probably named the carrots," he adds, and she talked to her beloved plants in the garden to get them to grow. The one thing she couldn't grow was money, always in short supply for farm families during the era, the height of the Great Depression.

Still, looking back, Paul doesn't recall poverty. The farm had no electricity and no indoor plumbing, but he never missed a meal. The family grew most of their food. The farm wasn't large, just eighty acres, not all of which was arable, but the Hilliards had a garden, fruit trees, chickens, and larger stock. It wasn't a "picture postcard place," he says, "but it fed us." Paul's own memory of life on the farm revolved around a single word: chores. There wasn't a lot of play time and hardly any money. But he and his brothers didn't realize how short money was. Like a lot of American kids in that era, they were poor without realizing it.

As the family watched their barn burn, eleven-year-old Paul must have been conflicted. A smart and imaginative boy, he used to lie under his bed covers for many a night, listening for the haunting whistle of a passing train. While he knew that the flames represented trouble to the family, they were also intoxicating to him. They signaled adventure—the first of his young life. They signaled, perhaps, liberation. The Hilliards could no longer stay on their failing family farm. They would have to move. In Paul's young life, new horizons beckoned.

Later in life, Paul had learned to put this entire dramatic episode into some perspective. Typically, he employed wit in describing it. Perhaps the fire had taught him to view everything in life through the lens of humor—a solid Midwestern character trait that helps you shake off misfortune and keep moving ahead. He noted the irony: the family had largely weathered the drought, which was in its last year in Wisconsin, only to be knocked down by fire. "What a blessing that was," he says. "It took the barn. If I knew we could escape that miserable farm, I would have handed Wally the matches a couple years earlier." Paul will nickname little brother Wally the "Emancipating Pyromaniac," whose inexplicable love of matches on that dusty July day sent the Hilliard family, and Paul along with it, off on another trajectory altogether.

Life on the Farm: "You Could Work or Starve"

Paul's later quip hid the bitter truth, of course. Although the loss of the barn was partially covered by a $500 insurance payment from the Fountain City Mutual Insurance Company, Paul was a smart young boy and could recognize a disaster when he saw one. He saw that the world he knew was gone forever. It hadn't been a paradise, but it had the comforting advantage of familiarity and gave Paul a sense of place. He also must have sensed that his poor family had just gotten poorer and that a new uncertainty loomed.

Then again, uncertainty has long been the lot of the farm family. Weather and nature are the undisputed kings on the farm, and they are not always benevolent rulers. Suffering comes in many forms. You can have too much rain or not enough, scorching temperatures or unexpected freezes, floods, or drought. Wildlife can eat your stock or trample your field, and the horde of insects can sometimes reach biblical proportions. Facing other impersonal forces like grain prices, laws, tariffs, and international competition, the farmer can often feel like the commandant of a beleaguered fortress, caught between the scissors of rising production costs and lower revenue. While the old folk song lionizes the farmer as "the man who feeds us all," farming is, by and large, not the kind of lucrative living that makes you a rich man.[3] In that sense the Hilliards were entirely typical of their time and place. The farm had challenged them all from day one, both mentally and physically.

But if life on the farm is tough, it also pays handsome dividends in terms of human character. Farm life toughens you, forces you to meet daily deadlines. It teaches you that there are no excuses, only duties. You've got jobs to do, and saying, "I meant to . . ." doesn't cut much ice, especially with the livestock. As Paul tells it, echoing the words of many farmers before and since, these were formative years, and they left him with a sense of values that has stood him in good stead in his later life. What does farm life do to a person?

You become flexible. You're captive to the animals. The cows, turkeys, and chickens have to be fed. You become conscious of the routine. It's snowing like hell? You still have to go out there. You become resourceful. You're ten miles from town, you can't just run to the hardware store. You can't rely on excuses. You can have the flu or a fever, but the cows have to be fed.

It was the farm, in other words, that forged much of young Paul's character. The remoteness and isolation of the farm led to self-reliance and resourcefulness, probably more than he realized at the time.

Was Paul "typical"? Yes and no. Living on a farm was much more common in the America of the 1930s than it is today. Just about 32 million Americans lived on farms, about a quarter of the national population of 128 million. While that figure may not impress the casual reader, it's important to keep in mind the situation today (in the 2020s). The farm population has been dwindling steady for decades, and today it might just crack the 1 percent mark, with a few million farmers out of a total population of 332 million. So, in that sense, Paul was both out of place—a farm boy growing up in a country that was already heavily urbanized—and also very much a product of his times, along with the other 30 million Americans who still called the farm their home. They were a hardy band, with certain traits in common: toughness, hardheadedness, and self-reliance.

Paul still remembers those days, as well as his life in the country. "We could make a living, we had food on the table," he would say more than eight and a half decades after leaving farm life for good. He stills carries memories of the weedy fields and the farm, where "we just grew a few watermelons and sand burrs." Even as a child he learned to do his job, the only thing that mattered. The need for water was never-ending, Paul recalls. "You didn't need money at the farm. You needed moisture." But water didn't come easy: you had to pump it by hand. His father even added six feet of pipe to the pump handle for greater leverage in pumping water. That single well served the Hilliards in a multitude of ways: caring for the farm animals, watering the garden, washing their clothes, drinking, cooking, as well as the occasional bath.

As early as 1930, when Paul was five, he remembers handling his share of the chores. He used his red toy wagon to haul firewood to the house and was responsible for feeding the chickens, turkeys, and hogs. "I didn't much like farming," he remembers, "I was a book lover, but we didn't have an option." The logic of his life was simple, perhaps even brutal. In the state of nature that was Sand Burr Coulee, "you could work or starve." A few years later, things got even tougher. He and brother Bill learned the hard art of using the crosscut saw, working together in rhythm, to cut firewood in late spring and early summer. Any farmer will tell you that cutting wood is one of the tougher jobs on the farm. Paul and his older brother then had to stack the logs carefully, storing them outside, uncovered in the sun. Age six brought a bit of a respite to the boy's hard labor, as he started school. In a story that sounds increasingly alien to those of us living in the twenty-first century, where the line of expensive cars dropping Junior off at school can extend for miles in front of the building, he and his brother had to trudge a couple of miles on foot, or even on skis when the thick snow lay on the ground in winter.

The backdrop for all this was the Great Depression, the collapse of first the American, and then the global, economy. Unemployment in the United States peaked at the frightening figure of 25.6 percent in May 1933. Misery was rife in the land, and extremist voices were at their loudest. The Left and Right alike—both communist and fascist sympathizers—were united in their belief that American democracy was obsolete. A product of the horse and buggy age, it had clearly failed the basic test of putting food on the table for the vast majority of Americans. The 1930s was the age of Father Charles Coughlin, the Catholic priest from Detroit, who was one of the first to realize the power of modern mass media.[4] His fiery radio sermons reached an unprecedented audience, sometimes estimated at 30 million listeners. The good Father praised German dictator Adolf Hitler and claimed that American Jews were behind an international conspiracy to spread communism and destroy the country. The "invisible empire" of the Ku Klux Klan wasn't as widespread as it had been in the 1920s, but it still spread its gospel of hatred, and it still held the balance of political power in many midwestern states.

On the other extreme of the political spectrum, there were equally vociferous voices who were just as fond of Joseph Stalin and who wanted to recreate an American version of the Bolshevik experiment on these shores. In Depression America, the redistribution of wealth and property appealed to many people who were in dire straits. Media coverage of what was happening inside the Soviet Union also played a role. It was a time, after all, when you could actually read Walter Duranty in the

New York Times whitewashing terror and mass starvation in the Soviet worker's utopia with the pithy phrase, "you can't make an omelet without breaking eggs."[5]

For a few anxious years, it seemed as if US democracy was hanging in the balance. Fortunately for the future of the country and the world, the American people elected Franklin Roosevelt as their president in 1932, precisely because of the general state of unease in the land.[6] Under his wise leadership, the political center managed to hold. "The only thing we have to fear," he told the American people in his first inaugural address, "is fear itself."[7] That was the enemy, the "nameless, unreasoning, unjustified terror," the one thing that could paralyze the American people and prevent them from rebuilding their lives. Americans are a naturally hopeful people. They believed him and began to look more confidently toward the future. The economy was still in a mess, but he promised Americans a "New Deal" that would serve all the people, not just a select few with power, wealth, or influence. A plethora of new government agencies, along with a bewildering array of new acronyms like WPA, CCC, TVA, and FERA, became the new face of the federal bureaucracy in Washington, promising to bring the country out of the Depression that had gripped it since 1929.

Global affairs mirrored the tensions at home. Americans have gotten used to sharing the world with some fairly nasty dictators over the years, but the 1930s were the darkest era of all. Hitler in Germany, Mussolini in Italy, the militarists in Japan: all three were on the warpath, building gigantic military forces and threatening their neighbors with war and conquest. They concocted bogus racial theories to prove their own superiority, trained their young children to handle weapons, and chanted military slogans by the hour. War was in the air, but no one knew where it might erupt, and a clear majority of Americans wanted to stay out of it no matter where it happened. Isolationism was still the order of the day on the home front, and while we like to pillory the isolationists today for being short-sighted—or perhaps altogether blind—to these grievous threats, their desire to stay out of war is hardly an illogical sentiment.[8] After all, the country had just fought a bloody overseas war, from 1917 to 1918, and had precious little to show for it except a ruined economy and revenge-minded enemies.

But, of course, all this talk of high politics and economy was for adults, not children. Paul and his brothers were too young to be affected by the ideological currents of extremism or by the threat of foreign war. The Hilliard boys weren't living in fear. Looking back, Paul says today that he does not recall worrying about anything as a child, except what was happening on the farm. He remained happily unaware of the economic downturn in the 1930s; he doesn't remember those days as being either "great" or a "depression" at all, and, like most American children, he didn't lose a lot of sleep over Hitler or Hirohito. Being poor, working hard, living the no-frills life: that was just the way things were up in rural Wisconsin.

Paul always took solace in the fact he and his older brother Bill—Wally was too young to notice one way or the other—didn't know the depth of their own poverty. They felt pretty much on par with their classmates, all of whom were farmers' children in Maxville Township and had a standard of living similar to the Hilliards'. It was in many respects a life untouched by modernity, or at least those technological advantages we equate with modernity. The Hilliards had no vehicle until they bought an old Chevrolet in 1934. The house had no running water, no indoor plumbing, and no electricity, the farm itself featured only a few machines and horse-drawn implements. Paul remembers a slight change in 1934, when his parents purchased a small gas engine for the water pump and a Maytag gas-powered washing machine. Gladys would kick-start the motor on the latter, and the agitator would wash the clothes while she could walk away. As subsequent generations of disappointed homemakers would later discover, however, the main effect of the new machines was to free her up to do more work.

For the whole Hilliard family, the workday began before dawn. The boys' first chores were lit by the glow of kerosene lamps and lanterns. "I had my first relationship with fossil fuels with kerosene lamps with metal reflectors," the future oilman says. "We had them in the kitchen, hung on the wall. The reflector amplified the light. We went to the barn with kerosene lanterns, slinging them around." For the most part, there was a division of labor. Brother Bill was the "outside guy" at the farm, helping out with the farm-specific chores. Paul was the "inside guy," washing dishes, cleaning, and often cooking. He was no gourmet chef. "We ate a lot of pancakes," he recalls.

But there were no specialists on the farm; everyone pitched in to do everything. Paul remembers a rhythm to the work that aided their sense of teamwork and responsibility. In the winter they handled the snow, and in the summer, the dust. "Some of the things we did as kids they'd put our parents in jail for today," Paul says today. He and Bill handled "all sorts of dangerous stuff" while carrying out their farm chores—yet survived. "I shudder at it. But we needed labor on the farm." The chores were endless: "Feeding the livestock, cleaning the barn, cutting wood, planting, harvesting, canning, curing, preserving, milking: it never ended." Paul remembers the gift he got on his tenth birthday. It wasn't a toy or bicycle or a scooter. His parents gave him a "practical gift": a Keen Kutter double bit ax, a sturdy tool that can fetch a handsome price on today's secondary market. On the farm, everything—even your birthday—was about work.

Certain events, even seemingly minor ones, can sum up the farm experience for young boys in the 1930s, how everything seemed to be hanging by a thread. There was that day in 1934, for example, when Bill told Paul he wanted to show him something. Paul was nine and his big brother was eleven. It was something, all right: a shotgun, an 1897 Winchester Model 97 that belonged to their grandfather Clate Kees. Paul didn't remember how Bill got it—the eternal question we ask after a firearm accident—but Paul does recall that they were outside the house, standing barefoot, with the barrel of the gun pointed down between their feet. Bill was holding the gun with the hammer back, when suddenly it went off. The shell blasted a black hole in the dirt, missing their toes by inches. Paul doesn't remember any grown-up running to them wondering what that loud noise was all about.

That's not surprising. Folks are busy on a farm, and hearing the occasional blast of a gun isn't all that rare out in the country. But he does remember the gravity of their close call. Even years later, he shudders at a day that could have ended so tragically. "It could have blown off my foot or Bill's. And life would have been changed in an instant," he later remarked with some understatement. "We never told anyone of our folly," he added. Several decades later, Paul's Aunt Aggie, sister of Gladys, presented the shotgun to Paul as a gift. He mounted the century-old weapon proudly on a polished cypress plank. Even today, it hangs over his fireplace mantle in his North Carolina home.

If a shotgun blast was an anomaly, battling with the weather was the everyday reality. Looking back, Paul can recall brutal winter storms with snow, sleet, or freezing rain ripping through the area and shaking the childhood farmhouse to its very foundation. "Our home was not weather-proof," he says. In many ways even worse than the blizzards, because they were so unexpected, were the summer dust storms. The wind whipped sand and grime into the home through cracks in the walls, and more than once the family had to scramble to close all the windows, even during the sizzling heat of the summer. As the dust storm passed, they would all have to grab brooms and start sweeping. The sand billowed up in clouds and settled in their nostrils, eyes, and hair. He also recalled Grandma Kees having to keep the thick plastic wrap on her new store-bought lampshades to keep them clean. Paul grew up thinking everyone did that. Like a lot of children, he viewed the universe from his own small perch in it. He accepted his own life as just the way things were, even the unpleasant things.

What left the greatest impression on him as a boy was the most depressing sight a farmer can see: parched and wilting plants. It's common farm wisdom that corn "should be as high as your eye by the Fourth of July," and given the use of modern fertilizers in our own day, it can often be a great deal taller than that. There's another brutal principle, however, that governs life on the farm: "No water, no crops." The drought of the 1930s had a devastating impact on the growing cycle. With rain in short supply, crop yields plummeted. In some regions of the Great Plains, corn production dropped more than 75 percent. Diminished crop yields, in turn, meant underfed or even starving livestock. For families already skating on the bare edge of subsistence, the results were potentially disastrous.

Moreover, all of this was happening in the midst of the Great Depression, which had crashed not only the New York Stock Exchange but also the price of grain. Thousands of farmers had gone bankrupt under such conditions, and there are tales—too many to be dismissed easily—of families burning corn in their stoves rather than coal, since corn was cheaper. Sometimes, old-timers remembered, the countryside smelled just like popcorn.[9] Many farmers even did the previously unthinkable: slaughtering their own livestock in the hopes that scarcity would raise prices. One observer, New York journalist Paul de Kruif, visited the region in 1934 and painted a dire portrait in words: "I'm sitting here watching the pleasant brown waters of the Wisconsin River this mock June—with horses dying by the hundred for lack of pasture, with farmers' wives lying awake nights listening to the bawling of starving cattle, with many farmers' children pinch-faced for lack of bread."[10] Things were especially bad in central Wisconsin, the area known as "the Sands," where the fine grain of the soil was a poor agricultural medium even in good times.

Dry spells, droughts, and failed crops had been the lot of the farmer from time out of mind, of course. What was different this time was the political context. The collapse of the economy had led to the election of a new reformist president, and FDR's New Deal was now the law of the land. An increasingly activist federal government was determined to step in and help solve the problem. By the 1930s, agronomy, the science of crop production and soil management, had become a well-established scientific field. To agronomists and other agricultural experts working for the government, the Dust Bowl wasn't completely weather-related. Rather, the drought had had such a devastating impact because of improper and unsustainable farming practices that had brought the relatively water-poor region to the brink. The "Report of the Great Plains Drought Area Committee" (August 1936) put it succinctly: "The agricultural economy of the Great Plains will become increasingly unstable and unsafe, in view of the impossibility of permanent increase in the amount of rainfall, unless over-cropping and overgrazing and improper farm methods are prevented. The future of the region must depend on the degree to which farming practices conform to natural conditions."[11]

It was a message with a certain logic. In the 1920s, low crop prices and the high cost of machinery had led farmers to place more submarginal lands into production, and the need to get more land into production meant abandoning many soil conservation practices. Marginal land, soil erosion: these factors were as important to the Dust Bowl as the drought itself. Wisconsin was already feeling the pinch even before the weather turned bad. As agriculture had spread across the state, old-growth forests had been cut over and young sand soils had been depleted of nutrients and moisture. But of course, farmers needed new lands to cut, plant, and graze precisely to keep their heads above water, given the meager prices their produce was fetching in the Depression era.

At any rate, the federal government recognized the environmental damage to Wisconsin's rural counties, as well as the threat that the drought imposed to the state's livestock. The initial government response was to offer farmers loans, money that could be worked off to pay the debt, but with such depressed conditions in the region, loans weren't the answer. Contrary to the mythology of a rapid recovery—tales nurtured and sustained by New Deal supporters and historians alike—relief was slow and sporadic. Many farmers in Wisconsin took government loans, certainly, but they remained on their substandard land for the simple reason that they had nowhere else to go, and to paraphrase another old saying, "there's no submarginal land, just submarginal farmers."[12] The government identified these diehards as "isolated settlers" whose ancestors had been there since the frontier days, "the hapless and the helpless," who needed more drastic emergency measures to survive.

Histories of the Dust Bowl are filled with impressive data points about the government relief effort, in dollar amounts, in projects, and in something else that Washington always seems to have in abundance: advice. New zoning ordinances for rural districts, resettling isolated or remote settlers, dams to conserve water, the transformation of some submarginal lands into wildlife refuges, planting thousands of miles of shelterbelts and windbreaks: the New Deal was on the march in America's farm belt.[13]

But not in Paul's world. Paul says he cannot recall government aid coming to Buffalo County during the 1930s. County officials rejected federal aid programs in order to keep local governments from having to pay the required matching funds. Both Buffalo and Pepin counties were adjacent to others judged to be either primary or secondary drought counties. Local farmers, including the Hilliards, might have been able to use the aid made available elsewhere in Wisconsin for emergency feed, for seeds, or for a program in which the government would purchase lean cattle for slaughter. But local culture cut against accepting handouts from anyone, including Uncle Sam. "It was not an entitlement society," Paul recalls. "Government aid didn't show up until the mid-1930s; by 1937, even FDR was saying we were going too far with welfare." Paul's views on the topic haven't wavered much over the decades. "Give people free stuff, the demand gets insatiable."

Paul remembers a single, heartbreaking incident that captured the quiet desperation in which people lived during that decade. He saw his mother, Gladys, who was so skilled at handling (and juggling) the family's minuscule budget, weeping in the kitchen. An envelope from a relative with two or three dollars in it had been accidentally tossed into the wood burning stove and was gone. While Paul still maintains that "being poor is a relative thing," and that "we didn't know anyone with money, so the absence of money was not deprivation," these were tough times indeed—probably the worst period in the history of the nation's heartland.

Without money, without much in the way of a workable farm, and now without even a barn, the Hilliard family had a decision to make. Not long after the embers of the destroyed barn had cooled down, they relocated. With Gladys driving, the three boys climbed into the back seat of the family's 1927 Chevy, riding low with the weight of all their worldly possessions. The family was making for the small town of Durand, Wisconsin, some ten miles away and the Pepin County seat. Paul remembers barely glancing back at the family's dead-end patch of land, that "Mickey Mouse farm," he called it. Gladys's younger sister, Bess, was married to a truck driver, Clayton Tollefson, who brought his truck to the farm and transported the Hilliard cows to a rented pasture on the outskirts of town. Gladys was an optimist—you had to be in these conditions—and she told everyone who would listen that she would soon operate a small dairy business. As in so many families of the era, the future of all of them would depend on mom's drive and acumen.

"What My Mother Accomplished Was Miraculous"

When they arrived at their new home, Paul remembers thinking that his mother must have hit the lottery to get a place with indoor plumbing. And electricity! The small town of Durand, situated on the banks of the Chippewa River, had little more than 1,500 residents in 1936 (and not many more today, about 2,000). While a mere village by any reasonable definition, it might have looked like a bustling metropolis to Paul. It had stores, barber shops, a dentist, a doctor, churches, a high school, even a bowling alley. Most attractive to the eleven-year-old boy, however, was the public library filled with books.

Gladys set up her small dairy operation immediately. Although she had completed only eight years of school, she proved quite capable in her new role as entrepreneur, proving to be a sensible farm woman who kept close watch over family operations. As ever, she worked long hours while taking care of her husband William, whose health continued to deteriorate. "He did work in the sense that he could innovate," Paul says of his ailing father, and he was particularly adept at the precision tool work involved in repairing pocket watches. Unfortunately, Paul remembers, "he was always short on energy and oxygen. Physical exercise was beyond him."

In many ways, the move to Durand was more of the same for Paul, reflecting the unchanging nature of farm life. In a culture where everyone chipped in, Paul's list of chores grew continually. He washed the many dozens of milk bottles by hand and peddled fresh garden vegetables and ripe berries door-to-door with his wagon, selling them for ten cents a quart. He earned credit at the Farmer's Store, where the family would trade for much-needed staples such as flour, sugar, and salt. There were, he says, "a thousand varieties of work," and all of it needed to be done. These were the days before commercial refrigeration, and his family had huge blocks of ice delivered on a regular basis, which they kept in the barn. The blocks were covered in sawdust in a pit, with the bottles of milk packed next to them to keep the milk chilled and fresh before delivery. Sometimes they bought ice blocks, strapped them to the front bumper of their car, and then hurried home as fast as they could before the precious cargo melted.

Through it all, his mom's business kept them alive. "She was a humble lady," Paul recalls, "but self-confident." In an environment where every penny counted, "she could balance the books." She was also a figure of respect and affection in Durand. "Everybody I knew liked my mom. She was unobtrusive, inoffensive, ambitious, and caring." Gladys herself was the eldest of eleven children, but she would be the only one of her siblings who had children graduate from college—all three of her sons, in fact. That was no accident, however. The boys pursued higher education, Paul recalled, was because of their parents. Both Gladys and William combined parental love with exacting standards and discipline. "We enjoyed the blessings of example," he stated. "I was fortunate to have the background I did. Dad was a tough disciplinarian. Mother never talked about it, but she expected it."

Looking back on his father, Paul remembers a stern figure, but also a very intelligent one. "A high IQ guy . . . every now and then he would get philosophical." He demanded the best efforts from all his sons. "Don't even spit," he'd say, "unless you're going to do a good job." Even today, Paul still recalls a saying William Hilliard passed on to him one day:

> This is the law and the law shall run
> 'til the earth in its course stands still;
> that he who eats another's bread
> shall do the other's will.[14]

Independence of mind was the key; "eating another's bread" meant, in the end, loss of freedom. But given William's health problems—he "coughed all day long," as Paul remembers him—it was Gladys who did most of the heavy lifting in raising the boys and teaching responsibility by example. Her gentle disposition aside, Gladys showed strength, determination, and even stubbornness when she needed to. She was a woman who would not accept failure. "Mom was in charge," Paul says.

Besides the benefits of mother's new business, Durand also allowed Paul to meet his relatives, the extended family he hadn't really known up to now. Ruth Lillian ("Lila") Hilliard, for example, was his paternal aunt, twelve years older than Paul's father. A former schoolteacher in her late forties, Lila moved home to Durand to take care of her widowed mother, Paul's grandmother. The cliché "spinster aunt" comes to mind, but we should recall that in those days, teachers would lose their jobs if they got married. Lila had made a deliberate choice to remain independent and in the classroom. She was a "career woman," just a bit ahead of her time. "She was a wonderful lady," Paul says, someone who contributed to his sense of adventure and his desire to learn. Lila was wont to give Bibles as gifts, and Paul credits her with recognizing and encouraging his intellectual curiosity. She once told him, "You got your love of higher education from us Hilliards." The ambitious side of Paul's persona, the drive, that came from his mother's side of the family, the Kees. Both were going to play their part in Paul's life.

Given their relationship, it seems fitting that Aunt Lila took him to see his first motion picture. In the darkened movie theater, he settled down in the plush seats, enjoying the first run of Walt Disney's greatest animated feature, *Snow White and the Seven Dwarfs*, the film that defines the Disney empire even today. Paul's ticket cost a dime, a bare fraction of what it costs today. We can say the same about a soda pop and a Hershey chocolate bar (a nickel each).

Aunt Lila was also the one who took Paul shopping for his first pair of long trousers. In the 1930s, as it had been for time immemorial and would be for decades more, a major rite of passage for a preteen boy was to exchange his knickers—his "short pants," as they said, replete with a buckle or elastic below the knee—for long trousers. Indeed, it was part of the language. "Still in his short pants" was a code word for childhood. Paul was no longer a child. The perils of adulthood soon became evident, however. He remembers riding home on the train, feeling all grown up, when his new tweed pants caught on a sharp metal strip under his seat and ripped an "L" shaped slit in the new wool material. Aunt Lila, always on task, quickly summoned the porter, who hammered the metal piece back into place so that no one else would be hurt. That done, she then examined her crestfallen nephew's knee. "Don't worry," she said, "we can patch it." And she did.

This road trip was perhaps the most dramatic, eye-opening moment of Paul's life. The destination was a real metropolis: the big city of Minneapolis. He'd heard those train whistles in the distance his whole young life; now he finally got to hear one up close as he hung his head out the passenger car window to feel the wind on his face. It was the first and only trip he took away from home as a boy. The next time Paul Hilliard left home on a long train ride, he'd be doing so courtesy of Uncle Sam, and the world would be a very different place, indeed.

Walking down the busy Minneapolis sidewalk, young Paul marveled at what he was seeing. A kid from rural Wisconsin couldn't help but be awestruck by the towering buildings, especially the thirty-two-story Foshay Hotel, the massive Basilica of Saint Mary, the hectic crowds, the honking cars stopping for the automated traffic lights, and the stores with shelves brimming with goods. And in a harbinger of things to come, Paul's Minneapolis trip would also include his first up-close-and-personal look at airplanes, sitting low and sleek and modern on the tarmac at Wold-Chamberlain Field, now the site of the Minneapolis-St. Paul International Airport.

Growing up in the 1930s, planes weren't so much the present as the future. Flight was still so novel in the American heartland that Paul has distinct memories of stopping his work in the fields at their approach.

In the Wisconsin of the day, this was something incredible. "As a young-ster on the farm," he recalls, "no aircraft came overhead without being subjected to the eyes of everyone who heard that strange sound." Cabins weren't pressurized yet, so most flights came in low, somewhere around 12,000 to 13,000 feet, and their primitive electronic systems meant that flights could only proceed in clear weather. As a result, hearing an airplane overhead usually meant that you could see it. These planes weren't "airlin-ers" yet. Commercial passenger flights wouldn't be common for another two decades, post-World War II. As young Paul looked up into the skies, he mostly saw crop dusters or mail planes, small single-engine craft. But now he'd had a close encounter with these craft, and the experience clearly marked a turning point in his young life. Later years would find Paul soar-ing through the wild blue yonder in a variety of aircraft, some military, some civilian.

Another of Paul's beloved relatives was his mother's father, Grandpa Clayton Kees, or "Clate." Paul's maternal grandparents lived up on a bluff, a couple of miles from the local Maxwell Bluff School. Paul re-members them having "a much better farm," including a tractor and "a big barn with electric lights." In perhaps the ultimate small-town luxury, they even had "a windmill and water." Paul described Clate as a hard-working Scots-Irishman with a frugal streak. He famously owned a single necktie, and his sons, as a joke, would take it to town, have it cleaned, and wrap it for him each year as a Christmas gift. In Paul's memory, Clate is always working, just like his daughter Gladys. Paul also remembers the homespun wisdom his grandfather imparted to him: "Life is simpler if you plow around the stumps."

From Boy to Young Man

Paul's schooling didn't change much from Sand Burr Coulee to Durand, even though the former was a one-room schoolhouse and the latter a larger and more crowded institution. Both schools, he believes, set him up for success. By his own admission, he was a good student but not an exemplary one. Oftentimes, his mind wandered from the subject at hand, and he would follow his own interests in reading, nearly always history. His early education in that one-room wooden schoolhouse af-forded Paul a chance to compete. A lonely farm boy accustomed to doing his tasks in isolation, the combined grades let him take his own measure and compare his skills to those of older classmates. His teacher would sometimes oversee arithmetic or spelling competitions—"spell downs," they were called—in which the assembled sixteen students could challenge each other, regardless of grade or age. "She'd hold up flash cards and everyone had to get their answers down," he recalled. "What a great competition: if a third grader could beat a seventh grader, what excitement that was!" But along with the fun came discipline. There was "no such thing as misbehavior at school," Paul says. "Nobody misbehaved. You were in trouble if you did. No one wanted to bring a note home." And certainly not Paul, who well remembered how strict his father was.

While Paul's school years don't appear to be all that unique, one thing separates his education from the one most American youngsters get today: a heavy dose of patriotism. In the 1930s, classroom learning did more than instill a grounding in the academic basics and a sense of order, it also stressed love of country. Morning exercises included raising the flag and reciting in unison the Pledge of Allegiance.[15] Holidays meant patriotic parades and John Phillips Souza's marching music. Paul is unabashed, even today, in his patriotic beliefs: "Our country was the land of opportunity," he says, looking back his lessons in school and what they instilled. "We were taught we should treasure our country." And in language which has resonated down through the ages, Paul remembers being taught that, "we were the 'City on the Hill,' the New World country that saved the Old World in 1917 and 1918."[16] For that reason, civics and history were his favorite classes at Durand High. "We were taught a lot about patriotism and by the late 1930s began to feel we were an exceptional nation, although I never heard that term used. We were aware of what we did in World War I: young people in the New World go across the ocean to save the descendants of their ancestors."

While Paul was coming of age intellectually, he was also entering the world of work. With the family's dairy operation thriving, twelve-year-old Paul found himself driving the family truck to deliver products to about thirty or forty area customers. "We were able to sell milk right away," he says, but Gladys soon expanded her offerings to include cream, cottage cheese, and seasonal vegetables and fruit. The local police knew that the boy, sitting on a stack of Sears and Roebuck catalogs in the front seat of the truck, rumbling down the town's streets for the early morning milk deliveries, was not of legal age to drive, which at the time was fifteen in Wisconsin. But in a small town, the police are usually aware of the family's circumstances, and the police never bothered Paul. Even if they had, "you had to do what you had to do" was a rule Paul that already taken to heart.

He was also able to land a paper route. Before school, young Paul delivered the *Milwaukee Journal* and metropolitan newspapers from Minneapolis-St. Paul. Local coverage in Durand was handled by the *Courier-Wedge*, a weekly. His wages didn't amount to much, he recalls, something less than a penny a paper. But there was a benefit: if a customer failed to pay for his subscription—not uncommon in the Great Depression's waning days—Paul could keep their newspaper. The end of the day would often find Paul sitting and eagerly devouring each edition, front to back.

So, while the job required little more than an accurate throw from a moving bicycle, the paper route was yet another window opening into a broader world. The opportunity was especially helpful because his parents never subscribed to any newspaper, news magazines, or even bought a radio. Before the arrival of television—still more than a decade in the future—most families in Durand and across the country gathered around the big family radio console at night. Shows like *The Lone Ranger, The Jack Benny Program*, and *Burns and Allen* dominated the ratings, and even the president of the United States was getting into the act with his famous "Fireside Chats." Radio brought an intimacy to American politics, a one-on-one connection between elected officials and the public.

When Paul thinks back on the radio of the era, he doesn't think about an entertainment program. Rather, he remembers pedaling by a house in town one day in 1936 and stopping to greet the neighbor and his wife. Their friendly conversation was suddenly interrupted by the voice of a radio announcer, coming from inside the house. King Edward VIII had abdicated his throne in order to marry a twice-divorced American socialite, Wallis Warfield Simpson. Paul got off his bike to listen, perhaps the first moment when we can clearly say that Paul had awakened to the world of politics and international affairs.[17]

The Approach of War

Timing is everything, they say, and Paul's entrée into global aware-
ness could not have come at a more exciting, or ominous, time. We
might say the same for his entire age cohort, his "generation," if you
prefer. Consider a few key events from the era that we might label, "the
road to World War II":

1931: Japan invades the Chinese province of Manchuria. When
the League of Nations protests this act of aggression, Japan walks
out of the organization. Paul is six.

1933: Adolf Hitler comes to power in Germany, quickly establishing a Nazi dictatorship and building concentration camps for
his political enemies. The persecution of German Jews also begins
in earnest. Paul is eight.

1935: Hitler rearms Germany, thumbing his nose at the Treaty
of Versailles ending World War I, which limited the size of the
German military. He begins to build a powerful army and a new
air force. Paul is ten.

1937: Japanese forces invades China proper, rapidly overrunning
northern China and brutalizing the civilian population. Paul is
twelve.

1939: Germany invades Poland, starting World War II in Europe.
German forces swiftly crush the Polish army, displaying the efficiency of their new tank forces. A new German word enters the
world's military vocabulary: *blitzkrieg* ("lightning war"). Paul is
fourteen and just entering high school.

1940: German armies overrun France in a matter of weeks, de-
stroying the French army and driving the British army off the
European continent in a humiliating retreat from the port of
Dunkirk. The fall of France gives Hitler almost complete control
over the European continent. Paul is fifteen.

Up to now, these events have all transpired overseas, in Europe or far-off
Asia. America still seems like a safe haven. But President Roosevelt knows

that a world in which the dictators have trampled on democracy and human rights will be a very dangerous place for the United States, indeed.

In a December 29, 1940 speech, he tells the American people that the country has to be the "arsenal of democracy" against the dictatorships, prepared to come to the aid of any free people fighting for its liberty. The three fascist powers known as "the Axis" are on the march. The United States must now take a stand. "For us," Roosevelt proclaims, "this is an emergency as serious as war itself. We must apply ourselves to our task with the same resolution, the same sense of urgency, the same spirit of patriotism and sacrifice, as we would show were we at war." Appeasing the dictators is impossible—it has been tried, over and over again, and it has failed.[18] "No man can tame a tiger into a kitten by stroking it," Roosevelt tells the American people. "Democracy's fight against world conquest" depends upon "the rearmament of the United States." These, and many more, were the stories that Paul was reading in those leftover papers every night or hearing in snippets that were being reported on the radio. War was in the air, and it seemed increasingly unlikely that it would not spread to America's shores.

Paul admired President Roosevelt during this period, patiently trying to prepare a recalcitrant public for a war that he knew was coming. Even more, however, Paul developed a lifelong admiration for Great Britain, then standing alone against the Nazis, and especially for the resolute war-time leadership of the country's prime minister, Winston Churchill. He remembered Churchill's voice on the radio. "I had access to the news. I loved the news and geography. By 1940, I was convinced that Winston Churchill carried the whole world on his shoulders," he says. And no wonder. During Britain's darkest hours, with Hitler standing astride the European continent as a conqueror and planning the invasion of the British Isles, with the German "Blitz" pounding its cities into rubble, Churchill employed the power of words. Eloquent words, inspiring words that went into combat as surely as guns or tanks. Some of his phrases have become immortal, "the gathering storm" and "their finest hour," for example.[19] But reading more deeply into his famous speeches, as Paul has, can be illustrative of a great orator, and a great leader, at work. Consider this piece of Churchillian rhetoric, as Britain stood alone against the Nazis:

The whole fury and might of the enemy must very soon be turned on us. Hitler knows that he will have to break us in this island or lose the war. If we can stand up to him, all Europe may be freed and the life of the world may move forward into broad, sunlit uplands. But if we fail, then the whole world, including the United States, including all that we have known and cared for, will sink into the abyss of a new Dark Age made more sinister, and perhaps more protracted, by the lights of perverted science.[20]

"In the early years of the war, most of the news was bad," Paul remembers. "I just remember some of the caricatures about him. For two years, he was carrying the free world on his back. I remember cartoons where he looked like a bulldog. I saw him as a heroic figure."

And even as the British strategic situation stabilized and the United States joined Britain's war as a close ally and supplier, Churchill was still working his oratorical magic. Looking back in late December 1941 on the darker, early days of the war, he recalled that naysayers were predicting that, "In three weeks England will have her neck wrung like a chicken." Churchill knew he would have his audience—the Canadian Parliament, in this case—eating out of his hand when he paused for effect in the middle of his speech and declared, "Some chicken; some neck."[21]

That one is a favorite line of Paul's. Long into his nineties, he continues to read and study everything he can find about Churchill, whom he characterizes him as a "superhuman" figure. He still keeps a bust of Churchill in his home. "Our politicians come and go," Paul says. "Churchill is a permanent figure."

Paul began to learn more about the war as older students began leaving via draft or volunteering. Clearly, events were whetting his own appetite. "The world was so big to a kid then. You couldn't get your arms around it." But at the same time, that big world was getting smaller by the day. Paul calls himself "a contemporary of airplanes," and if the early course of the war—those German blitzkrieg-style victories—had proven anything, it was that the aircraft had become "the third dimension in warfare." Paul likens the situation the American Revolution. "There was Paul Revere and the lantern: 'One if by land, two if by sea.' But what if they came by air?"

These were the thoughts racing through his mind as he stood on the cusp of adulthood and also on the brink of a war that would find young Paul Hilliard soaring aloft, very much a part of that "third dimension of warfare" that he had first glimpsed as a teenager.

PART II
WAR

CHAPTER 2
PAUL GOES TO WAR

The Ties that Bind

Paul Hilliard's path into World War II began with the intersection of two timelines, where events in rural Durand, Wisconsin, crossed those taking place in faraway Tokyo, Japan. While people like to think that they make their own destiny, choosing their path in life and then following it, we must keep in mind that they are often subject to the whims of impersonal factors and distant decision-makers. While our own choices may appear to be free at the time, they also emerge out of a matrix of forces of which we may be only dimly aware. So it is with Paul, and with the other sixteen million or so Americans who donned their country's uniform in World War II. Small-town rural America, in particular, was about to change the world.

By 1940, the ties that bound Paul to his family and to Durand were beginning to fray. While he was keeping busy with his odd jobs and school, his father's health worsened. "Once we moved to town in 1936, I can't remember him being around," Paul recalls. William Hilliard was increasingly isolated and frustrated. His physical problems had grown in intensity to the point he had to be institutionalized for two years in Madison, Wisconsin. His chronic lung disease had led him down into the darkness of depression. Antibiotics could have treated his father's illness, had they existed at the time. After all, Alexander Fleming had discovered penicillin in 1928 at St. Mary's Hospital in London, the first proper "antibiotic." Its clinical use would not be widespread until the upcoming war created a heavy demand for it, however, and mass production of the drug was still in the research stage. "He suffered from depression because of his constant illness. If he was depressed, I understand it," Paul says. William

Hilliard died—too early—from pneumonia on November 6, 1939. He was forty-one.

"I was fourteen," Paul remembers. "When someone is sick for a long time [and then passes], there is a combination of relief and sorrow. Relief probably dominates." Although his brother Bill resented his father's authoritarian discipline, Paul remembers that their father "was not a big factor in our lives." Dad's concern for learning benefited the boys, certainly, but he was simply not present much of the time. When he was there, he tended to be emotionally remote, and his illness worked against his effectiveness as a father.

For day-to-day direction, the boys looked more to their mother. But Gladys, too, was receding in importance in their lives. Her older sons were growing and becoming increasingly independent, and consequently, their need for Mom's constant attention was diminishing. By the time Bill and Paul reached the ages of sixteen and fourteen, respectively, they were considered grown young men in the hard 1930s world. Less than two years after his father passed away, Bill graduated from Durand High School in the class of 1941. It was a day to celebrate. Gladys had her own news, however. A widow still in the prime of her life, she announced she was getting remarried.

Her new husband managed a hardware store in Pepin, some twenty miles from Durand on the Mississippi River. He was a widower, with a son and daughter of his own. By now Paul was sixteen, a junior in high school, independent enough that he and brother Bill decided not to move to Pepin. Only Wally, just nine years old, would go to live with Gladys and her new husband. As things turned out, the new blended family did not remain in Pepin for long. Gladys was as savvy and as ambitious as ever, and she soon recognized that war industries were gearing up in the industrial areas of America, providing better economic opportunities. The family moved for a while to Waukegan, Illinois, north of Chicago, and then back to Wisconsin, to Kenosha. Both Gladys and her husband found work in the defense industry. Paul could see the hand of history at work. "By 1940 and 1941, America was the arsenal of democracy," Paul explains, recalling the famous phrase from President Franklin Roosevelt. "Jobs were plentiful in Kenosha, Racine, or any other industrial area."[1]

For his own part, Paul stayed busy in his small town. There were plenty of jobs to choose from as more of the young men left for the war. President

Roosevelt instituted the first peacetime draft in US history in October 1940. The term of service was only one year, and Roosevelt also coupled the draft with a promise to America's parents (and especially mothers): "I have said this before, but I shall say it again and again. Your boys are not going to be sent into any foreign wars. They are going into training to form a force so strong that, by its very existence, it will keep the threat of war far away from our shores. The purpose of our defense is defense."[2]

As boys in Durand began to sign up or be drafted, Paul, too, began to get the itch. He was only in high school, but he couldn't help but notice the variety of military uniforms all around him. He remembers walking down the streets and, in his mind, he felt that he was getting long looks from the townsfolk. He imagined that they were questioning him as to why he, a healthy young man, was still in town and not in uniform, like their sons were. Perhaps they were wondering if he was good enough or if he was classified as 4F, "unfit for military service" due to physical, mental, or moral reasons. "You felt strange walking down the street," he says, "seventeen years old, healthy."[3]

Paul's high school years were not memorable for his social life. He always had to work and "we didn't have much of a car." But he relished his participation in high school team sports: basketball, baseball, football. "I played on the d-line," he says of his football career. "I wasn't fast enough but played quarterback when the guy got hurt. I played both ways." At five foot nine and 155 pounds, he realized he was probably not bound for the pros. As always, he summarizes his prospects with a characteristic quip: "I was not very big, but I made up for it by being slow."

As for classwork, well, that was hit-and-miss. Paul was too easily distracted by the subjects he enjoyed to extend himself to subjects he didn't. "As a student, I was as good as I wanted to be. Sometimes a C student, sometimes better. I was always distracted. I would read other stuff. I was too varied in my interests," he admits today.

After his mother's remarriage, Paul moved in with his grandmother and his aunt, Ruth Lila. The women fussed over him—probably too much. "Grandma was in her eighties; she wanted me in the house at dark." She was a "good lady," he remembers, and taught him her own version of homespun wisdom, old aphorisms such as, "Never even steal a pin; it's with small things you begin," but Paul had a hard time keeping to his assigned curfew. "You weren't going to change her way of thinking," he says. He held part-time jobs at local gas stations and at the bowling alley—then, as now, a popular haunt in small-town America—where he was a pinsetter. "That would go on until midnight sometimes, but it was a job," he says. He knew he had to work and earn a living, despite his grand-mother's concerns about late hours. "She cared for me, but it went beyond that. She wanted to dominate me!" When he finally came into the house each night, he was met with his grandmother's strict "lights out" rule. It never hindered his reading, though. He would form a canopy over his head with the bed covers, and, with a flashlight, read into the wee hours.

Eventually, the chafing got too much for him, and he moved in with his best friend and classmate Bob Heike. Bob's parents, George and Olivia, welcomed Paul into their home, letting the two boys share a room upstairs. One memory that still sticks with Paul is the day that Mrs. Heike joined the local war effort, becoming one of the 20 million women known to the American public as "Rosie the Riveters"—trading in their cookpots and rolling pins for drill presses and lathes.[4] Every day, Olivia rode in a car with five of her girlfriends from Durand to the Presto Aluminum Company in Eau Claire, some thirty miles away. The firm had just con-verted to wartime production, and the manufacturing of pressure cookers had given way to the production of bombs, artillery, and rocket fuses. She and her pals worked third trick, the "graveyard shift," as it's still called. All over America, moms and daughters from Main Street were arming the country for war.

Paul particularly enjoyed his new home because the Heikes lived right next door to the local public library. The librarian learned to appreciate Paul's visits and voracious reading habits and let him borrow all the books he could carry. They recognized his type, an avid youngster who always re-turned things quickly. Paul remembers reading a couple of Horatio Alger stories early in his time in Durand. Even though they were written for younger boys, he drank in the lessons of the main characters, young boys like "Ragged Dick" who achieved the American dream through honesty, hard work, and pluck.[5] He could not have suspected how the novels of Horatio Alger would eventually come to define his own life. Many twen-ty-first-century readers find Alger old-fashioned and accuse him of con-cocting a mythic America that has never existed in reality. For Paul and for many of his generation, however, Alger's portrayal of America—a land of opportunity, for those willing to grasp it—was the simple truth.

Books also took him to a wider world, places which he had not yet seen, but seemed to understand instinctively. Looking back, Paul remembers enjoying the works of Nathaniel Hawthorne and James Fenimore Cooper, especially Cooper's *Leatherstocking Tales*.[6] Cooper's seminal masterwork was a series of five novels featuring a frontiersman named Natty Bumppo. Known to European American settlers as "Leatherstocking" and to Native Americans as the "Deerslayer," Bumppo was a character who combined all those traits that had come to seem distinctively American. He is a young white man raised by the Delaware Indians: a woodsman, hunter, and interpreter. Brave, honest, and honorable, he seems to be the embodiment of the wilderness dweller, the frontiersman, an ideal American type who was vanishing by the time Cooper wrote, and a distant but still inspiring memory to young Paul Hilliard.

The public school system in the United States was a marvel to the world at the time, and Paul came to appreciate his classes and opportunities at Durand High. This was not a one-room schoolhouse, but a comprehensive institution with a student body of three hundred. He remembers the school as "a four-year deal, organized," with the standard class offerings of the day. The list was impressive. The students of Durand received instruction in algebra, geometry, English literature, history, and civics, plus a couple of years of Latin, featuring texts written by the Roman authors.

He learned to appreciate his good teachers, including a favorite English teacher, Ruth Grote, whom Paul describes as an "old maid," although we might quibble; she was thirty-six. She was a Wisconsin native, a graduate of Lawrence College (now University), had earned her degree in English, and taken courses for teacher certification. Working at the high school as both teacher and librarian, she knew how to handle her young charges. He liked her mannerisms, the way she talked, and her unique way of disciplining cocky students like himself: "If she wanted to punish you, she'd make you learn something. One time we were studying Shakespeare. A girl was reading something about a 'harlot.' I was probably a sophomore or junior. I asked, 'What's a harlot?' Ms. Grote said, 'Paul, I want you to learn by tomorrow and explain to the class.' I learned from that experience," Paul says today, dryly.[7]

At night when they had time, Paul and Bob Heike would often talk about their futures. To Paul, college seemed far out of reach, just like it was for most kids from Durand. Both boys knew that professionals—doctors, lawyers, and teachers—all needed higher education, but few of their friends could afford it. Durand wasn't alone. High school graduation rates in the country were less than 25 percent in 1940, and in fact they were about to drop even lower as young men left high school early to enlist in the military. Less than 3 percent of the population had a college degree, compared to 35 percent today. As Paul notes, however, "you didn't need a high school degree to be a mechanic or a radioman. How many men were involved in D-Day or in other World War II operations? All that equipment was built, maintained, and operated mostly by guys without a high school education."

The opening years of World War II paralleled Paul's high school career, beginning with Hitler's invasion of Poland in September 1939, the month that he entered Durand High School. The radio trumpeted news from the various battlefronts every day, and more and more local families were losing their sons from the farm as they signed up to serve or were drafted into the burgeoning US military machine. The specter of war hung over Durand—and the entire world—like a threatening thundercloud before a storm.

Decision Point: Tokyo

Turn on a radio back in the 1940s and you might have heard the song, "What a Difference a Day Makes." It's not the most memorable tune of the era, and its lyrics were never going to win a literary award ("It's heaven when you / find romance on your menu.")[8]

Still, even the simplest song lyric can hit a listener hard. Americans hearing Bing Crosby sing "What a Difference a Day Makes" on his wartime Kraft Radio Hour might have grasped a deeper meaning. All of them had been through a recent, traumatic experience. If ever a single day had made a difference in their lives, it was December 7, 1941. Pearl Harbor not only plunged the United States into war, it also changed the country forever. It divided the life of every living American into a "before" and an "after," and few of them would ever forget where they were when they heard the news.[9]

The Japanese attack on Pearl Harbor was at first bewildering. Those who were there remember the shock: aircraft careening in, attacking, then banking away to reveal the big red circle on their wings, the mark of the rising sun. Sailors on ships in nearby waters got the chilling radiogram, labeled "urgent": AIR RAID ON PEARL HARBOR X THIS IS NO DRILL. Back at home, many Americans didn't even know where Pearl Harbor was, or *what* it was, for that matter. Remember, Hawaii wasn't a state yet, not until 1959. Indeed, one common anecdote tells of a child who, on hearing that Japan had bombed Pearl Harbor, asked, "Who's she?"

How had it come to this? Perhaps the best phrase to describe it is to say that Japan had become desperate. In July 1937, Japanese forces launched a full-scale invasion of China.[10] This was all-out war, with the initial operations involving over six hundred thousand Japanese troops. The Japanese overran north China, then linked up with amphibious forces landing in the south, at Shanghai. The war's signal moment was an orgy of violence after the capture of the Chinese capital, Nanjing, where victorious Japanese troops butchered two hundred thousand civilians.

Japanese planning emphasized winning a quick victory in China, since Japan's own manpower resources would not sustain a long, drawn-out conflict. Instead of coming apart, however, China unified under strongman Chiang Kai-Shek, whose forces slowly retreated into the vast interior of the country, setting up a new capital at remote Chongqing. In addition, foreign supplies began to flow into China, with arms from the United States and Great Britain arriving via a new road that had been hacked out of the mountains from British Burma to Chongqing, the famed Burma Road. The US was also preparing to send a "volunteer" air force to China, the American Volunteer Group, better known, for the nose painting on their Curtiss P-40B fighters, as the "Flying Tigers."[11]

By 1941, the fighting in China had stalemated. Even with a troop commitment of more than one million men, Japan was no closer to ultimate victory. This was the context for Japan's decision to widen the war. With the Western powers tied down by their own war against Hitler, their prosperous Asian colonies were vulnerable. Japan saw a huge, once-in-a-century opportunity to seize the resources it needed: rubber from French Indochina, tin from British Malaya, and especially the oilfields of the

Dutch East Indies. These raw materials would allow Japan, once and for all, to finish its war in China.

There was just one power standing in the way of this plan: the United States, which would surely not stand by and allow Japan to swallow up all of China and the western Pacific, to boot. Roosevelt had already signaled as much. In 1938, he placed an embargo on arms sales to Japan. In 1940, he extended the embargo to scrap iron—a principal material for Japanese steel production—and he ordered the US Pacific Fleet to shift its base from San Diego to Pearl Harbor, Hawaii, as a warning to Japan not to ignore American interests in the Pacific. In July 1941 he extended the embargo to oil and also signed an order freezing all Japanese assets in the United States. Talks between the two sides were fruitless, as long as Japan was determined to proceed on its path of conquest. But Tokyo was growing impatient. Before the plan to conquer a vast Pacific empire could proceed, American naval forces had to be destroyed, or at least temporarily neutralized.

And that leads to December 7, 1941, as Japan launched its infamous surprise strike on the US fleet at anchor in Pearl Harbor. The attack was a giant gamble for Japan, and especially for the Imperial Japanese Navy. It was also a piece of skilled military planning, the work of Admiral Isoroku Yamamoto. With all six of its precious aircraft carriers sailing across three thousand miles of open ocean in total secrecy, the fleet arrived at its designated station a few hundred miles north of Hawaii. Launching their aircraft early on that Sunday morning, the Japanese caught US forces completely unprepared. In just ninety minutes, Japanese dive-bombers and torpedo bombers destroyed or damaged nineteen warships and three hundred aircraft, killing 2,400 US servicemen. Almost half of that total was from a single ship, the battleship USS *Arizona*, which sank within minutes after a bomb struck its forward magazine, igniting more than a million pounds of ammunition. The ship's remains still lie in the waters of the harbor.

With the US Navy temporarily out of the way, a massive Japanese offensive overran the European colonial empires in Asia: Hong Kong, Malaya, the massive islands of the Dutch East Indies, New Guinea, and more. US possessions also came under attack: the Philippines, the major American base in Asia; Guam; and Wake Island. On the Philippines, invading

Japanese forces completely outmaneuvered a combined US/Filipino army under the command of General Douglas MacArthur. The defenders retreated into the Bataan Peninsula and finally onto tiny Corregidor Island. MacArthur was evacuated, but his entire force of 75,000 men surrendered in April 1942, the worst defeat in US military history. Their Japanese captors now subjected them to a brutal sixty-five-mile forced march to prison camps in the Philippine interior, the infamous Bataan Death March. At least five thousand died (and perhaps many more), a grisly sign of what was to come in what the Japanese called the Great Pacific War.[12]

Decision Point: Durand

Meanwhile, at a kitchen table in Durand, Wisconsin, an American family is sitting down to eat Sunday dinner. Paul remembers his uncle bursting in and announcing that the Japanese had just bombed Pearl Harbor. At first, the gravity of the announcement didn't sink in. Then, the first question: "How many lives lost?" someone asked, incredulous that Japan would do such a thing. All those radio reports of fighting in Europe and Asia had seemed so far off. If there was a war raging, it certainly hadn't been America's fight. For Paul Hilliard and a lot of American boys, however, the clock had been ticking all along.

That initial sense of uncertainty was typical of a lot of Americans. Despite the mythology of American youth storming the recruiting stations to volunteer their services and wreak vengeance on Japan, most took a wait-and-see attitude. Roosevelt's draft, the one that was supposed to end in October 1941, had been extended indefinitely, and, in fact, the vast majority of Americans who fought in World War II were draftees. Paul remembers that his passion for geography gave him an advantage over many Americans that day. Unlike most of his countrymen, he knew that Pearl Harbor was in Hawaii. But he did not quite know where the attack was going to lead. "I didn't attach any great significance to it," he says. "At the time, it wasn't a war, it was an event. I didn't know I'd get involved in it."

No one knew, but virtually everyone wound up getting involved. By late 1942, brother Bill had graduated from high school and was in the Navy, a sonar operator on a submarine chaser, and was about to see duty in the Pacific. Growing up in the solid and landlocked Midwest hardly prepared Bill for the motion of the waves. Bill was "seasick every day" and hated it. A sub chaser was small, just 175 feet long, and was known to sailors as a "rough riding boat." At times, the name "Pacific" (from the Spanish for "peaceful") must have seemed like a cruel joke.

Bill wasn't alone. Young, able-bodied men in the classes of 1941 and 1942 were leaving "in droves" for the military, Paul remembers, either by enlistment or the draft. If you did not enlist by eighteen, Paul says, then you were subject to the draft, although some local boys were deferred so they could operate their farms. Paul's high school was small, and he knew all those boys who left for the military before him. More and more he began to think of enlisting.

As the war progressed, the far-flung actions of global war became more personal in Durand. All the boys Paul's age started hearing the stories of their older schoolmates. Some weren't coming back. "One went to a POW camp in Germany," Paul says years afterward, "and his health suffered. He died young. Another was killed with the Marines at Peleliu."[13] And still a third, a soldier in the Army, died in battle with Japanese forces on the island of Leyte. Paul's family members, too, were marching off to war. His uncles Kenny and George (Gladys's brothers) soon joined the Coast Guard and Army, respectively. Later, a third maternal uncle, John, joined the Army.

Paul turned seventeen on June 18, 1942, and he had made his decision. He wanted to enlist. But he decided against joining Bill in the Navy. Paul had his heart set on becoming a US Marine. The mystique of the Marine Corps has been part of American culture from the beginning of the republic, from fighting the Barbary pirates on the "shores of Tripoli" to storming the "halls of Montezuma" in the Mexican-American War. More recently, Marines had fought the first big battle for US forces in World War I, grinding ahead against a buzz saw of machine gun fire in Belleau Wood. Their ferocity and aggressive spirit earned them the nickname "Devil Dogs" (*Teufelhunde*) from their German adversaries.[14]

Now, in this war, they were already doing it again. The stirring defense of Wake Island in December 1941, when all the news from the Pacific front was bad, showed that US Marines still had the right stuff.[15] A handful of Marines held out against a vastly superior Japanese force for over two weeks, even defeating a first landing attempt. The Japanese arrived in force and eventually stormed by the island on December 23, but defense of Wake Island became another immortal piece of Marine lore. It even got the cinematic treatment, perhaps the highest honor our culture can bestow, in the film *Wake Island* (d. John Farrow, 1942), starring Brian Donlevy, Robert Preston, and Macdonald Carey.[16]

A little later in the year, the Marine mystique was back. Seeking to keep the initiative after the big naval win at Midway (June 1942), the Commander in Chief of the US fleet, Admiral Ernest J. King, drew up plans for a landing on Guadalcanal in the Solomon Islands. Success here would punch a hole in Japan's Pacific perimeter and serve as a sign that this young war had already seen its turning point.

And who to call on? The Marines, of course. The First Marine Division was new to the Pacific, and its commander, General Alexander Vandegrift, felt that it still needed more training. Virtually everything the Guadalcanal operation needed was in short supply. The landing was a colossal improvisation, concocted on the fly to take advantage of the recent dramatic turn in the Pacific war. The Marines, with their sardonic sense of humor called it "Operation Shoestring."[17] On August 7, the First Marine Division landed on Guadalcanal. They surprised the Japanese garrison, overran a partially finished landing strip they christened "Henderson Field" and set up a defense perimeter. The fight lasted for six months, but the Marines hung on. Army units landed in reinforcement, and mile by mile US forces overran Guadalcanal, driving the Japanese into an evacuation from the island's western tip.

Young Paul read and heard all about these campaigns and the crucial role played by the Marines, and he was as susceptible to having his imagination fired as any young man. The notion of landing on foreign shores, carrying the national interest and the flag, was a potent idea. All those patriotic activities of his youth, raising the flag up the pole outside his one-room schoolhouse in Buffalo County, reciting the Pledge of Allegiance, listening to Souza marches on the Fourth of July, had left an indelible mark on him, as they had his whole generation. He also heard not-so-glamorous reports from his two uncles in the Army, one stationed at Ft. Lewis, Washington, and one at Camp Polk, Louisiana. Both were languishing and had little good to say about their experiences. Paul made his choice: he would be a Marine.

There was just one problem. At seventeen, Paul was not old enough to join the Marines or any other branch of military service. Because he was underage, he needed his mother's permission to enlist. Gladys balked. With her three brothers and oldest son already fighting the war, she had no desire to send off her middle son. As far as contributing family members to the national cause, she believed she had done her part and then some. She dug in her heels stubbornly, giving Paul a resolute "no" to all Paul entreaties.

Paul was just as stubborn, however, a character trait he had probably picked up from his mother. He knew that he was fit for service. And although he was still just an adolescent, he held no doubts at all about the righteousness of the Allied cause. Few Americans did, especially after Pearl Harbor. Roosevelt had called the Japanese attack "a date which will live in infamy." It was a crime, in other words. Now, America had joined forces with Britain—Roosevelt with Churchill—in a dramatic struggle whose objective was nothing less than "preserving the world's freedoms." There was no gray area here. "There was a clear delineation between good and evil," Paul thought, and he wanted to be part of it—not later, but now.

With war news continuing to fill the front pages of papers across the nation, young men everywhere in America were being encouraged to join it. Wisconsin was no exception. Even the governor, Robert M. La Follette Jr., had become an ardent supporter of the war effort.[18] He was an interesting case. Son of the previous longtime governor, and originally a Republican, La Follette Jr. was on the political Left. He founded the Wisconsin Progressive Party in 1934, speaking out on behalf of workers and farmers in the state. Before Pearl Harbor, like many in the American heartland, he was a leading isolationist, demanding neutrality in the ongoing conflicts around the globe and accusing President Roosevelt of agitating for war. But the Japanese attack had changed his mind, as it changed so many Americans. Even La Follette, yesterday's isolationist, now supported the war. It was a savvy political move, since the vast majority of his constituents did, too.

If there was little antiwar opposition in the state, there was probably none at all in a small town like Durand. About half of the able-bodied, age-eligible men in America put on a uniform between 1940 and 1946, and all around him Paul could see that men and boys not much older than himself were stepping up to the challenge. "To my age group, uniforms were ordinary and commonplace—and expected," he wrote to a friend. More than ever, it troubled Paul not to be in uniform, and he was still reading disapproval and disdain in the eyes of even the friendliest citizen of Durand. The fact that Paul might have been imagining these sentiments just shows how powerful social currents were running in favor of the war back in 1942.

Paul waged a months-long campaign to gain his mother's consent to enlist. He tried every argument, but she was a rock. Finally, his Uncle Clayton, Gladys's brother-in-law, convinced her: if Paul did not enlist in the Marines before he was eighteen, then he would be subject to the military draft when he came of age and likely be forced to enter another branch of service instead. Volunteering brought benefits, allowing Paul to maintain at least some semblance of free will and control over his destiny, even during wartime.

Uncle Clayton's arguments were irrefutable, and Gladys finally had a change of heart in February 1943, four months shy of Paul's birthday. Paul could join the Marines, she said and signed a letter of consent. He didn't hesitate, mainly because he did not want to give his mother time to change her mind again. Carrying the precious document in his pocket, with a duffel bag slung over his shoulder, he hitchhiked in bitter cold temperatures from Durand to Milwaukee, 260 miles away, to join the Marines. It was his first big city trip since his Aunt Lila took him to Minneapolis six years before. "That was kind of an exciting day for me," he recalls, with some understatement. "That was my second trip to a big city." The Marines accepted him, swore him in, and gave him his orders.

It's a little over six thousand miles from Tokyo to Durand, Wisconsin, but the lines of decision had now intersected. Powerful statesmen had decided on their strategies, and now a small-town kid was about to deliver his response.

Paul Hilliard was going to war.

San Diego

While Paul awaited his paperwork, he took a temporary construction job, working as a water boy and timekeeper on a construction crew at the Great Lakes Naval Station in Chicago. Construction at the station was booming in a frantic effort to expand its training facilities. Within nine months of the start of the war, the number of Navy trainees there grew from six thousand to one hundred thousand, and the buildings were barely managing to keep pace.

At seventeen, Paul was not eligible to join the union but worked alongside its members until his orders arrived that spring. Later, he says, he was relieved that he had joined the Marines and not the Navy, because of the treatment the new recruits got around the naval station. He watched them get their inoculations and then step right into training. "It would rain, and the sailors had shots in both arms, then walked in the mud in their white uniforms to incomplete barracks," he says. Because of the ongoing construction, they had to walk through muddy streets and carry heavy duffel bags. "They looked miserable."

When his Marine orders finally arrived, he rode an electric rail line that ran from Milwaukee to Chicago, and from there he boarded a train to take him to the West Coast. It was a fast train and made numerous stops: Kenosha, Racine, Waukegan, and other growing industrial cities in the region. His mother insisted on coming along on the Northshore train with him and to meet the final train that would carry him on to California. And she kept her promise. There she was, Paul remembers—frankly, who could forget?—nicely dressed and boarding his train with tears in her eyes. "Other young guys had girlfriends. I hoped no one would remember me: 'Hey, this guy's mama took him to the station. She was crying about her baby!'" He worried about that first impression. Like the great majority of Marine recruits, he expected to be sent to the Pacific theater of operations. The Japanese military there presented an imposing threat—the soldiers of the emperor were tough, hardened, and ruthless. He knew that's where the Marines were in the thick of the hardest fighting. The morning of his departure, however, what scared him the most was not the prospect of fighting the fearsome Japanese, but rather that "someone would see me waved off by my mama."

Departing the station for the West Coast and for his training, Paul said his goodbyes and began his own personal war experience. In his 2017 book, *The Second World Wars*, historian Victor Davis Hanson notes that during his boyhood in the 1960s, World War II veterans in his family related wildly different personal perceptions about the war.[19] Although they had been "kindred soldiers in a shared struggle," they experienced the war in different service branches on various continents against enemies of different backgrounds, races, and cultures. Indeed, it was as if they had been in separate wars.

That idea rings true for Paul. "We each had our own version" of the war, he recalls. "I had my version; some other guy had a totally different version." Decades later, Paul began to study World War II and its countless battles all over the globe. He became a true, self-taught expert on the war. In 1943, however, like all soldiers in all wars, he could only see what was directly in front of him, and the time frame of his experience was rarely more than twenty-four hours.

And so it was on day one. Paul took a seat in the passenger car jammed with other eager recruits, three abreast in a seat. For three days the train crossed the country bound for the West Coast. The boy who relished the study of geography and who had at night listened to the haunting train whistles could now see a rugged American landscape flashing by his window. All his young life, he had read and dreamed about this, and now it was passing by in all its glory:

> I remember the magnificence of the West . . . the Rockies, that was stupendous for a farm kid. I was so impressed with the beauty and ruggedness in the American West. We probably went the central route through Nebraska, the Great Plains, into the foothills and into the Rockies. It was impressive for a seventeen-year-old. I was bug-eyed. . . . I remember watching it all day long, overwhelmed by the magnificence . . . the sheer size of the country, I had never realized the immensity of the world. A few months later I got to the Pacific and saw the endless ocean.

The westward train only stopped a few times to feed its hungry passengers. Naturally, the restaurants were Fred Harvey's, the first restaurant chain in the country, founded in the Wild West in the late 1800s to serve railroad passengers and then revived during World War II to serve military passengers. Harvey Houses served over one million meals in 1943 alone.[20] Paul was the typical "Private Pringle," the American servicemen featured in Fred Harvey ads. In going off to war, he had truly entered the mainstream of American life, and eating at a Fred Harvey's for the first time was one of the rituals of that process.

The train finally reached the Los Angeles Union Terminal, a station as beautiful then as it is today. Paul marveled at its cathedral ceiling and marble floors, and still thinks of it as the "crown jewel" of train stations. He and fellow Marines switched trains to San Diego for the short ride south. All around him, he recalled, people were in uniform. "The whole world seemed to be in uniform or en route to a training station," he says. It was an impressive first week as an active Marine. Others were less enamored by their experiences. The southbound train for San Diego carried draftees and newly enlisted men from all the military branches, and Paul learned another lesson about being in the service. Men grumbled for all sorts of reasons: not enough sleep, no privacy, hard training, constant regimentation. The Marines were no different in this respect from the other services, or indeed from soldiers in Napoleon's day or even Julius Caesar's. "You always had a few," he says, "who were reluctant to do what they were doing."[21]

Paul had joined the Marines, at least partly, for adventure. Once he arrived in San Diego, he discovered that adventure would have to wait. First he had to be processed into his new organization. The Marines treated the new arrivals "like dogs," he says. Recruits got their first Marine Corps meal, then they received medical checkups and inoculations, and then their dog tags, identification cards, service record books, and service number. The shot was an ordeal. "They made sure your arms were sore," is how Paul remembers it. Then came the haircuts, a key marker of military life. It served two purposes, the first of which was physical: with new recruits drawn from all over the country living in close quarters, it was critical to reduce the chances of disease or infestations, such as head lice. But the purpose of the "induction haircut" ran deeper, into the realm of the psychological. It stripped recruits of their individuality and promoted a "team" mentality. The individual had to take a backseat to the collective whole. You were not a "person" anymore, at least not primarily, and you were no longer living at home. You were a Marine and had crossed over into a completely new world. Only then, as part of the team, then did you receive your uniform, your gear, and your rifle.

Paul's first night in the barracks has stayed with him. "It was flimsy and badly ventilated," he remembers, but that was not surprising. What did surprise him was the sound. On that first night as a Marine, Paul could hear clearly men crying in their bunks. "I could hear sniffling going on. I wondered what was wrong with them. They fed us well; what were they crying about? Some were twenty-five-year-old married men. The Marines were slow to draft. I thought, my God, this improved my standard of living. Fifty dollars a month, a roof over my head, and three meals a day."

Paul's incredulity makes a certain sense when we think about his origins. His only point of reference for "standard of living" was growing up poor in rural Wisconsin. Seen through that lens, his new situation in life might have seemed a bit like paradise. After years of hard work and want, someone was suddenly feeding and housing him, a new world of "three hots and a cot," as Paul likes to put it.

Well, not quite paradise, perhaps. What he discovered—quickly— about Marine life was how similar it was to life on the farm. Each day was hard. No one cared whether you "did your best." No one got an award for trying or a participation medal. The Marines cared about completing the mission. On the farm, you either fed the hogs or you did not, Paul says. You watered the garden, or you did not. In the Marines, you had a mission, and you and your unit were "tasked" with fulfilling it. "If you don't, no one cares about your best. Complete your assignment, fulfill your mission."

In fact, growing up on the farm had prepared Paul perfectly for his Marine duties. Self-confidence, self-reliance, initiative, all set within a context of obedience to authority: these have been the ingredients for success in the military life for a long time. Just as on the farm, there were no specialists in the Marines. Farmers had to find their own solutions to problems and exercise their independent initiative, and so did the Marines. "The farm gave you a sense of resourcefulness," Paul says. "It adds to your confidence. Whatever job they gave me, I felt I could do it."

In other ways, Marine life was vastly different from what he had known. Paul had lived a homogeneous life up to now, growing up among people very similar to him in taste, temperament, and outlook. The population of Buffalo and Pepin Counties was made up largely of Northern European and Scandinavian stock. The Marines, on the other hand, included people from all over the United States, and for the first time, Paul met people vastly different from himself, from the four corners of a country whose size he was only just beginning to grasp. Among his fellow Marines, Paul discovered a particular liking for Texans. "They were always confident and optimistic. They were raised in a state with optimistic people." It was one of many data points he filed away for use later in life.

The diversity of his new peer group also made him realize the benefits of his own upbringing. In particular, he had a new appreciation for the Wisconsin public school system, which, in his view, had prepared him well. The more he met soldiers from elsewhere, the more he came to realize how his broad public school education in Wisconsin had prepared him for this new life. "I had been in a pretty tightly controlled school system," he says. "We had good teachers. It fed your confidence. For some of those guys coming out of the hills of Kentucky or from the Bronx, they didn't seem to be well educated." He knew now how much he owed to the teachers who "were tough on me."

At least a dozen Marines from his platoon were of Mexican descent, recruits from along the Texas border, and, because of educational deficiencies due to poor schooling, Paul says they struggled to keep up in training. "These poor guys, I felt sorry for them. They weren't as well educated as some of us were. I don't know what happened to them. I did not see them in skilled jobs." In fact, Marines who struggled to read and write were at a real disadvantage in a profession where a modicum of reading skill was absolutely necessary, if only to understand the regulations and service manuals that are so much a part of modern military life.

Farm life paid off in one other area of his new profession: firearms. His experience with hunting carried over into the marksmanship test, where he scored just two points below expert. It helped that he had once owned a BB gun and then, as soon as he was old enough to hold one, a .22-caliber rifle. He had honed his shooting by targeting rabbits and squirrels. "Shooting small game can improve your marksmanship," he says. "City boys didn't know anything about a rifle." If he thought he was going to get a pat on the back for his performance, however, he was dead wrong. He received no praise for falling just short of "expert," but instead had to endure a dressing down from the drill instructor, who told him off. "Damn it!" the Marine yelled. "All you needed was two more points!" Paul still remembers him to this day: "Corporal Sberna. He wanted to turn out good platoons and qualifying as an 'expert' fed his record."

The first portion of Paul's basic training in San Diego concentrated on getting him in good physical shape, and the schedule was just this side of murderous. The seven weeks included four types of training:

Weapons: 151 hours (46%)
Physical: 24 hours (8%)
Garrison: 93 hours (29%)
Field: 54 hours (15%)

It added up to a grand total of 322 hours. Note the weight assigned to weapons training. No matter what a Marine did (or does today), he is expected to be a rifleman.[22]

Paul's memories center on the physical side. He and his fellow "boots" endured endless hours of hiking and physical training at all times of the day and night, aiming to get the recruit used to a variety of environmental conditions. "We did calisthenics, marched here, marched there." Again, a farm kid like Paul probably endured the rigors more easily than a boy from the city. After eleven weeks of basic, he received orders to report for an aptitude test in "aviation, radio, and radar," three subjects about which he knew next to nothing. Paul protested, a bit naively. He didn't even have a radio in his house growing up. "They looked at me like I was hard of hearing," Paul recalls. He had learned a second lesson of Marine life: you follow your orders. Your desires didn't matter to the Marines.

He took the test, and although the corps never deigned to tell him his score, he must have done well. A few days later, the Marines shipped him across the country, once again by train, once again three Marines seated abreast in each seat, this time for five days, from San Diego to Jacksonville, Florida. On this trip he says he saw what he called the "back door of the South." As in his previous trip to the West, he noted once again the beauty and the sheer size of the country: "I saw some beautiful country for a kid who loved geography," he recalled. Those days when he had been a boy in Buffalo County, listening to the whistle of the distant Chicago-Northwestern line, now seemed increasingly distant, as if they belonged to a different lifetime.

Jacksonville

Arriving in Jacksonville, with its beautiful vistas of the Atlantic Ocean, Paul soon discovered that he had no time for the beach or creature comforts. Classes in his new field of radio and radar were six days a week, 6 a.m. to 6 p.m., with half days on Saturday. He got every fourth Saturday and Sunday off. "Otherwise, it was school, school, school," he says. "You talk about concentrated." The winter in Jacksonville that year was unseasonably cold. The prefabricated barracks were unheated, and Paul remembers sleeping while snuggled in his Marine heavy-duty overcoat under the thin blankets.

Beyond learning how to operate the radio, Paul spent additional months in Jacksonville training as an aerial gunner. Just as becoming a Marine gave him his first cross-country railroad trips, it now hurled him aloft for the first time. He was 1,500 miles from the Buffalo County farm, where he had paused in his chores to watch aircraft soaring overhead. Now, he was in the air and folks on the ground watched his plane, a massive amphibious Consolidated PBY Catalina "flying boat." The journey was not without its memorable moments. "The first time I got in unstable air and saw the wings flap a little, it terrified me," Paul recalls. "I didn't realize airplane wings could do that."

The Catalina was used for practice in a number of areas: anti-submarine patrol, gunnery, and radio. Paul remembers flying out into the Caribbean and to the Bahamas, and even to the southeastern side of Cuba at Guantanamo Bay. "That was an interesting experience: practicing radio, learning to use antennae, changing frequency." His radio, in this pre-transistor era, was the size of a large post office box. "To change frequency, you had to tune it in, tune it up. You learn how to do all that," he says. The plane could stay aloft for as long as fifteen hours. Training flights over the Atlantic served as scouting missions for German submarines.

Jacksonville, at that time, he says, was "jammed" with soldiers, sailors and Marines, either training or waiting for assignment. Now eighteen, he was still three years shy of the legal age to drink. Sometimes he could get a beer at the PX, but the bars were overrun with servicemen, "fifty men to every woman," in Paul's recollection. He opted instead to stay closer to home at the Naval Air Station, reading whatever he could scrounge up. With no library to slake his thirst for literature, he would usually grab training manuals to pass the time. "I read almost anything you could find," he recalls. "I wanted to do well. I was a sergeant by the time I was done training. A private got $50 a month, I got $78. I had almost a thousand dollars saved before I got out."

World War II in 1943

Saving his money, reading technical and training manuals, looping lazily around Cuba in a big flying boat: Paul's war had, so far, revolved around everything but fighting. Yet the broader war was raging at the business end of the vast US military machine.

By the end of 1943, America had been at war for two full years.[23] To observers then and since, the Allies had turned the corner from the very real possibility of defeat to an increasing probability of ultimate victory. US and British forces had prevailed in North Africa against Axis forces on that continent, trapping an immense bag of enemy prisoners, hundreds of thousands of them, at Tunis. Soviet armies had dealt the Germans a series of crippling blows on the Eastern Front, trapping the German Sixth Army at Stalingrad and again taking another huge haul of prisoners.

Victory was in the air in the Pacific, as well. The fight on Guadalcanal, begun in August 1942, had finally ended in February 1943 in total victory for US forces. That same year had seen further fighting in the Solomon Islands and New Guinea, part of General Douglas MacArthur's brilliant plan for seizing the vast Japanese naval base at Rabaul, on the island of New Britain. After a series of well-planned landings brought US forces ever closer to Rabaul, the Japanese navy evacuated the base for the island of Chuuk (formerly known as Truk), almost eight hundred miles to the north. MacArthur's drive on Rabaul triumphed, in other words, without having to storm its primary objective—a great savings in American lives.[24]

Things were a great deal messier in the last great Pacific action of 1943, the US landing at Tarawa in the Gilbert Islands chain. Tarawa was a tiny Pacific atoll, far different from the vastness of New Guinea (the world's second largest island). The Japanese force was not deployed on Tarawa to "win." They intended to kill as many Americans as possible and then die. The Americans did not have a lot of choices, either. Attacking a tiny island leaves no room to juke or dance around. They had to attack Tarawa frontally, and a frontal assault, even if it works, is guaranteed to be bloody.

The American assault, Operation Galvanic, opened up early in the morning of November 20, 1943, with a heavy air raid, followed by a sustained, three-hour naval bombardment. It did terrific damage, smashing the Japanese communications net, but the Japanese defenders were sitting in deep bunkers, and many survived to man the guns just as the first Marines hit the north shore of the atoll.

For the attackers, the wheels came off early. The main problem was the coral reef around Tarawa. The amphibious craft that carried the Marines ashore—"Higgins boats," they're called—draft four feet of water and need at least five feet for navigation. This day saw a neap tide, however, and the ocean stubbornly remained just three feet deep. The landing craft hung up on the coral, while Japanese gunfire pounded away. The Marines onboard hopped off, desperately trying to free their boats. When that failed, they decided to abandon their boats and wade ashore, over the coral reef and into the deeper water of the lagoon. They were eight hundred yards from shore, holding their rifles aloft, trudging forward in chest deep water. Enemy fire raked them the entire time, killing and maiming.[25]

Japanese fire was grim, merciless. At day's end the American force had barely gotten ashore. Of the 5,000 Marines who attempted to land, some 1,500 were killed or wounded. While the Marines went on to win this fight, the results were shocking, so shocking that the White House had to decide whether photos and video footage of the aftermath should be released to the public. Bodies floating in the water, bodies half-submerged, bodies contorted in impossible positions on the sand: the cost of victory on an obscure coral atoll.

Paul, and all those Marines training with him in Jacksonville, missed every one of these actions. He and his comrades in arms had no idea of the strategic situation in the Pacific as they prepared to deploy there. Mostly they trafficked in rumor and speculation, part of that famous network of military communication known as "scuttlebutt." One thing was certain: there seemed to be a lot of fight left in Japan's fanatical soldiers on those remote Pacific islands. And that was precisely where Paul Hilliard was headed next.

CHAPTER 3

"NOTHING BUT JUNGLE BELOW"

On the Great Ocean

Paul Hilliard's war began with another long journey, this one to San Diego by rail, then from San Diego by ship over the Pacific. It was late summer 1944, and he was now a Marine through and through. Trained as a radioman and gunner, he knew that he was most likely to be an airman. But where was he going? He had no idea. And on which type of aircraft? Once again, he came up empty. "In the Marine Corps, you expected to go to the Pacific," he says, but beyond that simple assumption lay a vast gray zone of expectations and rumor.

His first destination was Guadalcanal in the Solomon Islands, site of so much recent heroism on the part of the Marine Corps. The outbound voyage was Paul's real initiation into the theater of operations, and it certainly seemed to be an unusual place in which to wage a modern war. As he gazed on the vast expanse of the Pacific Ocean, it was as if Japan and America were struggling over the control of a great void. The ocean was endless, rolling by in a monotonous seascape, punctuated very rarely by tiny dots on the horizon that only gradually resolved into land.

Indeed, the Pacific is much more than a mere "ocean." It covers more than 30 percent of the surface of the globe. Sprawling over an area of 60 million square miles, its basin is larger than the landmass of all Earth's continents combined. Fighting a war in such an oversized environment meant big problems for everyone: the planners, the logisticians, the supply vessels, and, of course, the fighting men at the sharp end.[1] Since most of the islands in and around the Pacific were underdeveloped economically, both Japan and the United States had to transport everything they needed—every single bean and grain of rice, every single bomb and rifle, and, of course, every single gallon of fuel—from their home territories thousands of miles away to the forward combat zones. In the end, the side that performed this difficult trick more successfully and consistently, the one that managed to conquer these vast distances, would be the victor in the Pacific War.

And now Paul was in the middle of the void. He had to hand it to the Marines: they certainly were showing him the world. He had criss-crossed the country twice at their expense, from Chicago to San Diego and then back again to Jacksonville, and now they were sending him across the deep waters to follow in the footsteps of Magellan. Paul would later say that the long, practically eventless voyage made little impression on him, but that's only half-true. Once again, just as the war was broadening America's horizons, it was doing the same to the small-town boy from Wisconsin, breaking old patterns of observation and thought and forging a new global outlook.

The summer voyage took more than two weeks. Time weighed heavily as Paul and his fellow Marines spent the days watching the ship's bow slice through the rolling waves. They spent virtually the entire time on deck since the heat below was simply oppressive. Night brought no relief, just more sweltering temperatures and fetid humidity, and the entire complement bedded down on any surface they could find. It is a truism of military life that officers should keep the enlisted men busy at all times, even if it's only painting or repainting a rock, but there were plenty of idle hours on this outbound ship.

Paul does not recall writing home much on the trip, and in fact he was an infrequent letter writer for most of the war. He disliked wasting time and saw no reason to narrate the humdrum of his everyday life in the Pacific. If places and events did not seem remarkable, even in the most exotic locale, he didn't write much about them. He did write occasionally to his mother, but hardly anything beyond that. Hearing him speak of his time overseas and comparing it to the accounts of other veterans, Paul seemed to suffer less from loneliness than many of his comrades. Perhaps it was because of his maturity and the adult responsibilities he'd been carrying for some time now. Perhaps it was the considerable amount of independence and distance from his family he had already carved out back home. Writing is not only a personal act, it must be directed at someone, and there really was no "someone" in Paul's life at that time. In that sense, he made a perfect soldier for a modern expeditionary force.

It was different with family men. "Guys who were married wrote every day," he says. "I wasn't impressed enough with the events of the day to write." His reticence remained in place until he started corresponding with a girl whom he had met in Florida at a USO dance just before he shipped overseas. Her name was Sally Meagher, a USO girl who volunteered to dance with the soldiers. Paul stayed in touch with her throughout the war, and the two would see each other again when the war was over.

A last reason Paul didn't write is how little he was allowed to say. Neither the Marines, nor any other American in uniform, were allowed to divulge their whereabouts. Americans of all ages who were alive during World War II still remember the adage, "Loose lips sink ships," and while it's hard to imagine enemy agents poring through every letter home from an American fighting man without the use of a supercomputer, it is true that bits and pieces of precious intelligence could find their way into the wrong hands. Married couples often worked out a kind of code to evade the military censors. A soldier might write home and say something like, "They're treating me well here," which was actually the code he had agreed upon with his wife to tell her he was in the Pacific theater. One married Marine serving in the Pacific, Lt. Edward L. Newton, devised a simple way to keep his wife informed about where he was located. Before he deployed, Newton sat down with his wife, Helen, and placed two identical maps on the table. He then instructed her to place any letter she received from him on her map. He would stick pin holes in the letter that would match up to both maps letting her know where he was. But no method, no matter how ingenious, could convey much information. The real reason for a soldier to write home wasn't to relate the story of his day anyway; rather, it was to let his loved ones know he was still alive.

Even on the best of days, the news from the Pacific was spotty. Most Marines were stationed on far-flung islands or fighting deep inside steaming jungles or on jagged coral atolls, and regular mail service was a dream. The Marines themselves did not often know where they were. Paul was somewhat familiar with the geography of the region, more so than many Americans, who were far less aware of the expansive Pacific, with its myriad islands and tongue-twisting place names, than the continent of Europe. For most

Americans, Paul says, much of the Pacific was "too remote to be of much interest," and those who fought the war there labored in relative anonymity.

Yet that was changing during the conflict. Like Paul, most Americans had now at least heard the names Wake Island, Midway, or Guadalcanal. Even for Paul, however, an island like Bougainville in the northern Solomons was an unknown commodity. As for Buna, Tsli Tsli, Vella Lavella, Choiseul, or Pavuvu, the vast majority of the country, armed services and civilians alike, probably couldn't find them with the help of a map. Indeed, officers had a standard response when newly arrived Marines wanted to know just where in creation they were: "You're a thousand miles from where you've ever been, and a thousand miles from where you're going." That was all a Marine needed to know, and all the questions in the world wouldn't help.

Lack of knowledge and interest in the Pacific was reflected in US news coverage at the time. Paul suggests that it ran about 80 percent to 20 percent in favor of the European theater versus the Pacific theater. Americans were focused on war news from places they knew, not those they didn't and would likely never see. More Americans focused on Hitler than they did on Japanese Prime Minister Hideki Tojo. "They considered Hitler and his army more dangerous than the Japanese." And while American boys were dying on obscure beaches of the South Pacific, troops in the European theater were liberating the great cities of western Europe, like Rome, Paris, and Marseille.[2]

Consider, for a moment, the month of June 1944, while Paul was at the end of his stateside service and about to deploy overseas. By now, American military potential was unfolding in full measure. On June 6, US forces, in concert with our British and Canadian allies, launched the greatest amphibious invasion of all time—Operation Overlord, the long-awaited landing in western Europe.[3] The Allies deployed overwhelming combat power on that morning: almost 7,000 vessels, including 1,213 combat ships; more than 8,000 operational aircraft, including almost 3,500 heavy bombers; and they landed 156,115 men on the coast of Normandy on that first day alone. Within five days, they had brought ashore 325,000 men 54,000 vehicles and more than 104,000 tons of supplies. Within a week they were building artificial harbors (Mulberries) to supply this vast host, and there were even plans to lay a pipeline under the ocean (PLUTO) to bring them fuel from Great Britain. In the course of this operation, the Allies seemed to have entered another realm, bending time and space to their will in their drive to victory over Nazi Germany.

Even today, almost eighty years after the event, virtually every American knows something about that story. It's one of the most famous events of the war, known universally as "D-Day." The landing at the central beach, code-named "Omaha," has gained immortal status for its example of Allied heroism under fire. Even if you're not an avid historian or reader, chances are you've seen Steven Spielberg's film *Saving Private Ryan*, which, in its first twenty minutes, recreates the Omaha landing in shocking detail.[4]

But there is another wartime event that happened at almost the same historic moment as D-Day that very few Americans know about today. About a week after the Normandy landing, US forces launched an invasion of the Mariana Islands chain in the Pacific, an operation that in many ways equaled the size and scope of the D-Day landing, and in some ways even surpassed it. Operation Forager, too, involved a vast flotilla: the eight hundred ships of Admiral Raymond Spruance's Fifth Fleet, escorted by Task Force (TF, or "Taffy") 58, a sleek but muscular force of twelve fast aircraft carriers flying around eight hundred aircraft and accompanied by eight battleships and eighty other warships. The force carried 80,000 Marines and nearly 50,000 Army soldiers for the invasion of the Marianas, while Taffy 58 served as the strike force that would destroy the Japanese Combined Fleet if it tried to contest the US drive into the Marianas chain. Forager wasn't just a one-hit operation. Three separate islands were on the target list: Saipan, Guam, and Tinian.[5]

In many ways, Forager rivaled the Normandy operation. Naval historian Victor P. O'Hara put it this way:

Normandy was roughly a hundred miles from Portsmouth. The infrastructure of England was completely at the disposal of the Allies. Since a cross-Channel operation had been on the books as a major invasion since April 1942, the Allies literally had years to build the airfields, ports, roads, and support apparatus required.

The situation for Forager was the polar opposite. Saipan was 1,017 miles from Eniwetok, the nearest Allied anchorage, and

3,500 miles from Pearl Harbor, the closest major base. The landing force had to bring everything needed because there was no
quick resupply. There were no nearby bases for air support. The
wounded had to be treated on-site.

"In the event of disaster," O'Hara notes, there was no place to retreat.[6]

In a month of fighting on Saipan, US forces fought their way across
the island. The battle was a hard one, but superior US firepower was the
difference, driving back the Japanese defenders in a grinding and bloody
series of assaults.[7] The cost was enormous: some 16,525 US casualties
in all, including 3,426 killed in action. And in a grisly coda, Japanese
civilians on the island committed suicide *en masse*, leaping off the crags
at Marpi Point on the northern tip of the island, rather than surrender to
the Americans.

The conquest of Saipan (and later Guam and Tinian) was one of
the critical battles of the Pacific War. Once the Marianas were secure,
the United States could now begin the forward staging of its new heavy
bomber, the B-29 Superfortress. Possessing a range of more than five
thousand miles, a B-29 flying from Tinian could hit Japan and make it
back safely to base.[8] With these futuristic aircraft flying from their bases
in the Marianas, the systematic destruction of Japanese cities now began,
culminating in the great incendiary raid over Tokyo in March 1945 and,
of course, the twin atomic bombings of Hiroshima and Nagasaki that
ended the war in August.

As a Pacific veteran, Paul often notes that US forces fought two great
battles simultaneously in 1944. One, the D-Day landing, went on to become a legend, and the other, on Saipan, has disappeared down a version
of George Orwell's "memory hole," barely making a dent in the American
popular imagination. He thinks he knows why: "Normandy was about
the freedom of a continent." Saipan, by comparison, helped to liberate
a remote archipelago that Americans had never heard of at the time and
rarely think about today.

Keith Wheeler, a World War II correspondent for the Chicago *Times*
and author of the memoir *The Pacific Is My Beat*, one of the best journalistic accounts of the war against Japan, criticized the scant news coverage
of the American victory in the Marianas, and the Pacific War generally.[9]

Pacific reportage always seemed to lag far behind that of the other fronts, he felt: "My accusation, I admit, is based upon fragmentary evidence—upon the six clippings which I received yesterday and upon a few recent Honolulu and West Coast papers which have drifted in here. I know this story broke at a time when it had to compete with several other big stories: the investment of Cherbourg, the flight of B-29s to Japan, the Republican National Convention. The American press, with its stubborn refusal to recognize the Pacific, played it for a very bad fourth." Coverage of the Pacific, Wheeler wrote, was "one of the most disgraceful flubs in the history of American journalism."[10]

Paul didn't know any of these details: the strategic situation, the journalistic difficulties, or even the range of the B-29. He was in the midst of a months-long stay in the Solomon Islands, training for an as yet undefined mission. That was how World War II went for the enlisted ranks, particularly in the Pacific. Paul and his fellow Marines were kept in the dark about their assignments or the progress of the war. He didn't understand the reason for the mysterious secrecy at the time, but he does today. First, his immediate superiors were often just as much in the dark as he was. They didn't know which assignments the Marines were about to draw or where, specifically, they would all be assigned after the Solomons. Second, the military was tight-lipped with its enlisted ranks so that, if they were captured, they would not have much information to divulge to the enemy.

All a US prisoner of war was supposed to offer the enemy in case of capture was his name, rank, and serial number. The less American captives knew, the better. Paul and his fellow Marines often joked that they could tell the enemy "little more than their name, rank, or serial number, and what they had for dinner, because that's all they knew!" He adds, "While serving in the Philippines, we knew little or nothing about either strategic plans or tactical operations. We only knew about the day's assignment and very little about that. What I say here about events is based primarily on reading history." Paul and the other Marines often joked about their "Columbus missions": "We didn't know where were going when we took off, we didn't know when we arrived at our destination, but we made as big as mess as possible and left our calling card. When we returned, we didn't know where we'd been, and we did it all at government expense."

And so it was with Paul's time on the legendary island of Guadalcanal. While he faced little physical danger there, and never fired a shot, he could point to being "wounded" very early during his stay. The incident has stayed with him, and he can still recall the details. Shortly after his arrival on the island, he saw his first coconut, and a native explained to him how to get the husk off and drink the sweet milk. Paul tried to open the hard shell himself using his Marine-issued combat weapon, a Ka-Bar knife, and promptly slashed his finger. It was a painful and lasting lesson about handling the local fruit. It might also have served as a reminder of just how far he was from home.

The rest of his time in the Solomons consisted of mundane tasks and training on the island of Bougainville. The stitches in his finger healed enough to enable him to type reports. He was very grateful for learning how to type while he was a student back at Durand High School. "I found out there that sometimes you do things, unthinking things, that help you later," he says. He had taken a semester of typing at Durand to avoid a chemistry lab.

"Marines did not like enlisted men sitting around," Paul observes of those days. "They had to find work for you. Go dig a ditch or haul sand to the beach; do something." Paul's higher-ups asked if anybody could type. He could, he raised his hand, and he got a new assignment: the teletype. "I got out of digging and hauling. I handled messages coming in and going out," he says. From that point on, his fellow Marines nicknamed him "Scoop."

Most of his combat training on Bougainville focused on split-second recognition of ships and aircraft, both Japanese and American, a crucial skill in the long-distance, low-visibility Pacific War. "We'd turn out the lights to get tested. You'd get one-tenth of a second [to recognize the ship or aircraft]. We did no flying. We did a little shooting on the ground. But we had very little specific training." That split-second testing reminded him of the math flash card contests he had mastered in his one-room schoolhouse back in Maxville Bluff.

Handling messages. Looking at flash cards of aircraft silhouettes. Convalescing from an attack by an aggressive coconut. Wondering about the future and where it would take him. There is an old saying, perhaps as old as warfare itself, that war is months of boredom, punctuated by moments of sheer terror. Paul was drinking deeply of the former, but if he could only peer a small way into the future, he would have known that he was about to get all the wartime action a young man could handle, on the sprawling Pacific island chain known as the Philippines.

Dauntless on Luzon

The Philippines are gigantic in every way.[11] Consisting of more than 7,500 islands, the country contains just 120,000 square miles of actual landmass. In terms of overall size, however, the archipelago sprawls some 1,150 miles from north to south and some 700 miles wide from east to west—thus covering more than eight hundred thousand square miles in all. The islands are strategically located, sitting astride the trade routes from the Pacific to the rest of Asia, and would-be conquerors have long seen them as a desirable asset. The Spaniards had first colonized the islands, one of the dividends of Magellan's voyage of circumnavigation; they had later fallen into American hands after the Spanish-American War in 1898, although the United States had to fight a bloody counterinsurgency war to secure them.

Most recently, the Japanese had conquered them in their wildly successful opening campaign of World War II, in the process of which they smashed an outclassed and under-equipped American force under General Douglas MacArthur, then badly maltreated the prisoners they took. It still stands as one of the most humiliating defeats in US military history. For all these reasons—strategy, vengeance for the Death March, MacArthur's wounded pride—reconquest of the Philippines stood high on the list of US wartime priorities.

That third factor, perhaps, should be listed first. Every American who knows anything about World War II knows of MacArthur's stirring promise as he left the islands. "I shall return," he had declared, apparently oblivious to the fact that even the highest-ranking general is not the final arbiter of wartime policy and decisions. The president of the United States is—it was up to Roosevelt whether MacArthur "returned" to the Philippines, but MacArthur's promise had effectively tied the president's hands. It was neither the first nor the last time that this particular general would challenge civilian authority.

Those three little words had also determined the near-term future of young Paul Hilliard. In March 1944, the Joint Chiefs of Staff ordered

MacArthur to draw up plans for the invasion of Mindanao, the southernmost big island in the Philippines. Mindanao was the safe play, an island big enough to represent a major foothold, but remote enough from the archipelago's center of gravity that the Japanese wouldn't deploy their main force there. MacArthur, characteristically, had a bigger and much riskier target in mind, however: the principal island of Luzon and the capital, Manila. That was what he meant by "return"—to the seat of power in the Philippines. In September, after air raids by fast carriers of the US Third Fleet (Admiral William F. "Bull" Halsey) against the central island of Leyte revealed the weakness of Japanese defenses there, the Joint Chiefs changed course: MacArthur now received orders to land on Leyte—a medium-risk, medium-gain option. To take advantage of Japanese unreadiness, the operation, originally slated for December, was advanced to October.

Rescheduling an operation this size inevitably leads to scrambling, and in MacArthur's case, it had to do with his air support. The usual solution for an island campaign, carrier-based aircraft, wouldn't work here. The Philippines campaign was going to be too large, and take too long, to keep aircraft carriers on permanent station where they would be sitting ducks for Japan's intensifying *kamikaze* effort. Squadrons from the Army Air Forces were available, but were going to need augmentation, given the scope of the campaign. The improvised solution was to employ land-based Marine aviation, battle-hardened units that had been in almost constant action for twenty-two months. Marine aviators, about five hundred pilots and gunners in all, would therefore fly in the Philippines campaign in the "close support" role for Army troops on the ground.

On October 20, 1944, elements of the US Sixth Army, commanded by General Walter Krueger, landed on Leyte.[12] MacArthur followed soon afterward, wading ashore and declaring that he had, indeed, kept his promise and "returned." The landings were without incident; Japanese strategy by this point in the war was not to contest the water's edge, but to lure US forces into the interior and into a killing zone of hidden Japanese emplacements on jagged outcroppings and ridges or in deep ravines and caves. For the next two months, US forces—Marines and Army units alike—ground forward against heavy Japanese opposition. Losses were heavy on both sides, but superior American logistics and massive firepower, both on the ground and in the air, proved to be the difference. US forces had become highly efficient killers in the course of this war, and the totals for "killed in action" by the end of the battle for Leyte in December 1944 show it: about 3,500 Americans, and nearly eighty thousand Japanese.

And now, finally, the moment had finally come. MacArthur's promise to return to the Philippines was about to intersect with the timeline of a kid from small-town Wisconsin. The general's next target was the great island of Luzon, and on January 9, 1945, the Sixth Army under General Krueger landed at Lingayen Gulf, high up on the northwestern coast. The landing took the Japanese by surprise, since they had not expected MacArthur to strike this far north—MacArthur had a real eye for these operational possibilities. As they had on Leyte, the Japanese withdrew in front of the American advance, scattering into the interior. But even in flight, the enemy still had formidable forces on the island. Luzon is huge, and although the Americans quickly gained the upper hand and held on to the initiative, progress was slow and casualties high. Indeed, US forces would be in action on Luzon until the very end of the war in August 1945.

And Paul Hilliard would be in action virtually the whole time. Like MacArthur, he too undertook a long voyage to Luzon, some three thousand miles. The accommodations weren't quite up to the general's, however. Starting at Bougainville, Paul and his buddies shipped out to Milne Bay off New Guinea. The ship was a converted Australian cattle boat, and the stench was terrific. "I could smell it immediately," the former farm boy says. "I stayed on deck all day." The ship was packed with men and equipment of every sort, and each marine only had a single canteen of water per day. In the blazing heat, other smells started taking over the ship, whose shower facilities were a "length of pipe with numerous holes drilled in it, secured to the rigging and connected to a fire hose pumping sea water." As young men often learn, the gap between their glorious expectation and the quotidian reality of war can be wide.

Paul spent Christmas Eve 1944 at Milne Bay and then departed for the next leg of his voyage, to the coral atoll of Ulithi, where he would spend New Year's Eve. Ulithi was so tiny it didn't even show up on some maps, but in the final year of World War II, it became for a brief time the most powerful naval base in the world: the staging area for the final assault on Japan, the invasion of what the Japanese call their Home Islands. It was an unforgettable sight to Paul. "The first time I saw that type of naval force—ships as far as the eye could see, was at Ulithi," he says.

From Ulithi, it was on to Luzon, and yet another adventure, this one less fragrant but far more dangerous. En route to the Philippines, their transport ran into the tail end of a monstrous typhoon in the South China Sea. They faced sheets of rain and gigantic waves. That, Paul says, was the "scariest part" of the voyage. "It is unforgettable to this day," he says. "You could see the stern of the ship disappear underwater. Ships were towing barges with bombs. You could see some ships' props come out of the water. Fortunately, I don't get seasick; I was one of the few." Paul quips that, in this "vomitorious" atmosphere, it was good to know "the difference between upwind and downwind." It was another miserable journey, once again emphasizing the difference between the glory and reality of war. "We must have been in (the vessel) for three or four weeks. We rarely took a shower. It wasn't a pleasant deal," he remembers. He also remembers a lilting female voice floating from a radio onboard. It was Tokyo Rose, the Japanese propagandist, assuring the men over the radio that "they would never get to the Philippines."

The convoy arrived at Luzon on January 23, 1945, coming ashore at Lingayen unopposed by the Japanese. Navy construction engineers were already on-site and had prepared an airfield between the villages of Dagupan and Mangaldan, putting marsh netting over a rice paddy. "We had taxiways and runways," Paul recalls. "It was dusty, or it was muddy, I remember that," he says today, before returning to the customary Marine Corps lament in the Pacific War: "We didn't know where we were." Now, finally, he got the answer to all his questions of the past eighteen months. Paul was going to war as a Marine aviator, flying as the radioman and gunner, the back seat, in other words, in a Douglas SBD Dauntless dive-bomber.

There was just one problem, however. He hadn't received much training in the plane; "none at all" might be a more accurate descriptor. In fact, Paul says he had *never* flown in a Douglas SBD dive-bomber before facing his trial by fire in the Philippines. He also remembers a fellow gunner griping about the lack of training for shooting the .30-caliber guns located in the rear of the plane. "The sergeant told him to learn on the way to the target," Paul says today.

While it sounds counterintuitive for a military force to throw unprepared men into combat, especially to have them serving a machine they have never met, the manpower demands of a global conflict like World War II all but guaranteed that such things happened. Marine aviator Colonel John Howard McEniry Jr. flew the Dauntless on Guadalcanal, and he, too, wrote that none of the pilots in his squadron had made a dive-bombing run before their first mission.[13] Some of them had only made a "checkout" flight. "None of us had ever fired the machine guns on the SBD. None of us had ever dropped a live bomb. None of us had ever flown the plane at night. None of us had ever flown the plane on instruments," McEniry said:

> As an example, one of the pilots, who will be nameless, came to me after we had been at Guadalcanal for some time and asked me to go over with him how to fire the two .50-caliber machine guns which were fired by the pilot forward through the propeller. He told me he had never been able to get his guns to fire and that ordnance had reported they were in working order each time. We went to one of the planes, and I asked him to show me what he did. He showed me how he charged both of the guns, turned on the gun switches, and then pulled the trigger, which was on the stick. That was all he knew. He did not understand that in order for the guns to fire it was necessary for the master arming switch to be turned on.

McEniry's evaluation of his squadron's training was critical, but fair: "We were far from well trained."[14]

Now, in the middle of the Pacific Ocean, a nineteen-year-old Marine boarded his SBD for the first time. This was the same plane that had turned the tide of the Pacific War at Midway, sinking four Japanese aircraft carriers in just over twenty-four hours, and it sank more aircraft carriers in the course of the war than any other plane in the American arsenal. By 1945, the Navy and Marines considered the Dauntless obsolete and were phasing it out in favor of a new model, the Curtiss SB2C Helldiver. In war, however, a vast gulf separates "obsolete" from "useless," and the Dauntless still had a role to play in the Philippines campaign. Even in its twilight, the Dauntless could still deliver the goods.

Paul and his fellow Marine aviators, seven squadrons totaling about 105 planes with two-man crews from Marine Aircraft Groups (MAG)

24 and 32, were pressed into action shortly after their arrival. As so often in war, they had no choice in the matter, and the schedule was tight. In this case, Mother Nature was in charge. The spring rains were going hit in April, and that would call a halt to operations. Landings and takeoffs would be nearly impossible. The time to attack the Japanese was now.

Paul's missions were all during daylight hours, never at night, so the pilot could acquire the target visually. Paul rode in the rear seat, facing the tail, and wearing a flight suit, goggles, helmet, and boots. Gloves were not part of the outfit, so his fingers could easily work all his devices: the radio and two machine guns. The seat was U-shaped and large enough to make room for his parachute, which he sat on during the flight. And to remind him of how potentially deadly his job was, the SBD was also equipped with a rubber life raft and a survival kit with minimal food just in case the plane went down over hostile land or water.

Paul looks back on his flying missions Luzon as a lesson in extremes. Sitting on the airstrip and waiting to takeoff was a time of oppressive tropical heat. Takeoff and ascent soon flew you into chilly air, and your body simply wasn't ready for the slap of it. The temperature dropped into the high fifties at 12,000–13,000 feet above sea level, and the open cockpit provided no relief. "You never stopped shivering," Paul recalls. The Dauntless conducted high-precision, high-risk attacks, plunging onto their target almost vertically. Several planes usually flew together in formation and then peeled off, seconds apart, to bomb. Diving from 13,000 to around 1,500 feet, the point at which the pilots delivered their bombs, brought quick relief from the cold. "I didn't mind the dive at all; you got down to where it was warmer."

Was there fear? Of course. "None of us had ever flown in a dive-bomber before," Paul says. "We were somewhat apprehensive." Perhaps the worst moments came while the planes were circling the target area. "That was the anticipation. You had no idea what was happening and when," he says. While the plane carried a crew of two, each man was alone, in a sense, focused on his own task and skills, and communication between the two took place only by intercom.

The most remarkable thing about his first flight, he remembers, was that they were in the dark. "We didn't know what we were doing." He recalls the strange feeling of getting into the back seat of the dive-bomber. "It was like being in a small tub. The leadership assumed that since you were assigned you must be trained," Paul says. Pausing, he adds, "They had high expectations." He also recalls a certain trepidation from those first missions. "You could look down there and see nothing but jungle and Japanese, and I didn't consider either one of them appealing."

Nonetheless, Paul soon came to love and appreciate the Dauntless. The plane had long range and good handling, was rugged, maneuverable, dependable, and strong enough to survive the "Gs" when it pulled out of the dive. Like all crew members, he wished it had a bit more speed and firepower, and airmen often joked that the SBD stood for "slow but deadly." (It didn't.) Like everything in Paul's life, however, he soon acclimated himself to the Dauntless. On his first mission, he spent a lot of time "fiddling with the guns"—he had only had a couple of hours' practice prior to his debut. But he soon got used to it all. He got used to facing backward, he got used to being confined in his space, the "tub," just large enough to accommodate his body and operate the .30-caliber guns. He got used to firing them, swinging them side to side using his whole body, rather than just his arms, since the twin guns had a 270-degree traverse. All in all, it wasn't much different from learning to use a shovel or pickax back on the farm.

If the Dauntless had one special problem area, it was making sure the gunner didn't shoot off the plane's wing or tail. This was the age before automated or smart weapons, and the possibility was real. Paul remembers crew chiefs at the airbase making sure to warn the crews in clear and profane language to "not return with a plane damaged by your own weapon." The highest level of risk came from firing the guns while the pilot made a sudden swooping maneuver. "If a pilot made a sudden move and you were firing, absolutely you might hit the plane," Paul says. "If you got carried away, you could shoot your tail," and that would mean lights out. "You tried to do things right," he says of his radioman/rear gunner experience. "You didn't want to be the only screwup in the deal." That "big, ugly master sergeant," the crew chief, always reminded them before they took off, "If any aviators return from their missions with holes made by anyone other than the Japanese, you boys are going to be on the flight line all night patching."

Success in battle always revolves around intelligence—making sure it's correct and having enough of it. Dive-bomber missions required two things: good intelligence plus visibility over the target. The two were an inconstant combination at best. Aviators usually got up early and ate early, he says. They remained on standby alert until called. Then the moment came, and they boarded a truck and drove out to their planes. "Sometimes they briefed us, sometimes not," Paul says. "We were airborne artillery for the Army. We would have three to fifteen airplanes and would have Army forward air observers [FAOs] on the ground." Success depended on a three-man team: the FAO identified targets and reported them to ground communications, who then relayed them to the flight leader. "They sent planes down, one by one, to bomb. The Army (or, in some cases, the Marine spotter) would observe with field glasses and tell the next guy where to bomb from there. We kept radio silence so we had no idea when or what we would bomb. We stayed off the transmitter. The conversation was with pilots, not the gunners."

The uncertainty level was always high. "I'm not sure sometimes we even knew what the mission was (at the outset)," he says. They were searching for the target. And not infrequently, nothing happened at all. If the terrain was too rough to circle the target, he says, the pilot would just get out of the area and return home.

If things went well, the mission was simple. The crew awaited instructions for attacking the target, flew toward it at a level speed of about 150 knots (173 miles per hour), bombed it, then returned to base. A dive from about 12,000 feet would take 25–30 seconds at roughly 250 knots (300 miles per hour), with the plane diving down at a hair-raising 70-degree angle. The dropping point was 1,500 feet, low enough for accuracy but just enough altitude to give the bombers sufficient time to pull safely out of their dives.

Even "safely" is a relative term, however. No one emerged from a dive unscathed. McEniry said it outright, perhaps the dirty little secret of the dive-bombing fraternity. At some point, everyone blacks out:

> On any run on any ship, everyone pulled between nine and twelve
> Gs and went into some stage of a blackout. This was long prior to the
> G-suit, which was designed to help prevent them. Blackouts come in
> stages. First you have a hard time seeing; then you cannot see at all.
> At this stage you usually released some pressure on the stick and your

sight returned shortly . . . Normally, when your sight returned, the nose of the aircraft was above the horizon and you then pushed the stick forward so as to go right down on the water."[15]

Caught between exhilaration and unconsciousness, those magical twenty-five seconds of dive were the payoff of the entire mission, the most exciting part of the flight, and the dive-bomber's entire *raison d'être*. Make no mistake: you had to have a strong stomach for these missions. Paul usually did. Only once did he make the mistake of drinking milk and eating two grapefruit before going up. He never did that again.

Outside of those magic seconds, your mind could wander. With the early morning starts and the long return flights home, the rear gunner could sometimes nod off to sleep. But pilots had a way to wake them, Paul remembers. "About halfway home, pilots would switch tanks and let the engine sputter. They knew damn well . . . that we would jump in the back seat. That would wake you up. You listen very carefully to the sound of the engine, especially over the jungle or open water." Indeed, the undercurrent of danger was never far away. Over the ocean, he says, he would imagine sharks circling below, looking for something to eat. And then the aircraft would cross the dense green jungles below—with all their attendant danger.

Looking back, Paul knows he was lucky in the Philippines. Consider what happened to Second Lieutenant Kenneth G. Pomasl, a classmate of Paul's brother Bill back in Durand. A Marine aviator in the Philippines, Ken failed to return from a mission on January 23, 1945, on the eastern Philippines island of Samar, just about the time Paul began flying over Luzon. Pomasl got separated from his fellow fliers due to bad weather and was flying on instruments. He lost radio contact and couldn't break out of the overcast. Running out of gas, he had to make a water landing, and came down tail first.

He exited on a wing, lowered himself into the water, and inflated his rubber raft. A friendly group of Filipinos paddled out in canoes to assist him, but Japanese soldiers spotted the group and opened fire. Although the bullets fell short, the frightened Filipinos swam away. Hours later, Pomasl abandoned his rubber raft and came ashore. He sheltered for two days before he met another group of friendly Filipinos again, who nursed and fed him a welcome meal of rice, boiled chicken, and bananas. They eventually arranged for him to meet a boat back to Leyte, where he flew back to the airstrip at Guiuan. Pomasl returned to his Marine comrades six days after his odyssey began.[16]

Paul never dove that deeply into the heart of darkness and generally takes a modest and matter-of-fact view of his missions. "It was long hours of boredom with a few seconds of excitement," he says. The dive-bomber crew "would circle and shiver for a couple of hours, the pilot would dive and deliver the bombs, and we'd strafe it and hose it down real good with those twin .30s and go home and get something to eat."

The Raid on Santo Tomas

If there was a moment in which Paul "made history" in the Philippines, it came early during his assignment on Luzon. On February 1, 1945, he participated in a close support mission for a column of the First Cavalry Division—the raid on Santo Tomas. The operation was, in words of one division historian, "part of a series of four rapid-fire prisoner of war liberation raids in the Philippines." They numbered four in all: Bilibid, Cabanatuan, Santo Tomas, and Los Baños, and all took place in a brief time span of one month, from late January to late February 1945.

MacArthur had ordered the cavalry to make a high-speed "dash" to Manila, about 110 miles away, to free 3,700 US civilians who had been interned by the Japanese and held for more than three years at a camp near Santo Tomas University.[17] By its very nature, a "raid" is a quick strike. The idea is to catch the enemy unawares and keep him on his back foot. Forces usually are a single column, moving light, and the niceties of the art of war—march security, firm lines of communication, and flank protection—are the first thing to go. So it was with the Santo Tomas raid. The commander of the First Cavalry Division, General Walter Mudge, had to move fast, nearly 100 miles from south of Lingayen to his objective near Manila; he had to face fierce Japanese resistance the entire way; and he had open flanks on both sides. He had to improvise.

The solution was to rely on Marine aviation. By now, the SBD squadrons had earned quite a reputation for efficiency, with the press dubbing them the "Diving Devil Dogs of Luzon," an homage linking these Marines to their fierce predecessors at Belleau Wood in World War I.[18] Marine

Corps historian Robert Sherrod argues that since Marine aviators had trained originally as riflemen—as all Marines do—they had a more intuitive understanding for the complexities of air-ground coordination than Army pilots. Marine aviators were more likely to accept a more limited role, not as soaring flyboys on independent sorties, but as "an additional weapon to be employed at the discretion of the ground commander": "The concession was not as difficult for Marine aviators to make as Army and Navy officers had found it. Before the war nearly all Marine aviators had served as company officers. The senior fliers knew the problems of the men on foot, and they were therefore more likely to have a sympathetic understanding of the man who had to assault a pillbox or a hillside cave."[19]

They were, Sherrod says, "Marines first, aviators second," and that was the lodestar that helped them transition so smoothly into their role of ground support for the Army. It was, he notes, "of secondary importance that the troops in the Philippines happened to be soldiers rather than Marines."

A single example will suffice. While Army fliers balked at answering to forward spotters on the ground, the Marines embraced them, stationing Air Liaison Parties (ALPs) on the ground. They communicated directly with bombers in the air to guide into precise attacks on enemy positions. The opposite was true, as well. Marine aviators flying ahead of ground forces could radio precise information back to the ALPs. It was a classic informational feedback loop.

While a column of the First Cavalry under Brigadier General William C. Chase drove for Manila, at least nine SBDs were in the air at all times, looking for signs of Japanese positions, while nine more were on alert. The planes flew thirty miles ahead or echeloned twenty miles behind the left flank. When needed, the dive-bombers immediately destroyed the enemy by bombing or strafing, but often it only took a "dummy run" to scatter the Japanese, who by now had developed a healthy a fear of the "little planes that dive."[20]

At 4:30 a.m. on February 3, the first soldiers of Chase's column made the last push for Manila, covered by Marine SBDs. According to the Marine battle record: "Just after sunset, the soldiers reached Santo Tomas University and liberated more than 4,000 prisoners who had been there for more than two years." The "dash" had lasted just sixty-six hours, slashing its way through Japanese opposition without cease. General Mudge wrote its success "depended solely on the Marines to protect my left flank against possible Japanese counterattacks": "The job that they turned in speaks for itself. I can say without reservation that the Marine dive bombers are one of the most flexible outfits that I have seen in this war. They will try anything once, and from my experience with them, I have found out that anything they try usually pans out in their favor."[21]

The Marine Corps has many great slogans. *Semper Fideles*, sometimes shortened to "Semper Fi" is the exemplar, but there have been others, such as "First to Fight," "A Few Good Men," and, perhaps best of all, Captain Lloyd W. Williams's retort in World War I when a French commander advised him to retreat during the battle of Belleau Wood: "Retreat? Hell, we just got here!" Perhaps we ought to add a new slogan to this inspiring list, one that seems particularly on point for the life story of Paul Hilliard: "A Marine will try anything once."

As always in this war, Paul did not fully recognize his own squadron's participation in the action until official histories of the campaign were published well after the war. It was the same old thing in the Marines. The commander did not explain the broader context of the mission to the crewmen and never related details that the Dauntless crews did not need to know. "All they told us is 'you're going to be on patrol.' We did not know."

The raids on the Philippines saved nearly four thousand prisoners at Santo Tomas. Ever since the fall of the Philippines in early 1942, the Japanese abused their POWs and civilian internees alike, holding them in filth and squalor and barely feeding them. Now, as US troops began their rapid advance toward Manila, the Japanese were murdering their captives wholesale. Manila, once the "Pearl of the Orient," was now a desperate city. It wasn't only the captives who were short of food and supplies. So were the Japanese, whose supply lines back to their Home Islands had long been severed by US naval victories. Filipino guerrillas reported back to MacArthur about the depth of misery in the city's streets and the maltreatment the Japanese captors were inflicting upon civilians. Doctors at Manila's San Lazaro Hospital estimated five hundred civilians a day were succumbing to starvation in December 1944. Indeed, of the 90,000 Filipinos and Americans captured in 1942 when MacArthur evacuated

Corregidor and Bataan, only a third were still alive when the General returned to free them.

The raid on Santo Tomas, then, almost certainly saved these captives from being murdered. What happened next in Manila confirms that judgment. With their plan of conquest a failure and their Greater East Asia Co-Prosperity Sphere an illusion, Japanese soldiers holding the capital engaged in a month-long frenzy of destruction and violence, involving the slaughter of thousands of civilians, including women and children; the wanton rape of Filipino women; and the destruction of Filipino cultural treasures and iconic buildings in the central districts of the city. This savage activity continued over the month it took to secure Manila. Estimates suggest that as many as one hundred thousand civilians were killed.[22]

Paul may not have known exactly what he was doing in the Santo Tomas raids, but the evidence is clear: he was helping to save thousands of lives.

Missions on Mindanao

After the rescue, Paul continued to participate in missions around Clark Field, forty miles northwest of Manila, which was the major Japanese airbase on Luzon. He also took part in bombing raids near Manila, part of the US offensive against the remaining Japanese military in that city who were determined to lay waste to it. Targets in Manila were "very specific and we were focused on them," not on watching the overall battle or action unrelated to his mission. From 12,000–13,000 feet, he says, it was impossible to see well enough to comprehend what was happening on the ground. He still remembers how his vision and perspective were skewed for a few seconds by the speed and sharp angle of the aircraft as it entered and exited the dives. Paul is sure of one thing, however. There were civilian casualties in the bombing in Manila. "Manila was a city of half a million to a million people," he says. "It was difficult to use bombs or artillery without killing civilians."

With Manila secure by late March 1945, MacArthur devised a series of five operations (code-named Victor) against eight major islands in the southern Philippines. Strictly speaking, he had achieved everything he had set out to do in the islands through the operations on Leyte and Luzon. He had broken Japan's hold over the Philippines, and the action in the Pacific was about to shift to the north, toward the Home Islands themselves. This third phase, then, was more of a mopping-up than a true strategic thrust.

Nevertheless, it wasn't a cakewalk for any of the troops involved. Paul's next destination was Mindanao, the large island at the southern tip of the chain. After the US Forty-First Infantry division landed on Mindanao on March 10, 1945, a landing made immeasurably easier by fact that island was crawling with pro-American Filipino guerrillas, the Americans quickly built two airstrips: Moret Field at Zamboanga, on the island's narrow western peninsula, and Titcomb Field near Malabang to the east, with the two separated by a steep mountain range.

Paul flew from both. From Titcomb, he took part in a handful of missions against Japanese positions in central Mindanao and the large town and port of Davao. The Japanese were dug in deeply here, and "mopping them up" required some of the most sustained tactical bombing of the entire war. One aviator in Paul's Marine Air Group (MAG-24) called central Mindanao "the most heavily bombed area of any in the whole Philippine campaign." The defenders were "dug in underneath trees and in foxholes so well that we had to blow up the whole area before the Army could advance": "Our Marine observers, who were with the ground liaison party in this area, said the damage was terrible and almost indescribable. Flight after flight of planes bombed and strafed this small area for days. When we began it was a heavily wooded area and when we finished there wasn't . . . anything left but a few denuded trees."[23]

With fewer and fewer Japanese planes in the sky, American aviators—Paul's MAG and all the others—had a field day, demonstrating the kind of havoc you can wreak once you've achieved air superiority over your enemy. Paul could tell that the Japanese effort, both in the air and on land was slackening: "By early 1945, our Navy carrier pilots, and our Army fliers had decimated Japanese aircraft. They were so short of fuel they had many aircraft that couldn't get off the ground. We had very little air opposition. All they had was ground fire, which I don't think was either intense or accurate. A dive-bomber coming at you with a thousand pounds of bombs, if the enemy had any sense, they were looking for cover."

From Moret, he flew numerous missions to the Sulu Archipelago, southwest of Mindanao, and toward Borneo, including raids on the volcanic island of Jolo. These missions were flown over open water, a new and not completely comfortable experience for Paul. "I didn't like those, out of sight of land," he says. The island missions were "scary," flying over Japanese-held waters. "We were over the ocean in single-engine airplanes." Paul remembers listening intently to the sound of the engine during those flight, vigilant for the slightest sound of trouble. Years later, when Paul himself flew airplanes, he always stayed attuned to the sound of the engine. "If it wasn't right, I could tell," he says.

For Paul, the pace must have been hectic, but as always, the overall context was obscure. The purpose of the air attacks from Moret was to strangle Japanese supply lines and, in particular, to cut off the supply of oil and minerals from Southeast Asia to Japan. "I can read about it, and it makes good sense now," he says. "When you are there, you don't know anything except what you can see. You have rumors and your line of sight." The men talked, wondered, and pondered their role, but that was about it. "We always would compare notes in bad weather and between flights. There was a lot of time to talk about it, speculate, and exaggerate," he says.

He thinks, to this day, that he flew more than fifty missions, although the official Marine count credits him with only forty-five. Having lost his flight book after the war, he could not counter their claim. "The way they kept records, they had a blackboard. Some guy on duty would get the aircraft tail numbers. I thought I flew more than fifty missions. They said forty-five." Paul got a certain amount of satisfaction in 2007, when he was on a panel at the Nimitz Museum in Fredericksburg, Texas. Here he met a Marine who had been a pilot in VMSB-341. "He said we all flew at least fifty missions," says Paul.

Save for his unsuccessful attempt to cut open that island coconut back on Guadalcanal, Paul sustained no injuries while in the Pacific. If Paul had any close calls in the gunner's seat, he could not remember them. He and his fellow pilot would only casually look over their plane when they landed. "I don't know if you knew what your close calls were," he says. "When you got back to the base after four or five hours, you were in a hurry to get in the truck, get to the bathroom, and get something to drink. I never looked back to see if we were hit. If there was a big hole, I would have noticed it."

Still, Paul notes, there was no shortage of danger for aviators on Luzon, and not only in the air. Perhaps his nearest brush with death was March 2, 1945, when the Japanese bombed his airfield near Mangaldan. The night guards heard the roar of an engine and soon searchlight beams were cutting across the dark sky. It was a lone Japanese twin-engine bomber. Blaring sirens disrupted Paul's sleep and that of his fellow airmen. Antiaircraft guns blasted away, and the sleepy Marines poured out of their tents to watch.

Paul still remembers this attack well. The Japanese still held the island Formosa (now Taiwan) and occasionally sent bombers from there: "The Japanese bomber would come over at high altitude. We didn't have a lot of antiaircraft guns. The alarm would go off, and we'd run for a trench so we could watch the show. We could barely see them up there. One night, while all attention was at high altitude, they sent in some planes at low altitude for anti-personnel (attacks). We heard it; we didn't know what happened."

While American fliers on the ground watched the high-flying Japanese plane, two additional bombers roared in at three hundred feet and dropped five-hundred-pound bombs, killing four and wounding seventy-eight on the ground. When the sun rose, soldiers were assigned to clean up the mess and attend to the dead and wounded. Operations then continued as usual. Typically, Paul says, he and his fellow aviators did not know the outcome of the fighting, the progress of Allied objectives, or anything about loss of life. Troops on the ground were closer to information about casualties.

Paul's squadron, the "Torrid Turtles" of VMSB 341, suffered no fatalities: "So far as I know we didn't lose any aircraft in our fifteen-aircraft squadron. The Marines gave you no information about that. There was no way to know if any information was true or not. It wasn't like the infantry, where you were up close. Our air group lost some. If a dive-bomber didn't get back, you didn't know what happened unless it was in your squadron or the missing man was your tent mate."

"In combat, they don't want you to know. They only want you to know what you need to know," he says.

During down time, there were few things to do or read on Luzon or Mindanao. Sometimes, Paul says, someone would come get him to work in the communications tent because he could type. For "Scoop," those typing lessons back in Durand were still paying dividends. "The rest of the time, I'd BS with other gunners and exchange rumors."

Perhaps Paul's most interesting mission was one he undertook on his own initiative. He wanted to learn a little about the country where he saw his only combat duty, and with his area of Luzon finally secure, Paul decided to hitchhike from Lingayen to Manila. He didn't have to go very far before he saw the immense destruction wrought by the Japanese, Americans, and the general mayhem of war. Manila had been founded in 1571, but now seemed to be a ghost town, a haunted place of shadow and ruin.

Among the wreckage and debris, Paul spied a group of Navy men hard at work at the Manila docks. Paul stopped and watched them, suddenly realizing he was receiving an unexpected lesson about capitalism. These men were US Navy Seabees (from "Construction Battalion," or CB). He watched as they sifted through stacks of scrap metal they had collected, the leftovers from Japanese planes that had been recovered or shot down, then processed them in a makeshift machine shop. Looking around, Paul saw numerous trailers filled with more scrap metal. The Seabees, seasoned and capable men with their hands, were transforming these fragments into souvenirs for sale such as necklaces, watchbands, rings, and other items. Some of the objects, he says, were decorated with cat's eyes. Paul purchased a watch band made from scrap for 50 cents.

Looking back on that experience, he still laughs. The Seabees—"old guys, thirty-five and forty years old," he says—were "working with government equipment on government time and making money for themselves." They were doing a brisk business. His sardonic comment today: "Government hasn't changed a bit."

On the coast of Mindanao, on the Zamboanga peninsula's coast, Paul also remembers an interesting encounter with an Australian, forty-five years old, who lived on a coconut plantation and who served as a "coast watcher." There, he kept his eye out for the enemy and pointed out any viable Japanese targets to the Allies. Three SBDs, Paul's among them, landed on a dirt strip near the plantation as part of a reconnaissance mission. The Australian greeted the Marines, and they talked a bit.

The Aussie was married to a "White Russian," a woman who was politically opposed to the Soviet Revolution and the bloody communist dictatorship in her native country. She had been working near the Russian border but had fled from there into the interior of China. Her vision of the world situation was bleak. "She told her husband that when the war was over, we may have to fight these 'Russian bastards,'" Paul says. Unbeknownst to him at the time, he was getting a peek into the near future. "She was describing to her husband—and he was telling us about— what would become known as the Cold War."

Assessing Paul's War

During the campaign to liberate the Philippines, Paul Hilliard had done it all. He'd flown cover over ground troops, helped pave the way for the liberation of thousands of prisoners at Santo Tomas, and hitchhiked across the country on his own. He dove from the sky to bomb the enemy, and he burrowed into trenches at night to escape the same fate. He bombed Manila and Mindanao and soared over the open waters of the vast Pacific in missions over the Sulu Archipelago. He'd even dabbled in cloak-and-dagger toward the end, in that final mission to the Australian coast watcher. He'd also become a typical Marine: grousing, dreaming about food, and sharing the latest scuttlebutt with his buddies.

In some ways, we may question just how "typical" Paul was. After all, anyone versed in the history of World War II who hears the word "Dauntless" immediately thinks "aircraft carrier," either taking off from an American vessel or sinking four Japanese carriers at Midway. Paul did neither, nor did he even set foot on an aircraft carrier during the war. He flew exclusively from land, and he bombed targets on land. Likewise, the word "Marine" conjures up beach landings, a frontal storm against fiercely defended Japanese beaches. Paul was in the air. Finally, the Marines were "the few, the proud," a self-conscious military elite who were never reticent in bragging about their superiority. Paul spent his Marine career, however, almost exclusively in support of a sister service, grateful US Amy units engaged in combat on the ground. Seen in that light, Paul's combat career was something of an anomaly.

Then again, World War II was nothing if not the land of anomaly. More than 16 million American men and women put on their country's uniform in the course of the war, a stupendous number if we consider that the country's population at the time was only 130 million or so. Each one of them has a unique story to tell, a tale of an individual life intersecting with the impersonal forces of history. As Walt Whitman wrote in his magnificent collection of poems *Leaves of Grass,* the American experiment is about ordinary people, individuals who blend into a whole that is infinitely greater than the sum of its parts.[24] Each one of those 16 million changed the war, sometimes imperceptibly, often dramatically, and so did the other 114 million Americans supporting the war by their hard work on the home front.

Paul may have been a small cog in a big machine, as he likes to say, but like every one of his brothers and sisters in uniform, he also had "a ringside seat to history," courtesy of Uncle Sam. In that sense, Paul Hilliard's individual war was also America's war, in all its courage, fear, and glory.

CHAPTER 4
BACK HOME

The End

Paul Hilliard's combat career came to a permanent end in July 1945. It was, he says, "totally unexpected." He certainly hadn't felt the end coming. Quite the contrary. Sitting out there on Mindanao, he was certain he was headed for even heavier action. "We felt the big battle was coming up, the invasion of Japan," he recalls. "We anticipated that." What he and his comrades did not anticipate was that the Marines had decided to retire the Dauntless from service in mid-July.[1] While it had been a success in the recapture of the Philippines, the plane was feeling its age by now, particularly in terms of its speed, and the Marines had a replacement ready. The new Curtiss SBC2 Helldiver had a bigger power plant than Dauntless, was equipped with a four-bladed propeller to the Dauntless's three, and was faster by 20 knots. It was also more heavily armed, capable of firing rockets, and able to absorb much more punishment than the older plane.[2] After six months of intensive combat in the Philippines, the aviators of MAG-24 and MAG-32 were sent home for new aircraft and assignments.

No one was very broken up about it. A combat deployment was just that—a place to fight—and none of the Marines had gotten too attached to Zamboanga. Paul remembers that the departing Marines were told they had "only thirty minutes to pack" for their return to the United States. One of the gunners responded, "Just give me thirty seconds to find my toothbrush." They flew off Mindanao that day. "They put us on a C-54 transport. We flew non-stop to Guam, a long flight, jammed aboard that thing," he remembers. All flights in the Pacific seemed long, and this one was no exception: Guam was a full 1,500 miles away from Zamboanga.

Paul and his Marine buddies carved out an impressive combat record in the grueling Philippines campaign. During the Luzon phase of
the operations, MAG-24 and MAG-32 flew 8,842 combat missions in
support of US Army units and Filipino guerrillas. They dropped 19,167
bombs and fired 1.5 million rounds of .50-caliber and .30-caliber ammunition. On Mindanao, Marine aviators flew more than 20,000 sorties in
10,000 combat missions, dropped 4,800 tons of bombs and fired nearly
1,300 five-inch rockets.[3] They delivered a formidable array of firepower,
and certainly represented a complete overmatch to anything the Japanese
could muster. The American commander on Mindanao, General Robert
Eichelberger of the Eighth Army, put it best:

> The value of close support for ground troops as provided by
> these marine fliers cannot be measured in words and there is not
> enough that can be said of their aerial barrages that have cut a
> path for the infantry. From all quarters, commanders down to the
> men with the bayonets, I have heard nothing but high tribute.[4]

Indeed, Paul and his fellow Marine aviators could brag that they played a
crucial role in one of the largest campaigns in the history of the US Army.

In Guam, Paul spent two days awaiting transport back to the continental United States. Just as he had observed at Ulithi, he could see
that Guam, too, had become a staging base for the impending invasion
of Japan. "As far as the eye could see," he recalls, he saw ships, aircraft,
tanks, and artillery. It was a massive assemblage of war-making material,
mass-produced by the world's most efficient industrial economy, all intended for one final blow: the destruction of Imperial Japan.

Virtually everyone deployed in the Pacific was talking about the invasion, and so were a lot of guys still deployed in Europe. This one time,
the scuttlebutt was accurate. An operation to invade the Japanese Home
Islands would be big, big enough to require just about everyone, and
the planning was by now well-advanced. As far as Paul was concerned,
however, Japan would have to wait. He sailed home from Guam aboard
the USS *Bayfield*, which had been used as the communications command ship off the coast of Normandy on D-Day, then later was sent to
the Pacific. Once again, he was not traveling on a pleasure liner. "It was

a decent ship," recalls, "but with no bunks. No one that I knew of slept below deck."

Ten days later, the *Bayfield* arrived in San Francisco. A photo captured Paul's image as the ship sailed under the Golden Gate Bridge, which had opened eight years earlier in 1937. For most American military personnel in the Pacific, it was the last piece of the country they saw as they deployed and the first thing they saw upon return. Paul remembers the sudden rush of joy he felt as the ship sailed under the bridge. He was glad to be back home at last. After the Marines and sailors went ashore in San Francisco, most of them headed immediately for restaurants in search of a decent meal. Paul recalls eating five green salads. The waitress only charged him for one, he remembers, a partial repayment, perhaps, for his faithful service to the nation.

Yet San Francisco wasn't the final destination. Paul reboarded the ship and headed to San Diego. Here, the men lined up for new equipment and new identification cards. Paul was just a month past his twentieth birthday, but he did some quick mental arithmetic as he stood in line. Stepping up for his turn, he declared his birth date to be June 18, 1924, exactly one year earlier than his real birth date. His new identification card reflected this little fib. He was now officially twenty-one, and therefore old enough to buy a beer. Thus equipped, he was well prepared for thirty days of leave.

He was on his way home, on the train back to Wisconsin, when he learned the breaking news. The date was August 6, 1945. The United States had dropped a new type of bomb on the Japanese city of Hiroshima: an atomic bomb. The detonation had essentially vaporized the city, killing 50,000 people instantaneously, and then many more from radiation sickness in the months to follow. It was a monumental moment in world history, the opening of an entirely new era, but he could not fully appreciate the import at the time.[5] While at his mother's house in Kenosha, three days later, he learned that a second atomic bomb had been dropped, this one on Nagasaki, with the same results as Hiroshima. Six days later, on August 15, Emperor Hirohito delivered a radio address to the Japanese people, the first time most of them had ever heard his voice. He told them the bitter news. Japan had been the victim of a "new and most cruel bomb," and now had no choice but unconditional surrender. We must, he said, "endure the unendurable and suffer what is insufferable."[6] And just that quickly, World War II was over.

It is hard to recreate today the scale and intensity of US military plans for the invasion of Japan, and what a hard struggle American planners expected it to be. Operation Olympic, scheduled for November 1945, would see US Sixth Army, with Marine reinforcement, landing on the southern island of Kyushu and securing it in a campaign of several weeks. Five months later, in March 1946, Operation Coronet envisioned two more US Armies, the Eighth and the First, landing on the big island of Honshu and securing the Kanto Plain, which was the heart of Japan culturally and historically and contained the capital city of Tokyo.[7]

Both operations, known collectively as Operation Downfall, were expected to face fierce resistance. Given the fight the Japanese had put up for the volcanic rock of Iwo Jima or the island of Okinawa, it was impossible to expect otherwise. The Japanese themselves had more or less stated their intentions outright, reinforcing the Home Islands with troops from their various conquests, arming the local civilian population of Kyushu, and announcing that there were "no civilians in Japan."[8] Each subject of the emperor, so ran the official line, had to be willing to die a "glorious death" in his name.[9] The prospects for a protracted fight were grisly. As President Harry S. Truman (who had succeeded to office after FDR's death) put it, Japan might well become "an Okinawa from one end of Japan to the other," by which he meant mass destruction and unacceptable casualties.

And now, suddenly, even miraculously, this frightening prospect had vanished. Japan had surrendered. While there is today in this country a vibrant debate over the use of "the Bomb" to end World War II—whether it was necessary and justified, whether it was the main cause that led Japan to surrender, whether we dropped it primarily to scare the Soviets into more docile behavior in the postwar world—don't count Paul among the doubters.[10] Like the vast majority of World War II veterans, he is convinced that the bomb "saved his life," or at least kept him from having to take part in the invasion of Japan, a campaign that was sure to be a mass casualty event. And like most of his generation, Paul sees criticizing the use of the bomb to be an example of *ex post facto* reasoning by people who were not there and cannot really understand the true gravity of the situation. When discussing this contentious issue, the opinion of the veterans cohort, at the very least, deserves a hearing.

Paul's thoughts range a bit more widely, however. By the late summer of 1945, he notes, US bombing raids had torched Japan's cities one by one, Japanese economic and industrial activity had come to a standstill, and the country's merchant marine—the backbone of shipping among the various Home Islands and thus the lifeblood of the economy—had been practically destroyed. Japan, in short, was facing economic ruin and imminent famine, and hundreds of thousands of people were certain to have died in the ensuing six months.[11] Such a horrible prospect does not even take into account the thousands of Chinese and other occupied peoples who were being brutalized and murdered by Japanese troops every day that the war went on. The atomic bombs at the very least shortened the war and for that, he believes, we should all be profoundly grateful.

There were few people asking questions in Kenosha that August when they heard the news that the war was over. Twenty-year-old Paul remembers that the town simply "went wild." Church bells rang. Fire engines blasted their sirens. People laughed, sang, wept. "Everyone who could make a noise made a noise," he says. The next morning, he woke up on his mother's lawn. He'd apparently enjoyed himself the night before, and no doubt he would have a very interesting tale to tell—if only he could remember the details.

The festivities out of the way, Paul faced a time of questioning, just like every other member of his wartime generation. Now that he had survived the great test, where did he wish to go with his life? Certainly, the Marines had taught him some lessons. He had spent thirteen months in the Pacific, six months in the successful Philippines campaign, and he'd even taken part in one of the largest urban battles of history's greatest war: Manila. He knew how to operate a military radio while aloft and how to blast away on twin .30-caliber machine guns. But so did a lot of guys.

He certainly had reason to be proud. He had done well at everything the Marines ordered him to do. Indeed, he'd been promoted twice during training while still a teenager, first to corporal and then to sergeant. He had even made pretty good money, $120 per month, including extra pay for combat and overseas duty. Typically, he still tends to downplay his success at such a young age. "We were all young," he says. "Mostly teenagers, as far as I know. I don't think we were a year or two apart. I was nineteen when I flew most of my missions. It was a young man's war—at least aviation was."

One thing he did know was that his Marine experience had lent him the cachet that comes from being a "gunner." In the public imagination, the job of tail gunner or rear gunner was one of the more dangerous roles in wartime aviation. For much of the war, it certainly was. By the time Paul went aloft, however, much had changed. By the time he got to Luzon, American dominance in the skies had made the job considerably safer. During his six months in the Philippines, he seldom saw a Japanese plane aloft. Still, Paul came to appreciate the romance and heroism associated with his wartime assignment.

Consider, for example, the meteoric political career of Paul's fellow Wisconsinite (and fellow US Marine with a record of service in the Pacific), a circuit judge by the name of Joe McCarthy.[12] He ran for Senate successfully in 1946 and soon carved out a national reputation for himself as a staunch anti-communist (to his supporters) and an unscrupulous "red-baiter," witch-hunter, and destroyer of reputations (to his detractors). Like many young politicians of his era, his qualifications for office consisted, at least partially, of his supposedly heroic wartime exploits. And how did McCarthy choose to present himself to the public? How could he most impress voters with his toughness and savvy? Easy: he called himself "Tail Gunner Joe."

McCarthy had actually served as an intelligence briefing officer for dive-bomber squadron VMSB-235 during the war, spending two and a half years in the Solomon Islands. His principal tasks were to take aerial photos and to study how pilots and gunners were affected by repeated missions. In the course of that perfectly honorable service, he also volunteered to fly twelve combat missions as a gunner-observer. While the missions do not appear to have been particularly dangerous, he did get to loose off a few rounds from time to time, the source of his later "Tail Gunner" moniker. Like many war stories, this one wasn't so much a lie as a mixture of the truth and the teller's penchant for self-promotion. McCarthy certainly would have had a harder time running for the Senate with the nickname "Intelligence Officer Joe."

Beyond the value a reputation as a Marine (a Marine should never use the phrase "ex-Marine"), Paul says that his service in the corps taught him a number of life lessons. He learned structure and the echelons of command, as well as the importance of teamwork. Marine service also encouraged lifelong habits of health and exercise, and decades later he could still bang out perfect, Marine-regulation push-ups. Paul says many times that the Marines "changed his life," and there is little doubt that they did. What remained to be seen, however, was whether any of the skills he had acquired in wartime could translate to success during the transition to peace. He wasn't alone. The entire country was asking the very same question.

New Beginnings

The sudden close of World War II did not bring Paul Hilliard home for long. The Marines had promised him thirty days of leave, and that's precisely what he got. Although the war had ended, his obligation to the Marines had not.

Like millions of other servicemen, Paul spent much of his leave attending to personal matters. His good buddy and former high school roommate, Bob Heike, had served as a radioman for the Navy in California and married a girl he met there. Paul attended the wedding. Also on his "to-do" list while on leave was visiting his relatives in Pepin and Buffalo counties and, perhaps most important, introducing his mother to the girl he had met at that USO dance back in Jacksonville, Florida.

Her name was Lillian Ellen Meagher. She was a "pretty little girl," he says, who had been working in Washington, DC. The middle child of three, daughter of a career military couple, she was born in the Panama Canal Zone on June 8, 1925, just ten days earlier than Paul. Her grandparents had been part of the great migration from Ireland fleeing the nineteenth-century potato famine. At some point in her childhood, Lillian had adopted the name "Sally" from a favorite line in an English nursery rhyme, "Sally McGundy, born on a Monday."

Paul and Sally's relationship developed over a long distance, as the two exchanged letters after his departure for the Pacific. When he returned home, they reconnected and married in the summer of 1946. Both were twenty-one. The couple eventually had four daughters. "I think what I wanted at that time was stability after the Depression, the drought, and the war," Paul says. "Like most of the men after the war, we married young." It was a national trend. Perhaps it reflected some elemental instinct on the part of returning veterans. Having faced down danger and the ever-present possibility of death, these young men now looked for something permanent, for a wife, a family, a home—a return to "normal" life. The "baby boom," the great postwar explosion in the American birth rate, had begun.[13]

But before Paul and Sally could tie the knot in 1946, Paul had one more obligation to discharge, and this was one he couldn't put off. The war may have been over, but Paul was still in the Marines. They now assigned him to duty at the Marine Corps Air Station Cherry Point in Havelock, North Carolina. Unlike the six months he had spent in the rear gunner's seat of the Dauntless, flying missions over the Philippines, he found the new assignment much more to his taste. You could even say it was glamorous for the first few weeks, as he operated radios on domestic flights, flying the C-47 and transporting show business personalities like movie star Virginia Mayo to entertain the troops.

One of the Marine pilots with whom Paul flew during his postwar service was Tyrone Power, one of Hollywood's best-known actors, a number one box office attraction, and the star of *The Mark of Zorro* (1940), *Blood and Sand* (1941), and many other films. When war came to the United States in 1941, Power joined up, and there is a movie newsreel showing him enlisting alongside fellow actors Jimmy Stewart and Clark Gable.[14] After joining the Marines, Power served as a transport pilot in the Pacific, carrying wounded Marines from Iwo Jima and Okinawa. Power was a respected pilot, but as Paul recalls with a smile, "When you got on a flight of his, you knew they were going to have a 'mechanical problem,' which usually resulted in a night on the town."

Paul could have accepted his discharge from the Marines in March 1946 with full benefits but opted instead to remain in the service for another three months. He received his official discharge on June 25, 1946, at the age of twenty-one. He also finished the coursework for his high school degree, and Durand High School acknowledged his completed courses and retroactively granted him graduate status for the Class of 1943. Just a week after leaving the Marines, he married Sally in her home state of New York, before returning to Kenosha to await the start of fall semester at the University of Wisconsin's Kenosha extension campus.

As Paul's personal life resolved into sharper detail, so too did his career plans. Like many returning veterans, he had decided to attend college. It was the last thing in the world a poor boy growing up on a farm during the Depression could have imagined, but World War II had changed all that. In June 1944, while the war was still raging but the issue no longer seemed to be in doubt, Congress began to worry about the state of the postwar economy. The last time the veterans came home from war, in 1918–1919, they had found the economy sluggish and jobs hard to come by. Within a decade, the situation had careened into catastrophe in the Great Depression. Many soldiers in World War II feared the same thing happening once their war ended. As the fighting dragged on and began to seem endless, many servicemen used to joke, "Golden Gate by '48"—a grim jest that the war wouldn't be over until 1948. The sardonic response was "Bread Line by '49," an equally dark joke that they would all soon be unemployed and on relief.[15]

To quiet such fears, Congress passed the Servicemen's Readjustment Act, better known as the "GI Bill." Its benefits were comprehensive: tuition and room and board payments to encourage veterans to attend university; low cost, zero-down-payment mortgages; low interest loans for business startups; one year of unemployment compensation as veterans transitioned back into the civilian economy, and more. These benefits were available to all veterans who had been on active duty during the war for at least ninety days and had not been dishonorably discharged. It was not for battlefield heroes only, but for all those who had done their wartime duty.[16]

Of the 16 million veterans who served in World War II, fully half, some 8 million, took advantage of the GI Bill's education benefits within seven years of the end of the war, and the number of college graduates in the country more than doubled from 1940 to 1950. College education was (and still is) a ticket from one world to another, from blue-collar hourly labor into white-collar salaried work or the professional ranks. Such a transition was a typical life-story arc for millions of veterans returning from World War II: a farm boy or central city tenement dweller in the prewar era now living in a single-family home in one of the gigantic prefabricated suburban housing tracts that sprang up soon after the war. Levittown, New York, was the most famous, but it was just one of many. Twenty million Americans moved to the suburbs in the decade after 1945, another colossal demographic shift, and perhaps the longest-lasting legacy of the war. Indeed, it is no exaggeration to say that World War II created the great American middle class.

Once again, Paul's experience paralleled that of the country almost exactly. Just as World War II changed his life, so too did the GI Bill. He was going to college at the University of Wisconsin at Kenosha. But why? To study what? The more he considered his interests, the more he wished to become a lawyer. It was a profession that ran in his family, specifically his grandfather Caleb Hilliard. Caleb attended the University of Wisconsin at Madison and graduated with a law degree in 1881. Until his death in 1928 he worked mainly as a local lawyer, first in the village of Pepin and then in Durand, where his office sat above the First National Bank. He was also, we might say, a local dignitary, holding a host of public positions: clerk in Pepin village, five terms on the Pepin County Board of Supervisors, three years on the school board, and time as supervisor of the first ward in Durand. From 1901–1905 he was justice of the peace, then served as city attorney for one year in Durand. In 1915, Governor Emanuel Lorenz Philipp, a Republican, appointed him district attorney. Paul decided a law career would continue the family tradition. Once again, returning veterans wanted, above all, to be grounded in something solid.

Going back to school proved to be no picnic. Images of veterans dressed in collegiate wear and attending classes in beautiful ivy-covered buildings were more mythical than real. Seven million American students enrolled in college in 1946 alone, straining campuses and facilities that were suited to serve about one million, Paul points out. With colleges frantically trying to ramp up to meet this unprecedented demand, classes took place wherever and whenever space was available. The facilities at Kenosha were, to put it politely, shabby. Blackboards, chairs, and desks looked like discards from the local public high schools. Buildings had limited cooling and heating.

Despite the broken-down appearance of the campus, classes in Kenosha were packed with veterans, many of them officers and most of them older than Paul. He discovered quickly that he was often the youngest and lowest-ranking veteran in his classroom. Always the competitor, however, he found that he could hold his own or better in his classes, despite the fact that he was also working outside the classroom to support his family—he and Sally were expecting their first child. After a few months, he also discovered that some of the former officers who were now his classmates did no better than he did, or not as well, and some, he claims, were absolute "knuckleheads." Education has always been the great leveler of American society, and Paul's experience at Kenosha was already confirming it.

Student dress was casual at the extension branch. In fact, because the manufacturing economy in Kenosha had been geared to producing military hardware rather than clothing, many veterans still wore their uniform or other military clothing to class. "There were no dress clothes" in stores, Paul recalls. "They didn't make any during the war." His mother, Gladys, proud her son was going to college, insisted on helping with Paul's wardrobe. "Sometimes my mother let her emotions overcome her," he recalls. Gladys went to a local department store and bought two white dress shirts for Paul as he was starting classes. The shirts were too large, but his mother was nothing if not resourceful, and she adjusted the shirt size. "She altered them, but the shoulders hung halfway to my elbows," he says. "They were the first white shirts I owned."

Paul found great satisfaction in his coursework and with his professors, especially in humanities and civics courses. At Kenosha, one of Paul's professors was Heinrich Friedländer, a scholar and refugee from Nazi Germany, who fled his homeland before the war and reached America by first obtaining a teacher's visa in Cuba. Paul took German lessons from Friedländer, who would sometimes wander from the lesson plan in class to lament the demise of the Germany he once knew and the destruction wrought by Hitler and his Nazi henchmen. He could get emotional. "When he talked too much he'd cry," Paul says. "He wept about what had happened to his precious Germany. I loved that guy." The experience will be familiar to anyone who has ever felt the exhilaration of encountering an inspiring scholar in class. "He was a wonderful man in his sixties; we were in our twenties. We'd get him distracted and he would talk about people like [poet Johann Wolfgang von] Goethe." To Friedländer, Goethe represented that "other Germany," a humanist nation that prized learning and literary brilliance above war-making, a land of *Dichter und Denker* (poets and thinkers). "He would quote Goethe in tears."[17] His exposure to quality professors like Friedländer appealed to Paul, who yearned to become not only an able and successful man, but an educated one. As in high school, he was both curious and competitive.

Apart from the classroom, this was a difficult time for Paul and Sally as newlyweds. To support his new family, Paul worked at Irving Polishing and Buffing Co. (today the Irving Polishing & Manufacturing, Inc.) in Kenosha, about a mile from the university. He often ran from work to the classroom and back. The exercise kept him in shape, he recalls today, but it could not have been easy at the time. He left home before sunrise and did not return until late at night. His new wife knew no one in Kenosha, and the couple didn't even own a car. For part of the time, they lived with Paul's mother, Gladys, who also worked every day.

Despite the pressure of work, school, and family, Paul says he was grateful to be progressing toward a college degree, one of millions of veterans across the country going to school and starting families: the GI Bill meets the "baby boom." He admits he was merciless to himself in his drive for personal excellence. One cold night, he remembers, he reached into his pocket for bus fare. He didn't find a dime there, only pocket lint. To discipline himself, he walked four miles to his mother's house that night, rather than ask for a ride or call for help. "That was my punishment for not having any money in my pocket," he says. "I have had that obsession ever since. I always carry a few dollars."

After a year in Kenosha, Paul decided it was time for a change. He transferred to Triple Cities College in upstate New York, a fledgling campus that drew most of its students from the cities of Binghamton, Johnson City, and Endicott. Paul and Sally had welcomed their first child, Diane, in March 1947, and Sally was glad to be closer to her aging parents. Triple Cities College had just opened its doors in 1946 with some nine hundred students and thirty faculty members. Initially, it was a two-year school with an affiliation to Syracuse University. It later became Harpur College and is today Binghamton University, part of the State University of New York system. The Hilliards sublet a bedroom in Sally's parents' rented apartment: her folks lived on the second floor; Paul, Sally, and their baby daughter had a room on the third.

Despite the GI Bill, the young Hilliard family was still short on money, and Paul had to work a variety of jobs. The first, before school started, was at a construction site. He had to join a union to work there and spent a few weeks standing at the bottom of a fifty-year-old landfill, digging with a shovel and building the footings for a planned warehouse. "We had to carry concrete blocks by hand, three or four guys, to a site where we would put them on the ground. I grabbed two—one in each hand—and the union steward told me, 'One at a time, son, one at time.'" His work on the building site left Paul with a sour impression about labor unions and their work rules.

His second job, which was also short-term, was more to his liking. He worked at International Business Machines (IBM) headquarters, the company's first manufacturing site, sometimes called Plant No. 1. The facility employed more than 7,000 people and operated under the guidance of Thomas J. Watson Sr., who had built IBM into one of the world's greatest corporations. Working there, Paul says, "was considered the best job you could get." He enjoyed the work: tending the golf course of IBM Country Club in late summer and fall of 1947, while attending classes at Triple Cities. His duties included watering the greens at night and using a "jerry cutter"—he described it as a "super Weed eater"—to keep the rough at the right length, as well as digging ditches.

Working at IBM even brought Paul an invite to the company Christmas party. It was a chance to get a free dinner and observe the legendary Mr. Watson up close. The boss, then in his seventies, was known for motivating and training his staff, and for paying well. Paul was less than impressed by what he saw, either the Watson legend or Watson the person. "It was in a big banquet hall at IBM. I got a free meal. It was one of the most boring, non-memorable moments of my life." His principal memory of the evening was listening to Watson speak. "Watson loved to talk. He limited his topic to the creation of the world and subsequent events," Paul says today with a smile.

What most interested Paul at the time were his classes. He reveled in taking courses in the arts and humanities. Among his favorite professors was Eric Brunger, who taught the History of England, replete with intimate and ribald tales of the British royals over the ages. "Brunger was so good. He had been part of a group sent to Europe in the 1930s to work on the causes and responsibilities for World War I," he says. Despite his heavy workload, Paul read Thomas Babington Macaulay's five-volume *History of England* under Brunger's direction and submitted a book report on it.[18]

In many ways, Paul found the experience at Triple Cities to be similar to his classes in Kenosha. The physical plant was inadequate, even wretched. "If you put those facilities today out for the public schools there would be riots," he says. "No air-conditioning, miserable heat, no central air." The pre-fabs were hot in the summer, freezing in winter. Snow drifted into buildings, which were heated by coal-burning pot-bellied stoves. Administrators sold students on the idea that they were education pioneers in the region, and to be fair, the veterans, many of whom had experienced far worse physical conditions in war, seldom complained. The bitter winter snowstorms with hip-deep drifts tried everyone's patience, however. "The winter of 1947–48 in the Susquehanna Valley was brutal. That weather was awful." It was so bad, he says, that he promised himself never to live in the North again.

Despite all these problems, Triple Cities College turned out to be suited for returning veterans like Paul. About 70 percent of the 1,100 enrolled students were veterans. Classes were held where space permitted: in Colonial Hall, donated by IBM, in prefab Army buildings, on IBM's corporate campus, and in an octagonal building called "the Casino," a local landmark in a park. Student morale was high; surroundings may have been primitive, but spirits were good. Alex Gilfillan, a music professor, said the mood on the Triple Cities campus was so good "that we have never [re]captured it again." Aldo Bernado, a student and later administrator at Triple Cities, said "there was a kind of learning atmosphere that I would call pretty darn close to perfect."[19] A campus history tells us, "The students enjoyed close relationships with the faculty. They wanted their degrees quickly, so they were on campus for longer hours." The students considered it a family atmosphere on campus and did not mind busing their own tables in the small cafeteria or carrying their chairs from one classroom to another. Paul enjoyed the school, but between work, classes, and family, he didn't have much time for casual friends. Years later, looking at photos in a history of Triple Cities and Harpur College, he can pick out perhaps six or eight friends he remembers from school.

With the earnings from the various jobs Paul was working, the Hilliards were finally able to scrape up enough money and buy a ten-year-old car, a four-door white DeSoto. But in the winter of 1947–48, Paul braked at a stoplight, turned the corner, and was hit by a truck emerging from a gas station, which took off the DeSoto's right rear fender. Repairs were not made for three months. During their lone year in Kenosha, he and Sally had weathered most of the winter with no car and survived. Now the family had to weather the elements with a damaged car. The Northeast was pelted by one blizzard after another that year. Paul began to ask himself why he should stay in such miserable conditions. The Marines had sent him to San Diego and Jacksonville for training, and he had learned to appreciate the warmer climate. He had left his home state of Wisconsin because of the cold. Now a New York winter was driving home that same message: "There are other places to live." His dread of freezing winters was driving him ever farther southward—a process that would continue.

Looking for a "change of venue," as it were, the future student of law met with a dean at Triple Cities to weigh his options for transfer. The dean told him of a program at the University of Texas in Austin that allowed admission to any military veteran who had completed junior year of college with grades of B or better. Paul had squeezed enough coursework into his first two calendar years of college study to rank as a junior, a benefit of his competitiveness and work ethic. He had also kept up his grades, always a point of pride with him. Paul could complete his undergraduate degree at Triple Cities retroactively by transferring his first-year law school credits back to the Triple Cities, in lieu of spending his senior year in New York. His intention all along had been to enter law school. Why not now?

The University of Texas law school was in the process of a concerted effort to upgrade its reputation nationally. Raising out-of-state enrollments was one way to improve the brand. To Paul, Texas seemed to be the right fit. While he'd never been there, he had met a lot of Texans during his Marine Corps career, and he discovered that he liked them. They were kindred spirits, in a sense. They were optimistic and friendly—and they put out lots of baloney.

"I had my sights on law school," Paul says. "I didn't know how to do it. But I was determined to go."

Gone to Texas

Back in the 1820s, the American South was filled with individuals seeking a new start. Maybe they had lost everything in the Panic of 1819. Maybe they had gotten into a scrape or two with the law. Luckily, they had heard about a sprawling territory lying to the west, a land with a big sky, where a man could make a fresh start, and where your opportunities were limited only by your ambition and hard work. At the time, the territory in question was a sparsely inhabited province of Mexico and the Mexican government welcomed settlers who could help to develop the land. Thousands did just that. For years afterward, you could ride past

abandoned farms in Tennessee or Alabama and see a brief message carved
into the fence or scratched onto the home. Three simple letters to let people know what had happened to the family who lived there, but without
providing too much detail. "G.T.T.," it said: "Gone to Texas."[20]

And so it was the Hilliard family. For a young man like Paul, with
ambition and a growing family, Texas seemed perfect. After complet-
ing his second semester at Triple Cities, Paul, Sally, and baby daughter
Diane left for Austin, driving in their used DeSoto by way of Kenosha.
As generations of settlers had learned before them, however, Texas was
a long ways away, and a lot of things could happen along the path. The
DeSoto developed engine trouble as they drove south through Missouri.
Paul got it repaired, but the unexpected expense meant that they were
running out of traveling money by Oklahoma. In the small town of
Atoka, Paul stopped at a bank, looking to cash a $120 GI check, but
the bank manager refused. He cited previous problems he had experienced when cashing checks for non-account holders. Paul assured him
his ID checked out, all the way down to the name on his Marine-issued
underwear, but the bank manager just shook his head. No meant no.
"You've got to understand," Paul recalls. "This was before credit cards.
That check was all I had."

Once they made it to Dallas, Paul stopped at a Prince's drive-in. He
wisely talked to the manager before ordering any food. Paul told the man
about his plight. He was out of money except for the government-issued
check he was holding in his hand. Would the restaurant cash the check
and let his family eat? As Paul tells the story today, the manager looked
at Paul's identification, then glanced out the window at baby Diane in
Sally's arms. Paul's money was good, the manager said. The family could
eat. In the course of his professional career, Paul later became a frequent
and very polished public speaker, and he still relishes the memory of this
moment, telling audiences what he had learned from it. "I could do more
business in a drive-through restaurant in Texas," Paul says, "than I could
at an Oklahoma bank."

A few days later at law school registration, Paul encountered new
problems of the bureaucratic sort. So far, he had pursued his education
in smaller schools. Now he was playing in a bigger league. A quick check
of his application papers showed that he was still three college credits shy

of being permitted to enroll in the law school under the early admission program. He tried to explain. He had taken a course out of sequence at Triple Cities, which left him short of the necessary credits to complete his junior year. Moreover, the University of Texas had not cleared his transcript for admission in Texas before he arrived and tried to register. Ever the optimist, he had simply shown up at school.

"The girl in the admissions office obviously thought I was some sort of screwball for driving from New York to Texas without being pre-admitted," he remembers. The registrar's office was more understanding, offering him an attractive option. Paul could take an advanced Reserve Officer Training Corps class for three college credits to gain junior status. The course would satisfy his admission requirement, plus pay him $30 a month while he was enrolled. That was three dollars a month more than the cost of his rent at Brackenridge Apartments in Austin, a deal that he could not refuse.

Paul duly enrolled in the Air Force ROTC program and stayed in it for two years. "I don't think I learned much," he says, but he did continue to earn money through the program and while in law school. Air Force ROTC made sense for him because he had already been bitten by the flight bug and had spent three years in the air in wartime. In summer 1950, he was commissioned a second lieutenant in the Air Force, and he spent six weeks on active duty in Illinois at Scott Field, an air base built in 1917 (now Scott Air Force Base). He also served at Carswell Air Force Base near Fort Worth (now Naval Air Station Joint Reserve Base Fort Worth).

His Air Force commission marked another transition in Paul's life, one that carried with it a certain tension. To accept the new commission, he had to resign from the Marine Corps Reserves, which he did. Two weeks after his resignation, however, he received a letter at home from the Marine Corps, calling upon him to report to Camp Stoneman in California. In was the summer of 1950, and US troops were already deploying to Korea. Paul was to prepare for overseas duty. By then, his second daughter, Paula, had been born, and an overseas deployment would have meant a real hardship on the family. Paul had to tell the Marines the bad news: "I told them I was already out of the Marines and in the Air Force on active duty," he says, relieving him of the obligation to serve in Korea. On August 5, 1950, Paul received his commission as a Second Lieutenant in the Air Force Reserve.

While admission to the law program at the University of Texas Law School was easy for Paul and many other veterans, staying in the program was another matter. Paul began by taking his general law classes: criminal law, legislation, property law. Like many first-year law students, he experienced something of a shock to the system. He quickly learned the difference between a "nurturing" system of education and an "attritional" one. While his professors at Kenosha and Triple Cities had done their best to help their students stay in school, law school professors seemed determined to eliminate their underperformers. And law, Paul soon discovered, was a subject about which he knew little. It was like learning another language, he says. He also understood hard work, however, and he had a good, basic education, a reservoir of knowledge from his early education through his junior year of college from which he could draw. He forged ahead into law school with a simple plan: "Read, read, read until you go blind."

He seemed to thrive on the competition from fellow law students and the demands from faculty and administration. He wasn't deterred by the professors who assured the class on day one that, "half would be eliminated academically before the end of the first year." The professors had to be ruthless, he says, because the law students had literally been "jammed into the college system," and many were not ready. Along with his natural competitive streak, Paul also had to work to support his family. In fact, daughter Paula was born on the morning of his criminal law final exam in January 1950.

Again, friendships and fun had to take second place to hard work. "I had no social life in Austin," he says. "I worked and went to school, and law school was hard. It was another world. I went to one ball game and one movie in three years in Austin." He also worked for the University Foundation, researching charitable organizations for potential fundraising. "The university was looking for money," he says. He also remembers what he was paid for his work at the foundation: fifty cents an hour.

Paul barely even saw his student neighbors living at Brackenridge Apartments. Most were graduate students and older than the Hilliards. Several of his neighbors were psychology graduate students, and he jokes today that "they were all crazy." But Paul and his neighbors occasionally shared cheap steaks and beer together. They were all in it together and could understand the shabby state of the married student housing where they lived. Housing was shabby for a reason: the Brackenridge Apartments, located on a lake, consisted primarily of two-story fabricated housing that had been built for the shipbuilding industry in Orange, Texas, near the Louisiana border. With the end of the war, these housing units were shipped to Austin to meet the needs of the burgeoning university student population.

One short-term job Paul took in law school still brings him satisfaction years later. The assistant district attorney hired him to build a rock wall. Even though he had no previous experience at bricklaying or masonry, Paul mixed the concrete, laid the brick, and built the wall. It was the Marine in him. You had a mission, you made no excuses, you did the job. To his considerable satisfaction and relief, the wall stayed intact.

But there was something about building that wall that pleased him even more: the work itself. His idol, Winston Churchill, had practiced the same craft. Back in 1928, during a tense moment in both his political and literary career, he had retreated to his country home at Chartwell. Here he built a brick wall with his own hands, as well as a cabin for his daughter Mary, which he dubbed "Marycot."[21] As Paul saw it, if it was good enough for Sir Winston, it was good enough for him. "Churchill learned to lay bricks," Paul says. "I had experience building walls."

As he approached graduation, Paul still had no set plan for using his law degree. "I didn't think that far ahead," he says. "I just wanted to go to law school. I thought I would go to work in a law firm." He still wanted to follow in his grandfather's footsteps. Caleb Hilliard spent forty years practicing law after graduating from the University of Wisconsin, but he never earned much money for his efforts. Durand was not the sort of place where a lawyer could get rich. He often accepted payment in kind from his clients when they couldn't afford the money to pay him. Paul remembers his grandmother showing him her muffin tin and eggbeater. She told her grandson that they were just some of the items her husband had received as a portion of his fee for providing his legal services. "My grandfather never squeezed anyone for legal payments," he says. Small-town culture was also at work here, however, "There was not much legal work because no one sued anyone. Lawsuits were unusual."

Finally, the day had come, and Paul graduated from law school. Despite the distraction of all those part-time jobs and his commitments to his young family, he did very well in school, graduating fourteenth out of his class of 114. While he fell just short of the coveted top 10 percent of his cohort, he had still achieved a lofty rank in a very good program. The law firms thought so too, and they came calling. Almost immediately he had set up interviews with a couple of Texas firms, one in the bustling city of Fort Worth and the other in Lufkin, a small town deep in East Texas.

Paul met with the former law school dean, Charles Tilford McCormick, about his options. McCormick had been at the forefront of establishing the UT School of Law's national reputation. A graduate of Harvard Law School, he had taught at Texas, the University of North Carolina, and Northwestern University in Chicago, and he had also served as dean at North Carolina. Author of the *Handbook on the Law of Damages*, at the time a standard text in law schools, he was a national scholar of the first rank.[22] He had numerous connections that could prove useful for a future lawyer, but what he gave Paul that day was something much more valuable: the hard truth.

Their conversation quickly got down to business. The interview for the job in Fort Worth had been delayed, he told Paul. "Very proper," but with a "twinkle in his eye," he explained why Paul's prospects in Fort Worth were not good. It seemed that the law firm there was looking for a young lawyer who "could marry the daughter of one of its biggest clients, thereby cementing the relationship between the firm and the client." As a married man, Paul was out.

The second job opening in Lufkin was equally complicated. The firm was led by Martin Dies Jr., a seven-time Texas congressman. He was tied up in an important case with national publicity, and it was taking up a great deal of his time. The local papers dubbed the case the "Marshall, Texas Housewives Rebellion," in which Dies represented a group of women from Marshall who refused to withhold taxes from the paychecks of their nannies and cooks. The women insisted that withholding the tax amounted to "forcing them to do the government's work without compensation." It was a complicated case, and Dies would be out of the Lufkin office for a month or more to work on it. As a result, he was unavailable to do any interviews for the firm's open job. That opportunity, too, seemed unattractive to Paul.

There was a third job possibility, McCormick reassured him. This one was with an organization called the California Company, and a recruiter was on campus ready to talk. Paul almost didn't wait for the dean to finish, agreeing to the interview. It went well, the recruiter offered Paul the job on the spot, and Paul accepted. Actually, he had little choice. He wasn't going to marry the client's daughter, as the Fort Worth firm wanted, and he had little desire to work with the fiery housewives of Marshall, Texas. Most important, he had exhausted his government funding through the GI Bill, and he was in need of a steady income to support his wife and two young daughters. The California Company it was.

Things moved quickly from this point on. Paul graduated with a bachelor's degree in law on June 2, 1951. Later that month, he took the Texas state bar examination, and soon thereafter the family left Texas for good. On August 5, he heard that he had passed the Texas bar. It was a moot point, as he was leaving the state.

Paul wasn't yet sure about the details of his new job with the California Company, but he was about to find out, and he was soon to get involved in a business that would become his profession, his passion and, perhaps even his obsession for the next seven decades.

It had something to do with oil.

PART III
OIL

CHAPTER 5
MOTHER NATURE'S TREASURE

In Cajun Country

Not for the first time, chance had intervened to change the course of Paul Hilliard's life. That recruiter from the California Company, Guy Daniels, didn't have to be on campus in Austin that day, but he was. Paul might have had other options, but he didn't. Of course, as the saying goes, the Lord helps those who help themselves, and we should remember that Paul had put himself in a position where luck could intervene by advancing through his coursework ahead of schedule. He had worked hard as an undergraduate, kept up his studies even while working multiple jobs, and attacked law school with all the grit and determination he had shown as a Marine in the South Pacific.

Now he stood at the threshold of a new career. Despite its name, which conjures up images of surfing and sun, the California Company was in the energy business and had been exploring for oil across the country for years. Indeed, it was a subsidiary of Standard Oil of California (usually shortened to CalSo or Socal at the time), and it is the company we know as Chevron today.[1] The company had been active in the southeastern United States for twenty years and had made its first big oil strike at Bayou Barataria in Louisiana in 1939.

Daniels gave Paul a choice of where to start. The company currently had five positions open, he said: Bismarck, North Dakota; Brewton, Alabama; Ardmore, Oklahoma; Denver, Colorado; or New Orleans. Paul remembers that the choice was easy. North Dakota and Colorado were out—too cold. Brewton and Ardmore? Too small. There was nothing available for him in Texas. The Crescent City looked like the right spot: an exciting city in a warm clime. "I had never been to New Orleans. It sounded like the place to be," he recalls. Big decisions often emerge from relatively minor considerations. As he often puts it today: "Texas was nine times bigger than Louisiana, but Louisiana was nine times more interesting."

Better still, the job paid $360 a month, about $100 more per month than the entry-level jobs at the law firms. The Hilliards arrived in New Orleans on July 1, 1951, and stayed at the Jung Hotel on Canal Street for two weeks at California Company expense. For Paul and his family, this was high living: a nice hotel, meals on the employer, the whole nine yards. Paul then bought his first home in the New Orleans bedroom community of Algiers, just across the Mississippi River from New Orleans, and remained a Louisianian for the rest of his life. Paul could not actually afford to buy the house, but the developer's superintendent was an old bachelor who was charmed by the Hilliard girls, and he fronted Paul $500 to help with the down payment.

Paul's new position was "landman," the public facing side of oil and gas exploration.[2] In formal terms, a landman interacts and negotiates with landowners for leases through which companies can explore and develop energy resources and minerals. Like a lot of things in life, however, that formal explanation doesn't begin to cover it. J. W. Beavers III, a longtime landman himself, explains that being a landman is "anything but specialized."[3] A good landman had to be part lawyer, part geologist, and maybe most important, a people person. In the course of his own career, Beavers checked and bought leases, ran titles, oversaw field crews, negotiated well trades, purchase agreements, and sale agreements, bought and sold minerals, and much more. His father had been a landman for H. L. Hunt, one of the richest oil men in America, and he used to answer the question, "What does a landman do?" with another one: "What do you want done?" Beavers recalls one of the most unusual tasks: "Lamar Hunt founded the American Football League and the Dallas Texans football club in 1959. My father and Mack Rankin were land managers for Hunt Oil Co. at the time, but they spent their weekend traveling all over the country scouting college football players, talking to their coaches and parents, drafting the players, and getting them to sign contracts to play football for the Dallas Texans and, later, the Kansas City Chiefs."

"Is scouting college football players in a landman's job description?" Beavers asks. "It was for two landmen."

Such a profession seems tailor-made for Paul, with his inborn initiative and flexibility. "I was a landman and worked with the lawyers on titles," Paul says, but he adds, "It was more land than legal." Indeed, much of the job was personal, getting to know the locals, talking patiently with them about their land, about local traditions and culture, and as he got acquainted with in his new turf in southeast Louisiana, he also came to know one of America's most fascinating subcultures: "I liked the field," he says. "I liked getting out with the Cajuns. I became fascinated with the exploratory aspects and working with the geologists."

Paul soon found that his journey from Austin to Algiers was more than a new job. It was a form of culture shock. The California Company prepared him for landman's work by sending him into the countryside to learn about the area. For Paul, these were months of tramping through bayous and forests in mud boots. His company guide, Joe Balmer, was perfect for the task, a man in his sixties who was always ready with a quip but who also had a deep knowledge of Louisiana culture. Paul, the former farm boy, could appreciate the agriculture of south Louisiana, where farmers grew sugarcane and soy, but he was also soaking in the local folkways. Once, as they were driving north on US Highway 61, they passed a cemetery, and Paul asked a very common question about the above-ground graves. "Why do they do that?" Paul asked. "High water table?"

Balmer's reply was classic: "This is Louisiana. When they get one of those statewide elections underway, and they need votes, they don't like to have to dig 'em up." Above all, Paul gained a sense that he had moved to very different place. Politics was not about governance, Balmer once told him, it was about entertainment. In a phrase Paul repeats to this day, he added that "in Louisiana, crime is not illegal."

And then there was the process of getting to know New Orleans, one of America's most fascinating studies in local traditions and cultural diversity. Driving in the famous French Quarter (simply "the Quarter" to residents), Paul saw an odd storefront and asked Balmer to explain it. The older man squinted at the shop, then told Paul that the sign was for a combination veterinarian/taxidermist shop. "Either way," Joe told him laconically, "you get your dog back." Another time, while passing through vast fields of ripe strawberries in Ponchatoula, north of New Orleans, Balmer said that in the Quarter, local merchants preferred tourists to strawberries, "because the former were always in season and easier to pick."[4]

Paul's new neighborhood in Algiers was also full of colorful drama, very different from the academic community in Austin. His backyard neighbor was a butcher and did not believe in cutting his lawn. He let the grass grow knee high. Then, one day, his wife found a snake in their home. The butcher's viewpoint changed suddenly. That night, his neighbors aimed their cars headlights into his yard so that he could see to mow. Another neighbor sold city directories to earn a living. Paul remembers a large disturbance one night. The police were at his neighbor's door. Although the man was selling the directories and collecting cash, it turns out he had stolen the directories in the first place. Caught red-handed, the culprit tried to escape out a window, but his bare feet couldn't handle the jagged oyster shell road as he struggled to run away on foot. Then there was the Navy officer and his wife, who routinely went to the Officer's Club at night and got "soused," as Paul recalls it, then would return home and stage some "pretty tough fights" while under the influence. All these were new experiences for Paul.

Algiers was a unique place, with some of the bawdiness of New Orleans, yet just enough separation from the city. With the Korean War going full bore and a military base nearby (Algiers Naval Station), both Algiers and the nearby town of Belle Chase were thriving. Since there was as yet no bridge between Algiers and the New Orleans Business District— that landmark wouldn't be built until 1958—California Company employees had to carpool to the ferry, cross the Mississippi River, and walk the eleven blocks to their workplace at 1111 Tulane, an experience of almost surreal heat and humidity in the summer months. He now knew why people did not live in Algiers unless they had no choice. Later, he says, he would look back at his living conditions and laugh.

Paul diligently worked territories in south Louisiana, including part of what was later identified as Acadiana, all the way north to Rapides Parish. He made trips to Houma, Thibodaux, and southwestern Louisiana. The California Company also made some passes at exploration west of Alexandria, in places like Allen Parish, Rapides Parish, and Oberlin. Paul worked out of Alexandria for several months, including old timber areas. "It was cut-over timber land," he says, "and people weren't careful about their titles." He sought answers about property ownership at the court-house, but the answers were not always there, and he had to conduct detailed interviews with elderly folk to trace the details of the heirship.

Those timber parishes that he visited were home to some unforgettable characters, too. Among Paul's favorites were Elam and Maggie Stokes, both of whom chewed tobacco and had a repertoire of stories. Paul met with the couple numerous times to pursue their family histories and heirship. Elam, he says, was a great storyteller with a long memory, rich in detail. His father had been a saddler with the Confederate Army and took part in the siege of Vicksburg. Elam had numerous stories from his father about the siege, when the inhabitants had been so hungry they boiled down harnesses for food, not to mention eating cats and mice. He also told Paul that the Confederate cause was never as popular in timber country as it was in cot-ton country. Rebel patrols used to comb through the very area where Paul was seeking leases to look for deserters who had tried to escape into the woods. In later years, Elam said, the "revenooers" had moved into the area, looking for "white lightning" and illegal moonshine stills.

In a way, Paul had discovered a land that time forgot, or at least where it seemed to be standing still. He felt it particularly strongly on the oc-casions when he drove through the now-deserted Camp Claiborne. The camp was a sprawling, 23,000-acre facility north of Forest Hill. Claiborne had hosted the famous Louisiana Maneuvers in the September 1941, when the US Army was frantically preparing for war. Generals Eisenhower and Patton had cut their teeth as battlefield commanders there, as had most of the American generals of the war. The 1941 maneuvers are still the largest peacetime exercise in the history of the Army, and it is hard to imagine any future event topping them. From 1939–1945, Claiborne trained a half million men to fight the Axis. When the tide of war turned in favor of the Allies, the camp also housed German prisoners of war. Now: nothing. It was as if World War II had not happened, or perhaps had been some sort of bad dream. "It was like driving through a ghost town," Paul remembers, a reflection, perhaps of his own memories of World War II at the time.

As much as Louisiana posed a culture shock to Paul, it wasn't hard for him to get used to it. "I was a country boy from Wisconsin," he says. "I liked those people. They were plain, hospitable. They would talk about anything you'd want. They talked about the Depression, too, which marked them for life." Old man Stokes spoke to Paul about people who had left Louisiana during the Depression for better prospects elsewhere. "He talked about one family that moved to California but came back," Paul recalls. "The fritter tree died, and the syrup pond dried up," is the way Stokes put it—a reference to the old tree in folklore that was full of fritters or pancakes. People used the phrase when their dreams died, when they thought the grass would be greener somewhere else and found out they were wrong. To Paul, the story suggested that Louisiana folk preferred to farm their own land and feed themselves rather than go work in a factory somewhere. The story resonated with Paul because of his years on a subsistence farm.

As open and honest as they were, Cajuns could prove very difficult when striking a land deal, Paul discovered. Operating in southwestern Louisiana, Paul met many people who spoke only Cajun French, but who "knew how to say 'no' in plain English," as he puts it.

"There was a sentimental thing; they did not want to lose their land," he says. The oil business was coming into full bloom in the 1950s and Cajuns were always looking for a better deal.

"They were tough to deal with. Man, you had to work. If you could find a guy in the neighborhood and get him to lease, and he had some influence, it would help," he says. Some rural Cajuns simply enjoyed the company of a stranger from time to time. Paul recalls one man in Lafayette Parish who just liked to sit and chat. Paul wooed him for months without being able to close a deal. "We talked and talked," Paul says, smiling. When Paul finally asked him why he wouldn't sign an agreement, he said, "If we sign the lease you're not coming back."

Certainly, Paul encountered his share of cross-cultural difficulties. Sometimes the language could be a stumbling block, and he often had to hire a notary public to interpret for him if the landowner did not speak English. In some areas, such as the Atchafalaya Basin, serious issues could arise pertaining to possession of the land. Record-keeping in that region could be informal and loose, to say the least. Nevertheless, he found the work rewarding. "I got along with people fine," he says. "I was a farm boy. It was farm country."

Beyond exposing him to the exotic culture of the region, Paul's three years working in and around New Orleans taught him a great deal about the basics of the oil business. Working for the California Company taught him one other key lesson, however. He was ill-suited to work in a large corporation. Paul was honest enough about himself to think it wasn't all the company's fault. "It may have been my personality more than the company," Paul admits today. Long-ingrained habits of independence were simply too difficult to break. The boy who had been on his own since he was fifteen was never going to develop into that classic 1950s, eight-to-five "organization man."

At this crucial point in Paul's self-awareness, a new actor appeared on the scene. The Hunt Oil Company in Dallas called him in 1954. Hunt was a large corporation, a major player and well regarded in the industry. A representative of the firm, a geologist, contacted Paul and told him, "Hunt is looking for a land varmint in Louisiana. Are you interested?" Paul, as always, was willing to listen, but his decision depended on what Hunt Oil would be willing to pay. He had moved up the pay scale at the California Company, but he and Sally were now parents of three daughters—Diane, Paula, and Linda—and would soon be adding a fourth: Donna. After meeting with Hunt executives in Dallas, Paul liked what he heard and took the job. He was to oversee land operations in the entire state, and he would also have a good deal of autonomy. Both aspects of his job description seemed to harmonize with his personality and made the offer appealing.

Working for Hunt meant another move, however. In July 1954, after three years in New Orleans, he and his family moved to Lafayette, Louisiana, a couple hours to the west. Paul seemed to have it all, working for a good company, earning good money, marriage, and a family. This was the "American Dream" that we hear so much about, almost a perfect example of what the generation that fought World War II wanted. Paul Hilliard, by all appearances, had made it.

But remember that old adage: beware of what you wish for. Paul had no sooner relocated and taken up his new job as a "land varmint" and relocated his family, than he learned the unpleasant truth: management at Hunt Oil was mired in what appeared to be total disarray. The company's founder, H. L. Hunt was "up in years," Paul notes (Hunt was sixty-five in 1954), and in the course of the 1950s, Hunt's attention had drifted away from the oil business. More and more he had become enamored of extreme of right-wing politics. He was an ardent admirer of Senator Joe McCarthy, later providing financial assistance to Far Right groups like the Minutemen and the John Birch Society, and he even formed his own conservative foundation, the Facts Forum, to fight what he saw as the communist threat to the American way of life.[9] While dad's mind turned to other things, Hunt's three sons (he would eventually father fifteen children), Herbert, Bunker, and Lamar, were still in their twenties and not yet ready to grab the controls at Hunt Oil.[10]

The stakes were high, however, and plenty of other people were ready. Hunt Oil had a good thing going in Louisiana, with about a dozen rigs in the state. H. L. Hunt had operated in the state since the 1930s, when he found and developed oil near the central Louisiana town of Urania. At first Paul was pleased with his new boss, since he felt that the company operated in a more relaxed fashion than the California Company. If a landowner signed a lease, the company was ready to drill, just the way Paul liked it.

The chaos from headquarters in Dallas was another matter, however. On paper, Paul reported to a former landman who, he states, "moved his lips when he read a stop sign." Paul never got clear guidance or direction: "He would say, 'Go to Venice [Louisiana] or Thibodaux. Call in when you get there.' I'd call from those places, he'd say, 'Never mind that. Go to Shreveport.' I did a lot of running, eating up miles. Hunt had so many people and they all had their priorities. My boss was whoever made the most recent call." Paul's view today of the disorganization at Hunt Oil is typically philosophical. "I learned," he says, "what not to do."

He also discovered that while he had too many bosses to count, he had nowhere near enough support. One day in early 1955, Paul visited a business friend from New Orleans, John Laborde, who was with Richardson & Bass. "They had beautiful maps," Paul remembers. "And I was working from something not much better than a road map." Laborde also had an office, a secretary, and a company phone, and Paul had none of these things. To be successful in Louisiana, you couldn't simply be working out of a corner of your bedroom in Lafayette or from the trunk of your car. It was a pitiful way to operate in a complicated industry, he realized.

Paul decided he'd had enough. It was just turning spring in Lafayette and the oil business was booming. America was thirsty for petroleum.

The American auto industry was exploding, as the number of cars in the country jumped from 26 million to 40 million by 1950.[11] Transportation, which had accounted for just about 50 percent of oil consumption, rose to more than 70 percent. Global trends were following a similar arc. Europe, formerly a coal-burning economy, was transitioning more and more to oil.

Hunt Oil seemed be missing out on the bonanza, however. Paul sat down and wrote a two-page letter to his supervisor. Paul asked a pointed question: was corporate going to furnish him with what he needed? He didn't have to wait long a reply. Within a few days, he received a telephone call from the corporate office. Did Paul really think that he needed all those changes to be successful in Louisiana? Paul had already said so in his letter, and he had no intention of backing down now. "Then maybe we ought to call this off," his supervisor suggested. Maybe so, Paul replied.

The official written response from the H. L. Hunt corporate office in Dallas, sent by air mail, was swift and final: "Confirming our telephone conversation today, I am enclosing herewith a check drawn on H. L. Hunt in the amount of $398.39 representing your salary through March 23, 1955, and two weeks termination pay in lieu of notice and all other claims. I feel sure that you will have no difficulty in locating elsewhere, and certainly wish you well in whatever you undertake."[12]

It was the 1954 version of "don't let the door hit you on your way out." Paul also learned that someone from Hunt was already en route from Dallas to retrieve his company car. Hunt executives had made up their minds to get rid of "the dissenter" once and for all, Paul says. That letter still hangs in the hallway of Badger Oil, the company Paul founded and has operated for more than sixty years.

Even today, Paul relishes telling people this story, noting proudly that he has been "unemployed since 1955." And from now on, he bore a new and proud title: "independent oil man." How do you earn it? It's simple, Paul says. "You get fired."

"I read it. I slept it. I dreamt it."

Paul had been fired. Certainly not for underperformance, but for asking pointed questions about the operation and for demanding the opportunity to succeed. Where some men might have seen this dismissal as a setback, Paul saw just the opposite: an opportunity. He enjoyed working in the oil industry, and he could point to four years of experience plying the trade in southwestern Louisiana. He liked Lafayette, too. Finally, with the receipt of that last check from Hunt Oil, he had nearly $400 to get started in a new direction. Looking back on this decisive moment in his life, he says today, "I decided I will figure out a way. I like this business. I will do some things on my own." He admits that he was "totally intrigued with the idea of chasing oil and gas, primarily oil, because gas was just about worthless." Hunt Oil may have been a frustrating situation, but by the time he left that company, he had "learned a lot about the business," he decided. At least enough to get started.

Armed only with a naive confidence and that last paycheck, Paul decided to go into business for himself. He knew that he had to act quickly: his $400 was barely enough to last a couple of months. He began by meeting with a few independent geologists and put together some options near the south Louisiana towns of Donaldsonville and Napoleonville. He had long been an independent thinker, the captain of his own personal destiny. Now, suddenly, he had become an independent oil man. Looking back, Paul says it wasn't all that big of a deal. "In reality, the term 'independent oil man' meant you were unemployed and broke." His mature verdict about his younger self is typically perceptive: "At thirty years old," he recalls, "I was dumber than a doorstop. But I had high hopes and unlimited ambition."

Also a great deal of knowledge. His work experience, especially his exhaustive travel in Louisiana, had paid off. He had amassed some 30,000 miles of travel in eleven months. As a result, he knew the roads, he knew the oil and gas parishes, and he had built up valuable personal contacts across the state. He was especially knowledgeable about the Louisiana coastal regions and the southwestern parishes in and around Acadiana. So that's precisely where he focused his early entrepreneurial efforts, in the places he had come to know best. He had decided to commit his career to Louisiana. The decision made sense for all the reason listed above, plus one more: "I did not have enough money to move elsewhere, had I so desired."

Throughout this period of Paul's life, the sense that destiny was calling him into the oil business is strong. It wasn't so much a "choice" he made. "I was addicted by the time I was with the California Company a year or two," he says today. "I was looking for oil, looking for something elusive and romantic. I don't know how you get out once you get in." The oil business chose Paul, not vice versa. "I really liked it," he says. "I read it. I slept it. I dreamt it. I worked it."

His first big deal—at least it felt like a big deal at the time, he says— was made around Pierre Part in Assumption Parish near Lake Verret, about twenty miles west of the parish seat at Napoleonville. It was mainly a fishing community of some three thousand people. It took him many months to secure the land, including difficult negotiations with a fractious family of ten heirs who, he says, "did not want to get along." To make things, more complicated, one of the bunch was a nun, who intended to give her share of the project's profits to her religious order. "Everybody was trying to buy that lease," he says, but only one person landed it: Paul himself. In the end, he profited about $25,000 from the Lake Verret deal, a princely sum in those days. The windfall was especially welcome for a couple with four young daughters, and Paul built a house. He didn't pause for backslapping or champagne celebrations, however. He deposited the rest of the money in the bank and went right back to work, doing what he did best: making deals.

"I was still operating as an individual," he says. He enjoyed the freedom. "I had bought leases for the company before then. They would set a price and if you didn't get it, you didn't get it." This was different. Paul could set his own prices and his own limits. He could massage the deal, do what it took to get the thing done. If the deal succeeded, it was his doing. And if it failed, it was his responsibility.

Paul recalls these early years in oil and gas as "a different world." In the 1950s, "the technology was less exact," he says, and a "lot of wells were drilled on sketchy seismic." Paul remembers a saying that was in circulation at the time. Wallace Pratt, a pioneer petroleum geologist, declared in 1953 that, "Where oil is first found, in the final analysis, is in the minds of men."[13] An inspiring thought, perhaps, but Paul also found that the minds of men, intuition, and imagination often led to dry holes. While a good oil man has to have the soul of a riverboat gambler, always willing to go with his gut and trust his intuition, Paul also learned the value of geologists and advanced technology. Compared to today's technology, however, exploration in the 1950s and 1960s often seemed to be little more than a guessing game. Rather than deter him, however, the uncertainty of the industry worked on him like a charm. "I find the oil and gas industry like a detective story," he says today. "Sometimes you catch the bad guy. Sometimes you don't." Or, perhaps, as he puts it more vividly, "Sometimes you're the fireplug; sometimes you're the dog."

Along with the exhilaration of getting to be a detective (or a dog), oil was also hard work. Success required a real sense of dedication, long hours, and painstaking attention to detail. Family life doesn't always mesh well with such a profession, but Paul has done his best. His daughter, Donna Hilliard Phillips, recalls her father working long hours and sometimes taking her and one of her sisters on calls with him. The girls would ride in the back seat, happy and eager to spend time with their dad. When he would stop at a house to get a lease signed, property owners would sometimes offer an icy soda pop or a cookie to five-year-old Donna. She met many of her dad's Cajun clients that way. As they passed working oil pumps in the field, Donna says her dad taught his young daughter that the slow bobbing machines were called "donkeys." With his typical humor, though, he also told her to call them by a new name: "Thank-you-very-muchers."

Donna also got to spend time in his office. Along with typical kid behavior like collecting the hole punch scraps for confetti, Donna especially liked spreading her crayons out on the large desk and coloring Paul's Louisiana land maps. Dad would make a mark and Donna would color the rest of the area in. Oldest daughter Diane also remembers the public library across the street from her father's office. Just like her father when he was a child, she was an avid reader, and spent long, comfortable hours there. At home, parent Paul tried to make up for what he didn't have as a child. Diane says that the family had so many magazines and newspapers that even her sixth-grade teacher was impressed. "We had *Time, Life, Look* . . . you name it."

Looking back, Diane sees a broader purpose at work here. "I guess it was a way Dad could impress upon us that there was a whole world out there. And to reach beyond the boundary of the little southern town we lived in." In that same vein, Diane says that Paul encouraged her to travel. She studied abroad during her sophomore year in college and met her parents in Hawaii. Her World War II-veteran dad decided to channel his inner history buff and show them Pearl Harbor. As luck would have it, Diane remembers seeing three very scary aircraft flying overhead, clearly identifiable as "Japanese bombers." It wasn't some sort of time warp. A

William and Gladys Hilliard,
Paul's parents, on their wedding day
in 1921.

The Hilliards in front of their home on the farm in Sand Burr Coulee,
1932. *Left to right*: Paul, Aunt Aggie, brother Bill, mother Gladys
(holding brother Wally), and Paul's father, William.

Another look at the house on the farm in Sand Burr Coulee with the all-important water pump in the foreground, December 2020.

Paul's schoolhouse in 1936.

Top Row: Albert Sylvester, Neil Lunderville, Mr. Weix, Harvey Gifford, George Kees,
Bottom: Arden Atkins, Paul Hilliard, Jack Kins, Robert Heike, Sidney Lunderville,
         Robert Goodrich, John Manor, Horace Hougen

J U N I O R   H I G H   B A S K E T B A L L

FRANK Weix • COACH

The seventh and eighth grade under
the supervision of Mr. Weix have organized a junior basketball team which
meets twice weekly. The team also includes some of the lower classmen. The
boys have responded favorably and have
practiced diligently during these per-
iods. These boys have competed with a
number of the teams from neighboring
towns.

They find this training a valuable
outlet for the surplus energy all boys
possess, as well as invaluable training for the future. It is easy to see
that many of these boys are already working hard to make them worthy of a place
on the team, and the chances are that
they will be a valuable addition to the
high school team.

52

Paul's junior high basketball team photo, 1938.
Paul is front row, second from the left.

HILLIARD, Clayton P.
Enl   22Feb43.
Taken   10Jun43.

With the country at war, Paul enlisted in the US Marine Corps, shown here in his official enlistment photo, 1943.

Paul's Marine Corps unit, the 433rd Platoon, in San Diego, 1943.
Paul is in the third row, fourth from the left.

Paul with his proud grandmothers, Grandma Hilliard (*left*),
Grandma Kees (*right*), 1944.

Paul in a Douglas SBD Dauntless dive-bomber,
Luzon, Philippines, 1944.

Paul (*right*) with Jim Gwilym
in front of the "Dauntless
Dive," 1944.

Paul (*center*) pretending to drink with two other
underage Marines, 1944.

Paul (*left*) with Marine pilot
Ed Schafer, posing on the
wings of an SBD, 1945.

Ed Schafer (*left*) and O. J. "Doc" Koester (*right*), Marine pilots with whom Paul flew, 1945.

Paul (*back row, far left*) with gunners in the "Torrid Turtles," plus their local aide, (*front row, center*), 1945.

Paul (*left*), with his brothers Wally (*center*) and Bill (*right*), in 1945.

Paul back in the States, 1945.

Paul's daughters lined up in their Easter best, 1960.
From left to right: Diane, Paula, Linda, and Donna.

Oilman Paul (*right*) with colleagues in front of a "Christmas tree," 1975.

Lobbyist Paul on a plane to Washington, DC, 1976.

Badger Oil's Maximilian
(UT) Well, 1982.

Sabine Pass drilling rigs
stacked during slump,
1987.

PETROLEUM
INDEPENDENT
October 1989

1989:
IPAA's 60th An... ...the
50th Anniver... ...the beginning

...IPAA Chairman

Also in this issue...
■ Louisiana wetlands' threat to the independent
■ Barton of Texas on *The Clean Air Amendments*

Paul makes the cover of the IPAA's official magazine, December 1989.

Paul (aka "Godzilla") testifying before Congress during the fight over the Iroquois pipeline, 1990.

Paul with CBS newsman Ed Bradley
while recording a news story on the oil industry's slump, 1997.

Transporting the C-47 to the National WWII Museum,
against an iconic backdrop of Jackson Square and the
St. Louis Cathedral, New Orleans, 2006.

Paul and his daughters Paula Breaux (*left*) and Linda Dupree (*right*)
at the National WWII Museum's Victory Ball, 2007.

Paul (*left*) with former US Secretary of State Henry Kissinger (*right*) at the National WWII Museum's American Spirit Awards Gala, 2008.

Paul with daughters (*left to right*) Diane Hilliard, Paula Breaux, Linda Dupree, and Donna Phillips at the Horatio Alger Awards Gala, 2009.

Paul receiving the Horatio Alger Award onstage with Bill Dore
of Global Industries, Ltd., 2009.

Paul with Supreme Court Justice Clarence Thomas at the
Horatio Alger Awards ceremony, 2009.

Paul (*left*) with Gordon H. ("Nick") Mueller, founding president and CEO of the National WWII Museum (*right*), 2010.

Paul (*left*) with former Senator and Governor Pete Wilson (R-CA, *right*) at the National WWII Museum, 2015.

Paul (*first row, right*), wife Madlyn (*first row, left*), and family, after Paul's talk on World War II and the role that oil played in winning the war, Louisiana Oil and Gas Association meeting, 2015.

Paul, chairman of the Board of Trustees at the National WWII Museum, with former board chairmen in front of the museum's Higgins boat, 2017. *From left*: Jim Courter, Phil Satre, Richard Adkerson, Nick Mueller, Boysie Bollinger, Paul, Herschel Abbott, Pete Wilson.

Paul and Madlyn at the American Spirit Awards Patron Party, Windsor Court Hotel, New Orleans, 2018.

Chairman of the Board Hilliard speaking at the American Spirit Awards, 2018.

Paul, decades later, taking a ride in a Dauntless at the air show,
New Orleans, 2018.

National WWII Museum President and CEO Stephen Watson
presenting Paul with a bottle of scotch labeled "GLENHILLIARD" at
the Hilliard Museum Gala, "A Night to Honor Paul Hilliard," 2019.

Madlyn and Paul in front of Paul's home on the farm in Wisconsin, 2021.

Paul (*center*) with business protégés and partners Dave Etienne (*left*) and Art Price (*right*) at Paul's home in Lafayette, 2021.

Paul (*center, in white*) with the National WWII Museum
Board of Trustees at the new Higgins Hotel, 2021.

Paul and Madlyn (*center*) with LouAnne Greenwald, director of the Hilliard Art Museum (*left*) and University of Louisiana Lafayette President Dr. Joseph Savoie (*right*), 2021.

Good friends: the author and Paul Hilliard, 2022.

movie crew was on-site, shooting scenes for the film *Tora! Tora! Tora!*, which dealt with the attack on Pearl Harbor and opened to audiences in 1970.[14] If Diane was surprised to see those planes, one can only imagine her father's thoughts, as history and Hollywood came together in the skies over Pearl Harbor. Only in America, we might say.

Paul continued to learn the business and ride the roller coaster of the oil industry. He was an independent through and through, but he also knew how to rely upon the wisdom and counsel of seasoned oil veterans around him. Foremost among the veteran professionals whose advice he respected was Lyle Cummins, a man in his early forties. A native Kansan from the town of Emporia, he was fourteen years Paul's senior and a figure who was well-established in Lafayette oil circles, partnering with geologists to profit from successful exploration. When Paul and Hunt Oil parted ways, Lyle heard about it and invited Paul to work with him. He took the younger man under his wing and invited him to share his office. Lyle was "the first guy I worked with," Paul remembers. "We would work on (exploration) ideas together, put them together and sell them." Cummins had entered the oil and gas business with no special skills or strengths, but he had a passion for the business. What impressed Paul most was his ability to put together a deal. "Lyle was not a geologist or engineer or lawyer," Paul says. "He just liked the business"—perhaps the most important attribute of all for an oil man.

"Lyle was great to me," Paul says. "A little erratic, a little independent, but he knew a lot of people." The two men worked on ideas they formulated with the help of geologists, scientists who brought to bear the latest available technology. Wallace Pratt was certainly correct. Oil is "first found in the minds of men." But good machines don't hurt, either. In the 1950s, the best available technology was the two-dimensional (2D) seismic survey. It could draw a picture, a slice through the earth, and thus reveal the subsurface geology, making it easier to predict the success or failure of a drilling project. Unfortunately, 2D seismic was an expensive proposition for small operators like Paul and Lyle.[15] "I operated a lot on ideas and options," Paul recalls. "And on scarce 2D seismic information." And also on limiting his liability. "Some of the prospects we put together by purchasing options to lease and turning it to an oil company and keeping a little interest, in case they found something."

In his seventy-year career in oil, Paul witnessed tremendous changes in the industry and an explosion in oil production in the United States, thanks to computer technology and innovations such as horizontal drilling, clearer three-dimensional (3D) imagery, and more accurate data analysis. "Today, there are much more advanced seismic and computers. We had none of that. Unless you were there, it was hard to describe it," he says. "It's like talking with a Millennial about the Great Depression."

Lyle Cummins brought one other thing to his business partnership with Paul: wealth. Lyle's wife, Virginia Frances Wilkinson, was a native Texan, and her family owned a sprawling southeastern Texas ranch near Bay City. While she provided the original nest egg, her husband soon added to it, establishing his own reputation and moving to the front rank of Lafayette's independent oilmen. Lyle worked a lot harder than he had to, Paul notes, simply because he loved the business.

Lyle's wealth, hard work, and reputation also added up to something crucial: a reliable and established line of credit. Credit was essential, Paul explains, to option or buy oil leases on prospective acreage. Credit meant credibility, in a sense, giving the independent operator a foot in the door. Sometimes that was all it took. "If you had a good enough story," Paul laughs, "the banks might lend you $25,000." Lyle and Paul agreed to sell their proposed deals together, an important step forward for Paul.

In 1955, oilmen in Louisiana and Texas organized the Louisiana Gulf Coast Oil and Gas Exposition (LAGCOE), and the fledgling biennial trade show staged its initial event in Lafayette.[16] Lyle's reputation and popularity was evident when his fellow oilmen chose him to serve as the first "LAGCOE Looey," a character meant to represent the industry as an "everyman" oil worker. As ambassador, Lyle proudly greeted all the attendees. Fifty years later, Paul would do the same (serving as Looey No. 25).

The oil industry was growing exponentially in Lafayette in the mid-1950s, as the two men shared Lyle's downtown office. A typical plan of action included procuring the services of a geologist, securing the leases, finding a buyer, and reaping some portion of the final profit by keeping a piece, sometimes just a small fraction, of the deal they happened to be promoting. It wasn't always an instant success. "There were a lot of wells being drilled then," Paul says. "A lot of dry holes. I had my share of them. It was a humbling business. You could work on a deal for two or three years, pour your heart and capital into it, and find out how wrong you were."

"Nature," he says today, "is an unrelenting teacher."

Badger on the Bayou

While Paul's relationship with Cummins was comfortable, their casual partnership was beginning to dissolve. The older man was an excellent mentor, not only teaching the basics of the business but also how to interact with people. He was charismatic and community-minded. Paul was younger, hungrier, and more ambitious. He recognized that the oil industry in southwestern Louisiana was beginning to mushroom and that it was in the process of coalescing around Lafayette.

One of the key factors in the rise of Lafayette to regional prominence was the construction of the "Oil Center" in the early 1950s. Local oilmen, who were locating their offices on St. Mary Boulevard and along Pinhook Road, approached Maurice Heymann, a retail merchant, businessman, and landowner, with the idea of building a Petroleum Club for Lafayette, as well as office space, on the square acreage where Mr. Heymann was currently operating a commercial nursery.[17]

The idea caught Mr. Heymann's imagination. The city's population had grown from 19,210 in 1940 to 33,541 in 1950, and the Oil Center proposal was generating new interest among oilmen from a variety of companies. "Mr. Heymann was quite a visionary. He started off with covered walkways, all connected. But that didn't last. He discovered he could rent them (offices) just as well without covered walkways," Paul remembers. "When the Petroleum Club was built, the whole thing just kind of took off. [Businesses] synergized with each other. The Petroleum Club became an attraction and was far more active than it is today."

The centralization of the regional oil business in Lafayette also attracted related businesses. Law offices, copy machine vendors, liquor stores, cigar stores, and more, eventually even clothing stores and restaurants: all of them moved into the Oil Center. "It was pretty freewheeling for about forty years, very competitive," Paul says. In 1952, there were eleven tenants in Heymann's new Oil Center, and by 1959, there were more than 250. Lafayette had exploded and was probably, pound-for-pound, one of the wealthiest urban areas in America.

The Oil Center also had its secondary benefits. In 1956, using the money he had made in the Lake Verret deal, Paul built his first home in Bendel Gardens, within a mile of the Oil Center. At the time, it contained twenty office buildings; by 1959, the number had nearly doubled, to thirty-nine. The Oil Center itself expanded to South College Road and Coolidge Street. The Lafayette Chamber of Commerce also pitched in, promoting ways for the city to accommodate and encourage the city's growth. The Southwestern Louisiana Institute of Liberal and Technical Learning (later the University of Southwestern Louisiana, and today the University of Louisiana at Lafayette) also did its part, contributing resources from the engineering and chemistry departments to complement the needs of the burgeoning energy industry.

Small wonder, then, that Paul, a young and ambitious entrepreneur, wanted to be near the center of all this growth. He saw the movers and shakers of the regional industry moving to new offices in the Oil Center, and he wanted to be there, too. Lyle disagreed, however, preferring the office he already had on East Main, closer to downtown Lafayette and to his home. The disagreement was unbridgeable, and their long partnership was over. Paul moved alone to Bayou Street, renting rooms in a house located just outside the Oil Center.

By 1959, Paul felt that the time had come to give his fledgling company a name. On November 16, he incorporated it as "Badger Oil," named for the state animal of Wisconsin (and the mascot of the University of Wisconsin-Madison). The moniker seemed to fit. Badgers were short and squat mammals, with long claws perfect for digging. Like Paul, they hunted alone, but could choose to hunt with others. Wisconsin had adopted the badger as a symbol to honor the first "tough as nails" miners in Wisconsin who didn't have shelter in the winter and had to "live like badgers in tunnels burrowed into the hillsides." Paul liked being the only badger in town. When people heard the name, they inevitably asked a follow up question: "What's a farm boy from Wisconsin doing in south Louisiana?" And once a conversation had started, Paul was on his way to doing business.

Badger Oil was created as a "C corporation," separating the company's assets and liabilities from the individual's. This status provided Paul and his independent solo operation a few tax advantages, he says, while also limiting his personal liability. And "solo" and "personal" are perfect words to describe Badger Oil in the early years. Paul was the whole show. Not until the early 1960s was he earning enough money to hire an assistant, Mary Jo Tullos. With her hire, Badger Oil "doubled" in size. She stayed with Paul for eighteen years, and for most of that time she was his sole employee.

Lafayette turned out to be a good choice for his fledgling business, a place to mingle with others in the business. When he started, Paul found that the oilmen tended to gather in one spot: Toby's Oak Grove restaurant at Lafayette's Four Corners. The club, owned by A. E. "Toby" Veltin, was the "magnet," Paul says. The menu concentrated on thick rib eye steaks and hard liquor, all that was necessary to draw together like-minded and energetic oil entrepreneurs. If the city of Lafayette had become the epicenter of the oil business, then Toby's Oak Grove was the social center. Paul says that Toby's was Lafayette's petroleum club "before there was a Petroleum Club" in the Oil Center. "If you were an oil man and you were within twenty miles, you went there for a steak and to hang out," he remembers, sharing "rumors, lies, and speculation."[18]

Having a new modern business area encouraged collegiality among oilmen, Paul says. It wasn't uncommon for oil and gas men to socialize outside of work, hosting barbecues, shrimp boils, and crawfish boils. Deals and gossip were passed with the heaping plates of seafood, spicy potatoes, and corn. "I had some great friends," Paul says of that early era, "even though they might be competitors." Competitors they certainly were, but even as they all went head-to-head with one another, Paul sensed a "brotherhood" among his colleagues. "You felt like you were part of a fraternity," he says. "Oilfield service and supply companies were all over the place," even far from the Oil Center. Scott Road, near the airport, across the river, was one such spot. "One side of the river couldn't hold it," he says. Looking back from the perspective of the energy bust of the late 1980s, which greatly reduced Lafayette's importance to the oil industry, Paul has a rueful tone. "It's sad looking now," he says, "but oil exploration boomed in the '50s, '60s, through the '80s."

The same kind of camaraderie that Paul valued when he partnered with Lyle Cummins was repeated with other local oilmen: Fred Bates, a Princeton graduate and a wildcatter; Jay Wharton Jr., petroleum geologist; Alfred Lamson, a St. Landry Parish native, independent oil and gas producer and fellow World War II veteran. All these men were good at what they did, Paul says, but they were also public-spirited and community-minded. Lafayette's growth did a great deal to help their careers, and in return, their community spirit did much to bolster and increase the wealth of the community.

In those early days, Paul's world centered on the work and friendship of oil industry professionals. But as Lafayette grew and new professionals moved to town—physicians, entrepreneurs, academics—he began to appreciate what they brought to the community as well.

"The town grew because of the oil business," Paul says. "Mr. Heymann donated land for Lafayette General Hospital." Built in the 1960s, it grew rapidly and had become Ochsner Lafayette General Medical Center in 2021. "Lafayette is a great place to be. It is right-sized, right on the interstate, and has fair air service. It's still a pretty good place to live," he says.

Near the close of the 1950s, Paul decided to move his office into the Oil Center itself. Initially, he shared a three-room office with a lawyer from Bunkie, Louisiana. Paul had to seek out Maurice Heymann to rent his first office. "Mr. Heymann was a character," he says. "I looked around the Oil Center for his office and found only a maintenance shed, from where I was directed to Heymann's office at his retail store downtown," Paul says. "I asked him why he didn't have an office in the Oil Center." Mr. Heymann's classic response: "That's for you rich oil people. I can't afford the rent out there."

After he hired his office assistant, Mary Jo, Paul believed that Mr. Heymann was overcharging for the space he rented. The office, he explains, was advertised at 360 square feet, but he checked it one day and it didn't even make it to 300. He asked Mr. Heymann about the discrepancy, and the older man responded, "You want walls, don't you?" He was measuring the office by the outside, not the inside, an unorthodox technique, to put it mildly. That made a difference. Paul could have fought the choice but decided to let it slide. He held a great affection for the older man. Even now, in his nineties, Paul still refers to him as "Mr. Heymann," rather than by his first or last name.

Paul's affection for the oil industry and the burgeoning community convinced him to plant roots in Lafayette. As he freely admits, it also led to one of the many financial errors he committed in his young career. In 1956, he built his first home in Bendel Gardens, a new subdivision on what had been the historic Bendel Estate.

Paul's second daughter Paula remembers that she did not appreciate the jump in financial success that was required to build in Bendel Gardens and to live there. The family's standard of living seemed modest to her for most of the time she lived at home as a teenager. She recalled her father either working in the office alone or with his lone assistant. It was much later, she says, before he seemed to find greater success and was able to expand Badger Oil.

While Paul relished his move to Bendel Gardens, he also made key error in building the new home. He built the house using the profits on his Lake Verret deal, but he forgot one thing. Uncle Sam always takes a cut. He had failed to set aside any money for taxes. "Then came the income tax bill," he says. "Holy mackerel: what have I done?" Paul went to American Bank & Trust Co. and spoke with a seasoned bank officer by the name of Johnny W. Hutchinson. Mr. Hutchinson looked down at the bill and then up at Paul. He had only one question, he says. In words that have echoed down through the ages in financial institutions throughout the land, he asked Paul, "What in the world were you thinkin', boy?"

Paul still recalls what happened next. "He told me what an idiot I was," Paul says, without disputing the point. Nevertheless, Hutchinson gave him the loan with generous terms, spreading the payments over the next three or four years. "I'll never forget him," is Paul's final verdict on his friendly neighborhood banker. And in the "all's well that ends well" department, rising real estate prices soon brought Paul out of debt and into the wonderful world of home equity.

In general, however, Paul agrees with his daughter's recollection. His progress in business was initially modest. "I had no large successes in the early years," he says. "I'd get a piece of a deal here, a piece there. The goal was to become self-sustaining in your household and office. That was your big step." Paul made money on buying leases and selling them to oil exploration companies. All the major oil companies had representation in Louisiana, and midsize companies were everywhere. He never feared failure, he says, because if worse came to worst, he could always work on day rates for other oil and gas companies. While he loved the hands-on aspect of operating the company alone (or with the help of Mary Jo, who handled the office), the business climate had changed dramatically for the better by the mid-1970s, and he could, for the first time, grow his company.

Trouble at the Wellhead?

They say that in life, timing is everything. And "Exhibit A" in proving that proposition is the oil career of Paul Hilliard and Badger Oil. Paul opened his business just a year after the Supreme Court handed down a decision in a case called *Phillips Petroleum Co. v. Wisconsin* in 1954, a federal case that utterly transformed the financial landscape for those who found, produced, and sold natural gas.[19] What sounds like a simple legal principle brought with it a multitude of real-world implications. "Being an independent in 1955 was not good timing," Paul says with some understatement. "The Phillips case said the government had the right and the obligation to regulate the prices of natural gas. That lasted about forty years. They gave bureaucrats the authority to set the price of our product." He had no idea, he says, that he had entered "a business that was so restrictive." Paul had buried himself in the details of the business at the time, and he admits he wasn't seeing the forest for the trees. "You can't see it when you're working every day. You don't see the trends until later."

Only a handful of states were substantial oil and gas producers and naturally benefited from high oil and gas prices. The rest of the states—the vast majority of them—wanted oil and gas prices to remain low. The federal government had traditionally kept its hands off the energy industry, trusting that a laissez-faire approach and the "invisible hand" of the free market would work more effectively to regulate prices. After all, if prices of any product rise high enough, consumers will not be able to afford the product, and producers will not be able to sell it. If they drop too low, then producers will stop producing, and consumers will have nothing to buy. Neither prospect is a very attractive one. But that hands-off policy was about to change.

The 1954 court decision allowed a federal agency to set prices for natural gas at the point of origin, the "wellhead," with the ostensible purpose of protecting the interests of consumers who bought gas that flowed on interstate pipelines. On the plus side, it ensured, or appeared to ensure, stability in pricing for consumers. Politics also played an important role. Consumers (i.e., voters) prefer to pay less for their energy, and politicians know that they can win votes on that issue in the short term.

In the long term, however, producers who aren't earning profits will stop producing. Low prices made the sale of interstate gas unprofitable for operators. In the oil and gas business, this means less exploration and fewer finds. That "cheap" natural gas whose price was regulated by *Phillips v. Wisconsin* was about to become scarce. Broadly speaking, *Phillips* hampered production and limited the supply of gas.

If natural gas were a luxury item or merely an esoteric byproduct of oil production, perhaps none of this would have mattered. Hundreds of years ago, gas was more of a curiosity than anything else. Ancient cultures from Greece to Persia to China had noticed bubbles popping out of the water or saw eerie flames shooting out of crevices. The Oracle of Delphi may have been constructed over a burning natural gas seep on the slopes of Mt. Parnassus, and native Americans ignited gas as it bubbled out of Lake Erie. Not until modern times did scientists positively identify the substance as methane (chemical formula CH_4), a colorless, odorless gas. One of its first practical uses was in lighting nineteenth-century urban streets (the famous hissing "gaslights" of Jack the Ripper's London or Edgar Allen Poe's Baltimore), but transportation of the stuff was so difficult that most people well into the twentieth century viewed it as a nuisance more than anything else, or perhaps even a danger. Think of the canary in the coal mine. His death was an early warning sign to miners that gas levels were dangerous and that they had better get out of the hole. As for oil producers, they usually just vented the stuff into the atmosphere or burned it off.[20]

World War II changed all that. New welding techniques allowed for the building of more reliable pipelines across America. The great expansion of US industry and the housing construction boom stimulated dozens of new applications for gas that went well beyond streetlamps. Today, gas heats our homes and operates our appliances like water heaters and cooktops. It powers our manufacturing and processing plants. It heats boilers to produce electricity. It is as important to the economy and to the quality of modern life as oil or gasoline. Finally, in our increasingly "green" age, gas has the advantage of giving a nice, clean burn. From a nuisance, gas has become a necessity.

Now, the search for gas and oil in America was about to go into a long, slow decline. Nearly seventy years on, Paul still talks about the "great timing," which saw him hitch his wagon to finding and selling a product that had just come under strict government price controls. The climate for his business had suddenly turned overcast, and the future of Badger Oil was very much in doubt. Paul likes to quote Shakespeare:

> Plenty and peace breeds cowards. Hardness ever
> of hardiness is mother.[21]

In other words, hard times toughen you. They nurture you as a parent would, hardening you, making you stronger, more flexible, and resilient. He was about to go through a period of his life that would test that proposition as well.

CHAPTER 6
HOME OF A THOUSAND MILLIONAIRES

Throwing it Away

Talk to Paul Hilliard for even the briefest of conversations, and chances are he will return to *Phillips vs. Wisconsin* at some point. "In later years, the depth of what they did sank in. There were unfortunate, unpleasant repercussions for producers and consumers," he says, labeling it "a perfect example of misguided intentions."

Consider this unintended consequence: at a time when demand for natural gas was skyrocketing all over the country, producers had no economic incentive to ship their gas across state lines. They knew that they could sell it at a much higher price to bidders in their own state ("intrastate"). By 1965, almost a third of the nation's natural gas reserves were earmarked for the intrastate market; ten years later, the figure had risen to almost half. This resulted in natural gas reaching consumers in the producing states, while the consuming states were experiencing natural gas supply shortages.

Or this unintended consequence: the *Phillips* decision, meant to help the consumer, led to an exodus of industries, including petrochemicals, from the northeastern states. These companies had depended upon a steady supply of natural gas and found more reliable sources by moving their operations to the producing states where natural gas could be sold at market price (and thus was still being produced in sufficient amounts). While it might cost more to buy natural gas at the wellhead intrastate, companies learned that at least they *could* buy it. Indeed, it was available in abundance. Many CEOs reasoned that if the gas couldn't come to them, then they had to go to the gas. Louisiana, with its abundant reserves of natural gas, was just one of many southern states that eventually welcomed northern industries that had decided to move south. Paul explains it: "When they built pipelines to New England (and supplies started to dry up because of low production), the industry moved south to get intrastate gas. Poultry, shoes, carpet, petroleum products—they all needed natural gas and they all moved south for cheaper prices. The industries moved out of Massachusetts and New England to the south."

Economist David Glasner echoes Paul's criticism: "The attempt of the large industrial states to continue consuming natural gas produced in other states at less-than market prices was ultimately self-defeating, because it led to a departure of major industries in search of more secure, even if higher priced, supplies of gas. . . . In effect, the court required that the FPC [Federal Power Commission] impose a virtual freeze on natural gas prices in new contracts."[1]

Glasner's analysis is useful in that it brings politics into the equation. Government regulation of gas prices did not benefit the whole country or all its people. Like virtually all government regulations, this one enforced the rules in a zero-sum game that benefited some (mainly in the northern industrial states) and hurt others (the relatively small number of oil-producing states, many in the South). In that sense, the law took money out of the hands of some Americans and transferred it to others.

Glasner also notes a repeated pattern. Government regulation leads to distortions or shortages of the regulated item. Eventually, a "crisis" arises, caused almost entirely because of regulation. Soon the public is angry, demanding that the government "do something," demands to which the government invariably responds with . . . more regulation.[2] And the cycle continues.

And one last consequence: *Phillips* turned out to be a bureaucratic and administrative nightmare. Boiled down to its essentials, the decision meant that each producer of natural gas—from the biggest of Big Oil to the smallest independent producer—was now treated as if it were an individual public utility. The FPC had unwittingly taken on an enormous burden. The FPC could probably have doubled or tripled its number of personnel and still not come close to being able to handle the paperwork, the compliance issues, the applications for exemptions, and more. A tremendous backlog soon developed. In 1959, to give just one example of many, the FPC received 1,265 separate applications for rate increases or reviews but was able to act on only 240 of them.[3] Moreover, not all natural gas was the same: some came from old (or "flowing") wells, some from newer wells, some from land-based wells, offshore fields, and more. Costs varied for all of them. Whatever price the FPC chose was bound to be unfair and whose only effect would be to hold prices stagnant and thus strangle any incentive for new exploration or increased production.

Paul still argues that the Supreme Court's 1954 decision was a fateful error that dealt a massive blow not only to the oil industry, but to America's global leadership role. The United States was the dominant power in the world after World War II. We often say it was "one of two superpowers," but the American economy was many times larger than that of the Soviet Union. And one of the reasons was our dominance in the field of energy. Our military power was unmatched, our global reach was nearly absolute. It was the height of the American Century. And this was the very moment, he believes, that an unwise and unfair political decision nearly threw it all away. "We're untouched," Paul says, "sitting on top of the world. Much of the rest of the world is still a wreck. And what does America do? Puts limits on the price of interstate natural gas. Of all times! Suddenly there was no real incentive to find gas."

Paul is a political conservative who believes in laissez-faire economics and the workings of the free market, and he makes no bones about it. For that very reason, he delights in pointing out the one dissenting Supreme Court justice in *Phillips vs. Wisconsin*: none other than that darling of the liberal cause, Justice William O. Douglas.[4] He preferred to have Congress, not the courts, resolve the issue. He also doubted that anyone in government had the expertise to regulate wellhead pricing, a prediction that proved to be accurate. "The regulation of the business of producing and gathering natural gas involves considerations of which we know little and with which we are not competent to deal," Justice Douglas wrote.[5] It may well be the only sentence Douglas ever wrote in his long career with which Paul would agree.

Paul's final verdict on what he sees as a mistimed, misguided, and harmful measure? It was, he says, a classic "and the government did what?" scenario, and it remains an example of the dangers of excessive federal interference in the economy.

One-Man Badger

Paul entered the energy industry at a time when American demand for oil was skyrocketing and when the country first became a net importer of oil. In the 1950s–60s, the available US production could not meet domestic demand, and so larger American oil companies began to expand their drilling operations abroad: Latin America, Africa, and, of course, the Middle East. Because of limits imposed on drilling and producing oil in the United States, Canada, and Mexico enjoyed special privileges to export there. Mexico, in fact, increased its oil exports to the United States sixfold.

Oil historian Daniel Yergin wrote that oil-producing countries (or countries that hoped to become oil producers) made concessions to American companies to drill in their homelands.[6] Many oil companies left US shores, where there were restrictions on domestic drilling, to explore and produce oil elsewhere. The result, Yergin wrote, was that American technology, money, and expertise traveled across the world. Nine American companies were working in the Middle East in 1946. In 1956, there were nineteen, and in 1970, eighty-one. Clearly, a small, independent company like Badger Oil (still barely more than Paul working solo) couldn't compete in the complexities of overseas drilling.

Another challenge to independents like Badger arose in the 1950s: drilling for gas or oil offshore in the Gulf of Mexico.[7] Against long odds, Kerr-McGee, a small Oklahoma company, drilled successfully from a platform in the Gulf of Mexico in 1947. Ship Shoal Block 32 was the first well drilled out of sight of land, some ten miles off the coast south of Morgan City. The well was sunk from freestanding offshore platform named Kermac 16, an engineering marvel including sixteen 24-inch pilings sunk over 100 feet into the ocean floor and a 2,700-square-foot wooden deck. The biggest test came just one week after drilling began, when Kermac 16 survived a Category 5 hurricane. Kerr-McGee was only drilling offshore because the firm's leaders knew they could not compete against the larger and well-established oil companies on land. Geology also seemed to argue in offshore drilling's favor; there was no reason to believe oil and gas deposits stopped at the shoreline.

Up to now, the largest petroleum reserves were in hands of the so-called "Seven Sisters," the elite of the oil industry: the Anglo-Persian Oil Company (APOC, the predecessor of British Petroleum), Royal Dutch

Shell, three of Chevron's predecessors (Standard Oil of California, Gulf Oil, and Texaco), and two of ExxonMobil's predecessors (Jersey Standard and Standard Oil of New York).[8] As the oil industry went global and drilling became more technologically complex, these companies—often collectively called "Big Oil"—grew into true global behemoths.

Kerr-McGee's oil strike in the Gulf began to change that. Innovations followed. In 1954, Alden "Doc" Laborde, a World War II veteran and marine engineer, designed a barge drilling platform that could move from place to place, the world's first mobile offshore drilling unit (MODU).[9] "Mr. Charlie" could drill "a 12,000-foot hole at a different location every month," and drill in water twice as deep as Kermac 16. Laborde had a hard time selling the idea. His own company, Kerr-McGee, refused to bite, telling him the idea "looked good on paper," but faced too many "unknowns" such as "ocean currents, shifting bottoms, hurricanes and many other factors that just would not allow this idea to work as planned." He eventually sold it to Shell, and his landmark invention drilled hundreds of wells in the Gulf before it was retired in 1986.

Other companies followed Kerr-McGee and Shell into the water. Drilling offshore was expensive, and still is, but Kermac 16 and Mr. Charlie were proof that an innovative idea (and deep-pocketed investors) could result in spectacular profits. The rush to drill in deeper water on the continental shelf precipitated a lengthy court fight between the states bordering the Gulf of Mexico and the federal government. The boundary dispute was over which entity, the federal government or the individual states, owned the minerals under the continental shelf and could therefore claim the oil revenues generated by drilling. The offshore drilling dispute took more than a decade to resolve, to Louisiana's eventual disadvantage. The state could lay claim to possession of three nautical miles off the state's coastline, a ruling that later came into some dispute because of ongoing erosion in Louisiana that has continued to move the coastline. Anything beyond the three nautical mile limit, the courts ruled, was the domain of the federal government.

Overseas exploration, offshore drilling, property disputes: none of these immediately affected Badger Oil, as important as they may have been to others in the state. Because offshore drilling was so pricey, complex, and risky, it was simply too rich for Paul's blood. Badger Oil did not drill offshore for another forty years. There were still plenty of oil and gas prospects onshore that were more accessible and affordable.

Clearly, Paul had entered the oil business at a time of serial disadvantages for small, independent companies like Badger Oil. From the time he started in 1955 until the early 1970s, he says, he never saw oil prices top $3 a barrel, and natural gas prices never rose above twenty cents per MCF (1000 cubic feet, yielding the energy of approximately 1,000,000 British thermal units, or Btu). "I remember reading the *Beaumont Enterprise* [Texas] newspaper headline about a ten-cents-a-barrel increase in oil prices. That was a big deal," he says. "Producer prices were stable," he notes, "but at a miserably low level." Under the right circumstances, stable prices can be a good thing, enabling prudent choices and long-term planning, but not if the price is so low it is strangling the producer. Thinking back on it, Paul puts it in stark terms: "The years 1955–1971 were difficult. Looking at charts years later, I am amazed that I survived."

Stubbornly, Paul forged on because he says he had no choice. He had to provide for his family, and he still liked the people in the business. That is a sentiment that has not changed in the more than seventy years he has been involved. "It's very much a people business," he believes. "There are some idiots and some who are unreliable. But in my life, I never found a better bunch of guys than independents, and the oilfield service and supply companies. I have nothing but the highest regard for these guys. They're reliable, honest, dependable, competent people."

Perhaps it's the nature of the oil business itself. "The drilling rig is in the field 24/7," Paul points out. "It's an unusual type of business. Offshore, it could be a million-dollars-a-day deal. You can't miss a screw or a valve in an operation like that. Many land rigs were in the boondocks. You need competence, reliability, and unwavering determination."

When Paul moved beyond being a landman to becoming an operator, he became increasingly dependent upon partners and contractors. "When you are operating as an individual—every day, all day—there are a lot of things going on," he says. "And I was an individual attempting to do all things at all times. Essentially, an amateur trying to do the jobs of a professional." But would he have it any other way? Probably not. Doing for himself was and is the single most salient characteristic of Paul's career: he loves the "hands-on" aspect that was the essence of being an independent oilman, operating "as a one-man Badger."

Not until the 1970s did oil prices begin to rise, and when they did, they did so in style. The cause was an oil embargo placed upon sales to the United States by the Organization of Petroleum Exporting Countries (OPEC). The OPEC countries banned petroleum exports to all countries that were giving aid to Israel during the 1973 Arab-Israeli War, what Israelis call the Yom Kippur War.[10] It was the first time that anyone had dared to use the "oil weapon" against the United States, which was Israel's primary supplier of weapons and military technology and provided it in abundance during the most difficult war in Israel's history. The attack by Israel's Arab neighbors, Egypt and Syria, caught Israeli military intelligence napping, and in the opening stages of the war, at least, as their army fell back before the onslaught, the Israelis were in a state of panic. They eventually righted the situation on the battlefield, with the help of massive amounts of US military assistance, including some of the most sophisticated weaponry then in the American arsenal.[11]

The results of the OPEC decision were not especially surprising. With the war less than a week old, the chairmen of the four American oil companies active in the Middle East—Exxon, Mobil, Texaco, and Standard of California—sent a letter to President Richard M. Nixon. They warned that US support of Israel would have a "snowballing effect," and the result might well be a "major petroleum supply crisis." They went on to predict that, "the whole position of the United States in the Middle East is on the way to being seriously impaired, with Japanese, European, and perhaps Russian interests largely supplanting United States presence in the area, to the detriment of both our economy and our security."[12]

President Nixon no doubt pondered the words of this letter. He was a serious man and understood the complexities of foreign policy. The note came from men in weighty positions of responsibility. But then, he received a second note, this one from Israel's doughty premier, Golda Meir, warning the president that war was in the offing and that her nation's survival hung in the balance.[13] President Nixon took the second letter to heart, even as he understood the first.

The embargo not only sent oil prices skyrocketing, it also came as a tremendous shock to the American public. Retail gasoline prices—the price at the pump—skyrocketed by 40 percent, literally overnight. Some gas stations were raising their prices as often as once per day, but that was if you could get gas at all. With the federal government enacting "one-time supply curtailment measures," gas was suddenly in short supply, and a new phrase entered the American lexicon, one that would have been un-thinkable just weeks before: the "gas line." For a public that had grown up with the automobile, the sign "Sorry, No Gas Today" might as well have been a harbinger of the apocalypse. Anyone alive at the time can remember lines at gas stations stretching out into the street for miles. Driving on the highway, traditionally a "flat out" pastime for American drivers, entered a much more sedate, even boring, phase, as interstate highways designed to handle 70 mph traffic now had new speed limits of 55 mph, courtesy of 1974s National Maximum Speed Law, a piece of legislation that openly declared that its purpose was not to save lives (which it did), but to reduce fuel consumption.

The oil shock of 1973 also led the federal government to reconsider some of its restrictions on US producers. To oil companies, from the largest down to the smallest independent, rising oil prices looked like an opportunity. Paul was trying to build Badger into something bigger and "more substantial." He could now assemble a staff and began to operate like a small oil company rather than a lone-wolf operation, hiring accountants, geologists, and landmen. He could begin to pursue a more conservative approach to doing business, splitting oil deals with other investors, but still pocketing impressive sums, given the new price levels.

Partnering on deals was a long-standing practice in the industry. Jimmie Owen was a famous wildcatter in the 1920s.[14] He coined a phrase that was as true now as it was then: "Eight-eighths fever will kill you!"[15] Essentially, the investor who risks the entire investment for a project stands to enjoy all the profits, but also has to suffer all of the potential losses. In this game, players face all-or-nothing stakes, in other words, and the odds eventually catch up with them.

"We always split the deals," Paul says of Badger and other independents. "A few times, Badger had all of it. I thought it was a sure thing—and it wasn't." Consider the time Paul was on vacation in Canada with his family. An enjoyable family road trip suddenly derailed when he got several messages from the office telling him that he had four dry holes in two weeks. He remembers driving, trying not to let the bad news get the better of him. It took all he had to keep looking happy for the sake of his four young daughters in the back seat. "I drove with a gorilla grip on the steering wheel," he recalls.

This moment in Paul's life encapsulates the oil business, especially from the perspective of the small independent. "You start with a geological idea you think is marketable," Paul explains today. "You're putting a deal together, you raise the risk dollars. These were four totally different types of deals." And then you wait. Perhaps you're in the field, perhaps you're at home. Maybe you're on the Trans-Canada Highway in a borrowed station wagon driving to Lake Louise with your wife and four daughters. Bad news never seems to come at the right time. Everybody gets some sooner or later, and for the independent oil man, you might say it's just the cost of doing business.

What really matters is how you react to it. Paul just kept going, seeking partners for his next oil project. Partners were always available. Plenty of independents were operating in south Louisiana. One independent oilman whose company and partnership Paul treasured was Sterling E. Little. "Sterling was one of the most memorable characters I worked with," he recalls. "He was always an optimist," something that is probably a prerequisite for success for an independent. "That never ceased, never wavered. I loved working with a guy who was optimistic and shared a sense of humor." Little, he says, could always handle adversity with equanimity and good humor. Like Paul, he was a Marine, a former transport pilot who "hauled the wounded out of Guadalcanal, hauled supplies in," Paul says. Little was a good geologist but also someone who treasured a good time, and he was single until he married at forty. "I think Sterling Little hugged every lamppost in the French Quarter," Paul laughs. "But once he married, that was it. He went straight."

The two worked on deals together for five years or so. On one occasion, Little and Paul put together a drilling deal in Allen Parish, west of Lafayette, on industrial timber land. The well was drilled under Little's name with high hopes for success, but very quickly proved to be a bust. At the time, the New Orleans *Times-Picayune* had an oil editor who published results of all oil exploration efforts in the region, and who wrote that, "the Little well was plugged and abandoned in ten days." Little joked it made him out to be some kind of a hero for "drilling a dry hole in only ten days!" A tart sense of humor was always a good thing in the oil business.

Little died before his time, but Paul never forgot his old friend. "Sterling," he says, "was another man who supplied the support and broad shoulders to encourage and teach me in the early days."

"Carter Lied to Me"

Almost two decades after the government imposed itself heavy-handedly into the oil and gas industry, the chickens came home to roost. Serious problems had begun to manifest themselves. There were "indescribable distortions in the market," Paul remembers. As prices finally began to rise in the early 1970s, profitability increased for everyone tied to oil exploration. But gas remained a problem. The 1954 decision regulating the price of interstate gas was still in effect, and interstate gas markets began to run short. Glasner notes with some irony the real results of the *Phillips* decision: "Beginning in 1968 total gas reserves in the United States (excluding Alaska, whose gas reserves are not accessible to the lower forty-eight states or Hawaii) declined each year until 1980. And because of the growing price disparity between the interstate and the intrastate markets, whatever new reserves were being found went almost exclusively into the intrastate market."[16] Those "new reserves" went, in other words, to the market where they could fetch a fair price. It was, he says, "a problem that had been developing for two decades."

"I remember well, more than forty years ago," Paul recalls, "Jimmy Carter was elected president and promised [Oklahoma] Governor David Boren that we would deregulate natural gas." Campaign promises have a way of disappearing into the mist once you're in office, and Carter did not follow through on his promise. Paul remembers one Oklahoma newspaper running a banner headline quoting Boren, reading "Carter Lied to Me."[17]

Soon into the Carter presidency, in January 1977, disaster struck. One of the worst blizzards in US history struck the northeast. Temperatures plunged to -60 degrees in some parts of the region, and thirty-eight people died. Carter declared the states of New York and Pennsylvania disaster areas and said that he was thinking of putting the nation on a four-day work week to conserve something that was suddenly in very short supply: natural gas. New Jersey Governor Brendan Byrne wasn't far behind: he invoked a wartime law and ordered residents of the state to set their thermostats to 65 degrees during the day and 60 degrees at night; he even warned violators they could go to jail.[18] All this happened in a country that is literally awash in easily retrievable natural gas. Paul doesn't mince words on this topic. He rarely does. "Nine days after President Carter took office, a blizzard hit: courthouses were open only one day a week in some places, and Carter wore a sweater on TV," Paul says, calling it "poetic justice." Many Americans either didn't know or wouldn't admit that the regulation of natural gas prices had backfired. Wisconsin, one of the northern states most in favor of cheap natural gas, was plunged into crisis.

The federal government had still not learned its lessons, however. In November of 1978, Congress passed the Natural Gas Policy Act of 1978. It took a bad situation, one plagued by administrative bottlenecks and backlogs, and made it much worse. Glasner criticizes the response: "Rather than abandon the controls entirely, the government stumbled around—modifying here, controlling there, and decontrolling elsewhere—until had it erected a patchwork of controls and regulation that continue to obstruct and distort normal market forces."[19]

This "patchwork" had disastrous consequences of its own. Natural gas prices varied wildly from well to well. Older fields yielded cheap gas, while the price of gas newer fields skyrocketed. "Badger was a small producer," Paul states, "but over a period of about ten years we experienced natural gas prices from eleven cents per MCF to more than eight dollars." As could be expected, not everyone was pleased, lawsuits over natural gas prices became more frequent, and the market remained uncertain.

Paul delights in pointing out the foibles of the system of the late 1970s, and the effect of price controls of oil and gas generally. "From a well in Acadia Parish, we were getting five dollars a barrel. The OPEC producers were receiving eight times as much for their oil as we were getting for domestically produced. Reportedly, people would take oil, put it on a tanker, take it to sea, and import it as foreign oil to get higher prices. It was typical of what well-meaning legislation can do."

Paul also remembers a visit he had with US Senator Ernest "Fritz" Hollings, a South Carolina Democrat, in Washington, DC, to discuss the Natural Gas Policy Act of 1978 and its many deficiencies.[20] To Paul, Hollings seemed clueless, especially when he declared that it was not

Congress's intention to draft and pass into a law a bill that created more chaos. "The statute was not designed to function like that," Hollings told him, shaking his head. Paul was too polite to issue a retort, but anyone knows him can guess what he was thinking.

By this time, the generally recognized need for growing supplies of natural gas changed how Badger Oil operated. Paul says that those who produced gas started looking for intrastate buyers where available. As Northern companies moved to Louisiana to set up their plants, Paul and Badger began to reevaluate the in-state market. "South Louisiana is a gassy area," he says. "We tried to avoid gas prospects until prices rose in 1972. With prices up, we chased gas."

That chase led Badger to take part in the drilling "frenzy" of the late 1970s. These were the years when Paul finally began to realize the fruits of his labor, an "overnight sensation" after twenty years. Skyrocketing oil and gas prices allowing operators like Paul to prosper, and he still looks back on this period as a time of expansion and newfound professional success. For all his hard work—or perhaps because of it—Paul's marriage to Sally did not survive. They split in 1969, just as the oil industry was to explode. He married his second wife, Eula "Lulu" Burton, in 1972.

Home of a Thousand Millionaires

Across the globe, with oil prices at all-time highs, ambitious individuals and companies were chasing oil. It was a global craze. Asked to characterize the mood of the times, an executive at Exxon didn't mince words: "It's just wild," he says. By 1978, drilling ships and rigs were bid up to double what they had been worth in 1973. Entirely new regions came into play: Alaska, Mexico, Norway, and eventually, the "biggest play of them all," the North Sea, where producers had to dig wells at unimaginable depths in some of the world's most vile weather, a "technological marvel of the first order," as one analyst put it.[21]

Across the nation, people were beginning to take notice of this small Louisiana town in the heart of Acadiana. Bankers noticed the accounts of their Lafayette customers swelling many times over. A landmark day in the rise of Lafayette to national prominence was March 8, 1981, when the *New York Times* ran a story headlined "Lafayette, La.: Home of a Thousand Millionaires."[22] William K. Stevens painted a portrait of a city that was not only the center of Louisiana's oil industry, but a burgeoning community for the nouveaux riches. Signs of prosperity were everywhere, he wrote, including folks who jetted around the world on safari and teenage girls dripping in diamond pendants and earrings: "At first, only scattered clues hint at Lafayette's new character and importance. A steakhouse puts $100-a-bottle Château Mouton Rothschild at the top of its wine list, and it becomes a frequent seller. A woman is overheard telling a coffee shop hostess how she is "getting ready for Acapulco." A Mercedes here and a Cadillac there zip along past fresh-faced new buildings."[23]

And there was no doubt what was driving this new wealth: "With oil selling at $37 a barrel, and investors consequently rushing to put money into drilling for that oil, once-in-a-lifetime fortunes are being made by those engaged directly in the oil business, and by those capitalizing on the prodigious, oil-induced growth of Lafayette itself."

Arthur Broussard, then-president of Guaranty Bank, appears in the article, estimating that there are "a thousand, perhaps more" millionaires in a town whose population at the time was only 85,000.[24] In 1981, Lafayette ranked ninth in the country in the value of retail sales per household—the shopping sweepstakes, we might call it. A waiter at the popular La Fonda restaurant, a Mexican place, tells the *Times* that "a $100 tip for a $50 meal is not unknown, but that 20 to 30 percent from a millionaire is more usual."

The *New York Times* is often highly critical of the rich—indeed, criticizing wealth often seems to be the newspaper's stock in trade. Stevens takes a very nuanced view in this piece, however. Sure, there are millionaires in Lafayette, but their behavior is very much conditioned by the locale. Lafayette isn't Anytown, USA. It sits in the heart of a Cajun country, and Cajun folkways don't tolerate people putting on airs. "At the Petroleum Club," Stevens writes, "you wouldn't know that so much money was seated in the velour chairs of the lounge or at the lunch tables, so informal is the atmosphere. Shirtsleeves and open collars prevail."

The appearance of the town mirrored the down-home nature of the men who lived there. "Outside in the Oil Center, a grouping of several streets where most of the oil companies' offices are clustered, it is just as plain. The buildings, generally one story high, are of subdued yellow brick, very functional." Lafayette could even work its magic on outsiders.

"Indeed, oilmen who move here from elsewhere tend to go a little bit native; to adopt the relaxed Cajun values and activities. Outdoor sports like hunting and fishing, for example, are extremely popular."

Paul's assessment on the piece: "Pretty much overblown." He suggested there may have been a couple of hundred millionaires in Lafayette then, most of them in the oil services industries, as opposed to the drilling for oil. Nevertheless, there is much that is accurate in the *Times* article. Stevens identified two concerns of Lafayette's wealthiest citizens. The first was income taxes, the typical fear for any high earner: "There seems to be little question that this is by far the biggest determiner of how the Big Rich use most of their money. As might be expected, they invest it rather than lose it. And not surprisingly, they tend to invest it these days in tangibles—houses, boats and condominiums."

The second, however, was potentially much more serious, since it involved issues of foreign policy, global stability, and especially the troubled situation in the Middle East: "Some [oil men] acknowledge that the current oil price bubble is to some extent an artificial one; that is, an arbitrarily inflated boom that is not that closely related to real scarcity of oil in the world. If prices can be raised arbitrarily by the Organization of Petroleum Exporting Countries, it is reasoned, they can be lowered just as arbitrarily. Furthermore, some oilmen worry that a future Administration in Washington might not be so friendly as the one in power now, and that price controls might someday be reimposed."[25]

This, too, was a true reflection of opinion in Lafayette at the time. Anxieties centered, in particular, on the Saudis, sitting on some of the world's largest oil reserves and some of the cheapest to extract, who could, at any moment they chose, flood the market and drive down prices.

Looking back, it is possible to read the signs that the Saudis were moving unilaterally to do just that. Such a move would crash oil prices overnight, and thus drive US competitors, whose oil was much more expensive to find and extract, out of business. In Lafayette, however, the spirit was still go-go. All the land and the cluster of offices in the Oil Center were in use by 1981. All told, Mr. Heymann had built 107 buildings, and by now some 450 oil companies or related businesses were located there. But beneath the veneer of high prosperity was an undercurrent of anxiety.

"Some people talked about it," Paul says of the local economy's dependence on stability in the Middle East to maintain prices. By 1983, seismic crew counts were in decline; fewer people were looking for oil. The Saudis kept oil prices high by voluntarily restraining their own production capacity, but OPEC was never a very disciplined organization, and other members were pumping more.

And then, suddenly, came the correction. The Saudis did what many had feared and rapidly accelerated their production in the mid-1980s. The reason actually had little to do with the United States, but more to do with relations among the OPEC states. In the mid-1980s, OPEC was handling a third or more of the world's oil. The organization had set quotas to keep prices stable, but some members were exceeding their quota, producing more, making an already serious "oil glut" even worse, and thus bringing down prices. At a June 1985 OPEC meeting in Taif, Saudi Arabia, Saudi oil minister Sheikh Ahmed Zaki Yamani read the member states a letter from King Fahd.[26] The king admonished his OPEC partners to stop their cheating ways, which, he said, were leading to "a loss of markets for Saudi Arabia." In blunt language, Fahd declared, "If member countries feel they have a free hand to act, then all should enjoy this situation and Saudi Arabia would certainly secure its own interests."[27] The warning was clear, or at least it should have been: Fahd would take measures if they didn't play ball.

They didn't, and he did, dramatically increasing production to 3.9 million barrels a day from 2.2 million barrels. Global prices immediately began to fall. This was the same stratagem that John. D. Rockefeller used to employ in the heyday of Standard Oil. If other companies were displeasing him in some way, he'd flood the market with oil and knock down market prices, forcing his competitors to cooperate, go out of business, or face the possibility of a takeover. He called it giving the market "a good sweating."[28] Now Saudi Arabia was doing the same. The kingdom's revenue was relatively unaffected by the price decreases, since it sold so much more oil than its rivals, but the revenue of other OPEC members was immediately slashed.

King Fahd's decision wasn't aimed at the United States per se, but the effects on the American oil industry were dramatic. By early 1986, the petroleum prices went into a downward spiral. The benchmark US rate for West Texas Intermediate crude plummeted from its all-time high of $31.75 per barrel in November 1985 to $10.00 a few months later. America had been shocked by skyrocketing oil prices in 1973. Now there was another shock, only in the opposite direction. Ponder this scenario for a moment: say a small oil company recently made a strike on the western slope of the Rocky Mountains in Wyoming, a 7,000-acre oil and gas field called Anschutz Ranch East. A barrel of oil costs the company $25.00 to produce. If they can sell it at $37.00 a barrel, investors are happy. When the price sinks below $10.00 a barrel, the company can't afford to pump the very oil it needs to sell. At that point, it isn't really a choice. The company closes up shop.

That's precisely what happened all over the United States. Paul puts it this way: "The oil industry lives on debt, and all of a sudden your income plummets 50 percent." No one knew where it would end. A dark question now defined the oil industry, viewed by most of the American public as the land of record profits and price-gouging: "How low would it go?" Paul is frank about the failure to anticipate the development. "We didn't foresee the Saudis opening the valve like they did."

With markets awash in Saudi oil, the oil industry swooned. "You talk about knocking the hell out of the industry," he recalls. Active rig counts in the United States sank from four thousand to six hundred. Businesses closed, and Lafayette's fabled millionaire economy faltered. Dr. Loren C. Scott, professor emeritus of economics at LSU, said Louisiana lost no fewer than 146,000 jobs over five years during the oil downturn of the 1980s. Lafayette itself lost 20 percent of its jobs, and Houma 24 percent. "It was a bloodbath," he said. The oil and gas industry laid off 100,000 workers in five months.[29] "You could buy a fourplex for what a single unit used to cost," says Paul.

Times were so grim, says Steve Maley, Badger Oil's manager of operations, that Charley G's restaurant in Lafayette linked its "lunch special" ticket to the price of a barrel of oil on a given day. "I remember getting lunch for $8.50," Maley recalls with a laugh. Charlie Goodson, the namesake and partner in Charley G's, remembers it being even worse: "The price got way down there. Something in my mind says it went to $5.40, but I know it was under ten dollars for a long time.[30] He started construction on the restaurant, which was located between two oil businesses, one with ninety employees, the other with four hundred. By the time the restaurant opened, both neighboring businesses had shuttered. As the local economy cratered, Scott remembers, gallows humor started making the rounds in Lafayette: "Have you heard? Louisianians are slipping into Mexico to seek work." Or one that Paul still remembers: "Walmart employs more geologists than Exxon."

For Paul, approaching his sixtieth birthday, the mid-1980s were a real learning experience, perhaps a wake-up call. "In '86, I got my lesson in debt and uncontrolled, unsustainable growth," he says today. By 1990, "I began to realize that when you have oil and gas production, every check you get for production is one less than you're going to get. It is not like a building that is still there after you use it. Oil and gas are finite resources to develop—they're a depleting asset."

"After the collapse of '86," he admits, "I realized that too much of a good thing is not good."

Paul's response was to diversify. In the early 1980s, he got involved in forming a bank, MidSouth, which opened in 1985. "I was one of the first ones in, one of the last ones out of the original bunch," he says. "The bank didn't do great during that early period, but [eventually] it was good to me. I loved every bit of it." Rusty Cloutier, a banker from St. Mary Parish, was hired to get MidSouth up and running in 1985.[31] At the start, the bank had a single branch on Pinhook Road. To save the bank money, he cut the lawn himself on Saturdays. Cloutier says the bank was troubled for at least its first six years. For those early years, board directors received no remuneration, and Paul still insists he did not deserve one. Banking was complex, he says, and he did not know a lot about it. But he enjoyed meeting other, established business leaders on the board and treated his board service, like everything in his professional life, as a learning opportunity. In 1987, MidSouth acquired Breaux Bridge Bank & Trust Co. Two years later, it acquired Commerce and Energy Bank of Lafayette. By the early 1990s, as the local economy recovered from the 1986 crash, MidSouth began to turn the corner. In 1993, the bank went public and the investors, including Paul, began to profit. "I learned about the power of compound interest," he says.

The bank's early doldrums reflected the local situation. With Lafayette dependent upon a brisk oil and gas industry, the local economy was in the dumps. "Lafayette wasn't on sale in the '80s, it was on super discount," is how Cloutier puts it. "About two-thirds of the original board members left because they were insolvent. They lost everything they had."

Most board members get paid for service, Cloutier says, but MidSouth was just the opposite. "We had 'country club' dues. Every month they had to bring a check to the bank."

But by the time Cloutier left the bank in 2017, shortly after Paul retired from the board, it had grown to more than sixty branches in Louisiana and Texas. In an ironic twist, Lafayette was once again suffering from the effects of an oil price free fall, and with the bank too tied to the energy industry, Cloutier was forced out at MidSouth. "Paul Hilliard was a very stabilizing influence," Cloutier says of his three decades at MidSouth. "No one had more knowledge of the oilfield than Paul did." It was precious knowledge, since the oilfield drove the local economy.

Cloutier says that Paul also had a keen business sense that helped the bank's leadership, especially the gift of attracting the right employees. His best advice, Cloutier says, was to hire people with a demonstrated work ethic and impeccable honesty. A "decent education" was important, Paul told him, but lofty credentials from elite schools did not always guarantee an employee would be up to handling their assignment. "Mr. Hilliard had a lot of belief in people. And he always had confidence in tomorrow," Cloutier says.

During his long career, of course, Paul learned that not every investment worked. He moved into the Oil Center in the late 1950s, for example, and over the years he outgrew four buildings. Certain that land and real estate was a solid place to invest, he learned instead that the real estate business offered no guarantees of success. When the oil industry went "into the ditch," he lost tenants in his building. Boom times encouraged the "greater fool theory," he says. People sometimes paid way too much for land. But overall, he made money from real estate investments.

The experience of the 1980s, he says in retrospect, provided an "era of wild expansion and an overdose of humility." When he thinks of the downturn in that decade, "I think of a thousand millionaires, but of a million idiots, too. I learned that you better be prepared for that black swan. I had no choice but to outlive all those problems. I couldn't trouble my wife and family with them."

"He's Not an Average Guy"

Paul could give wise counsel, as Cloutier testifies, but he also followed his own best advice. In the late 1980s, he hired two young men, one a geologist, Dave Etienne, who had been laid off twice during the oil downturn, and the other, Art Price, an accounting student at the University of Louisiana at Lafayette. The two young men helped Paul stabilize his company, turn Badger around, and prepare it for a new era of prosperity.

In a few short years, Paul developed a belief and confidence in both men as he relaxed his grip on the controls of Badger Oil and turned much of the company's direction over to them. The 1990s saw large energy companies make major cutbacks, disposing of properties with high depreciation, depletion, and amortization. Forsaking some of those fields gave independents new opportunities, as they could concentrate more intensely on fields that they believed had life left in them.

With fewer rigs operating, large oil and gas companies needed fewer people, and they laid off valuable employees. Many larger operations in Acadiana closed, some becoming parts of consolidations ordered from Houston. Many of their employees had settled down in south Louisiana and had no desire to move again. They became available to smaller independents, who gobbled up this new source of talent. Badger Oil raided many of these assets that larger companies left behind, both oilfields and people. Dave and Art were two good examples. Both men could see that Badger needed new strategies. Paul had the courage to allow new and capable hands to steer the ship that he had built with his own hands.

Dave saw that the oil industry in south Louisiana had changed remarkably in the three decades since Paul founded his company. Most prospects for independents in the old days, he says, were generated by subsurface work, not seismic studies, which were expensive. It was not as costly to get started in the 1950s. "Lafayette in the early days was a different town," Dave says. Paul would work with certain geologists in his early years at Badger, put up the money, sometimes at substantial risk, even to the point of mortgaging his own home. "You could do that if you were smart and savvy," Dave says, adding, "He has a different tolerance for risk than I do."[32]

In those days, deals were made with numerous partners and investors, each risking something to seek greater profits. Finding investors was not necessarily difficult because there were incentives, particularly tax advantages. "You could invest in oil and gas drilling because intangible drilling costs were 100 percent deductible in the first year," Etienne says. "It was very attractive to a lot of people. Everywhere in our business, people raised drilling funds."

Etienne adds that while geologists and landmen knew what might be sold as a plausible or attractive prospective package to investors, the real money for companies was in drilling the well itself. "The cost might be 10 percent land, 90 percent drilling," he says. "You own and control the prospect, then bring it to someone. You are promoting the deals. Investors pay a disproportionate share of what they earn. That was very common in our business. It remains common."

Dave gives an example of how Badger works its deals, based on the "third-for-a-quarter" philosophy developed by Marvin Davis: "I own the deal. I sell it to three people. They each pay one-third of the costs. For that, you [Badger, the operator] earn a quarter. The carried quarter belongs to Badger." That is how Davis, an innovator in the oil industry, did it, and that, Dave says, was a standard way to do business, with the person or company that owns the deal, the one with the idea and expertise, sharing equally in profits with those who invested their money.

Back in Paul's early days, there might be eight investors, the other seven whose investments would cushion the blow if a deal failed. If an investor did own the whole investment, he might reap all of the profits if the deal turned out to be successful; if not, he would lose his whole investment. The considered wisdom was that it was better to share the risk, even if you had to forgo the chance of reaping all the profit. "Exposure to a lot of things is good in our business," Dave says. "That's a way to spread the risk of ventures without having the capital to do it yourself." That was how Badger Oil modernized in the late 1980s and 1990s: keeping a quarter interest in the well, but not bearing all the risk.

Art Price joined the company while still a university student at the young age of twenty-two. While working for a local accounting firm that managed accounts for oil and gas independents and working on Badger's accounting software conversion, Art impressed the right people. Paul was advised to bring him on board, even though he was still a student. In his initial interview, Art recalls being surprised at how articulate Paul was about so many subjects and what a "voracious reader" he was. "His knowledge base is incredibly broad. He was someone whose respect I wanted to earn. I wanted to do everything I could to get him to believe in me. He did not suffer fools gladly at the time," Art says.[33]

"By the time I got on board, the industry had collapsed in the mid-eighties," Price says. "I missed the first renaissance. By the time I got there, over half the staff had been laid off. There were about forty people at the max; by the time I got there, it was down to ten people. Dave and I had a completely different vision for Badger."

By the time Art arrived in 1988, oil prices were at or near rock bottom. The downturn, he says, had been steep and protracted. His new boss, Paul, "had just completed working out his bank debt and narrowly avoided bankruptcy in the mid-1980s. He had cleared his biggest hurdle by sending some properties back to the bank," Art says. Among other cutbacks, Art says, were Paul's airplanes, the last of which was a King Air, a top-notch machine. The problem for the bank, Price says, was that Paul was using planes for business and pleasure. "When you own your own business, it's all business," Art says.

There were other cuts that had to be made. Badger had widely spaced properties in south Louisiana, Utah, and west Texas. Oil prices were low. Art says the goal was to "stop the bleeding" at a time when operating losses were substantial. He believed that Badger had to divest some properties, including most of those outside south Louisiana. Dave agrees: Badger knew Louisiana best, and it is always better for oil producers to work in the territory they know.

Another of Art's most urgent tasks was recovering uncollected receivables from other partners. "A lot of people had stopped paying their bills," he says, Badger worked out settlements for them. The goal in the late 1980s, he says, was saving the business, not growing it. "We were extremely cash poor," Art recalls. "We had to rob Peter to pay Paul, then circle back around."

For a while, he says, Badger styled itself in a different way: business promoter. "We might sell 100 percent interest in a prospect," he says. "We would manage the project, back-in after payout or get carried for some of the total deal. We earned money for managing the deal. We had intellectual capital; we could get it done. But we didn't have the cash to risk."

All these stratagems—sloughing off unwanted lands outside of Louisiana, working out payment deals for indebted partners, promoting and managing deals for others—had the desired impact: they kept the doors open. "It was an outstanding business model for cash-strapped entrepreneurs," Art says.

In the 1990s, Art Price and Dave Etienne became co-CEOs of Badger Oil. Price, the accountant, kept a tight watch over the money. Etienne, the geologist, developed a business plan that worked. "Dave said if we wanted to grow the company, we had to get beyond being promoters," Art recalls. "We had to increase our ownership in our prospects. We started off promoting the business model and returned profits into our next deal. By doing that, we increased our piece. You have to be believers. You are investing [risking money] alongside folks you brought into the deal. If you are promoting, if you are being 'carried' into the deal and not investing, if we were never willing to risk our money, we wouldn't grow. We shifted our focus."

The vision was Dave's, Art says, and Paul embraced it. "We were good at what we did," Art says. "Thank goodness, our successes outweighed our losses. Over the decades, we overcame the shortfall and built equity in the ground. That was a slow climb out of the depths of the depression in the '80s."

In addition to a new business philosophy, Badger embraced technology—especially 3D seismic—which by the 1990s had become more affordable for companies like theirs. Seismic technology provided a "picture" of the subsurface and helped geologists envision oil finds. It originated in the 1920s and was used for the first time in the Arbuckle Mountains of Oklahoma. Badger began originally to use 2D technology, which used explosives or sound waves to search for hydrocarbons. "We'd record data, read responses, which would tell where there were structures that could trap hydrocarbons. During 2D, we were looking for structures," Art says. "Two-dimensional seismic helped geologists know where structures might be. "Two-dimensional later became 3D depiction," he continues. "It was more fine-tuned. We got the poor man's version of 3D and embraced it. It revolutionized the industry. We became more knowledgeable and built value in the company."[34]

Three-dimensional or 3D seismic was developed in the 1960s but for many years was cost-prohibitive for small independents like Badger. That changed in the 1990s. Three-dimensional became less expensive, and improved graphics connected to the programs helped to add value to the results. A computer workstation that once might have cost $200,000 now cost about an eighth of that, as the new millennium dawned.

As "Big Oil" left existing fields in the 1990s, independents like Badger seized the opportunity to move in to explore bypassed zones the majors left behind. "Without 3D, the industry would not be able to do a lot of what it is doing," Paul says. "As large reserves became increasingly difficult to find, 3D made it possible to pursue smaller targets and produce them faster. Badger's batting average in the Gulf Coast and offshore is about 80 percent now. We don't do anything without 3D."

Art identifies the late 1990s and early 2000s as the years when Badger Oil began to grow again. As the majors started leaving the Outer Continental Shelf of the Gulf of Mexico, headed to international areas, independents moved in to buy up offshore leases. "We were making much bigger finds. When you were right, it created a lot more value, more impact for your punch. During that time, we became full-blown offshore operators," Art explains. For a decade, Badger reaped the benefits of an aggressive American energy renaissance. "At one time, we had the highest production of any single field on the Outer Continental Shelf [OCS] in the Gulf, 100 million cubic feet of gas per day from one field," Art says. "We developed that out of whole cloth. There was nothing there when we started." He likes to describe the change in the company from a "mom-and-pop" operation into NASA making a moon landing. Operating for the first time in federal waters off the coasts of Louisiana and Texas, the company was "fearless," he says.

Badger rode its successes right up until President Obama took office in 2009. The company perceived Obama and his new Secretary of the Interior, Ken Salazar, to be so hostile to oil and gas offshore drilling that Badger sold its assets in federal waters and turned back toward land. The decision, Art says, has proven wise, especially after the large British Petroleum oil spill in the Gulf in April 2010. An old drilling rig, the Deepwater Horizon, exploded and sank, killing eleven workers on the site and spilling 4 million barrels of oil into the Gulf until it was finally capped eighty-seven days later. It was the worst oil spill in history. The Obama administration responded with a moratorium on offshore deepwater drilling in the Gulf, and imposed new requirements for drilling in shallow water, as well. BP also had to pay unprecedented penalties: $5.5 billion under the Clean Water Act and $8.8 billion in natural resource damages.[35]

The first decade of the new century saw mixed results for Badger. Hurricane Katrina, the August 2005 monster that devoured New Orleans, did not damage the company's assets, but Badger still experienced protracted shut-ins, Art says, setting production caps lower than the available output. Damage to offshore facilities kept Badger from selling oil at higher prices. Hurricane Rita, which hit the following month, decimated southwestern Louisiana, and cost the company further production. One platform toppled, and once again, the company suffered shut-ins. Along with the setbacks came great successes, as well. Badger drilled about fifty wells with LLOG Exploration Co. in Lafayette. LLOG paid for seismic data, Badger prospected and drilled.

Dave notes that the company has played many roles in the thirty-plus years since he joined it—from one-off deals to buying its own fields to becoming an offshore operator. Under his watch, Badger Oil has become a seismic-based company and an expert at interpreting data, expanding to the Gulf of Mexico shelf. The newer model is to be opportunistic. Dave always maintains that Badger knows south Louisiana best. The challenge, he says, is that the prospect inventory has become lower. And many of their employees are older, grandparents with interests of their own. Some have gone part-time. "We are shrinking," he says, but always poised for the right opportunity.

Art sees the energy business as "dynamic," equally exciting and incredibly unforgiving." Both the industry and Badger enjoyed business growth "like we had never seen" over a fifteen-year spurt that resulted in the company's impressive success. He adds that Paul stepped back at a time when he believed his skill set was less suited to hands-on: he turned the company's direction over to Art, Dave, and others who were more specifically capable of taking the helm at that time. That, too, is a tribute to Paul. Many great men and founders find it incredibly difficult to step away when the time comes.

Art and Dave both agree that Paul remains an inspirational figure in the company, whose broad knowledge, blunt honesty, and boundless store of energy helps to focus their own mission. Paul likes to joke that, as he moved into his later years, he was "reduced from being the company's CEO to choosing the wine at company dinners." Art confirms that fact with a smile: "We've always had very good wine."

Art also points out that Paul's quip is just that, a laugh line. There is far more to him than that. Art joined the company during a time when Paul was already an industry spokesman, a leader in the Independent Petroleum Association of America, the national organization that spoke for independent oil producers. In that role and in others, Art says, Paul has been dynamic. "When I started, I was twenty-two. Paul was sixty-two. What I remember about him then was his limitless energy. He is a vibrant guy," Price says. He also says that Paul was not the "cuddly guy" then that people encounter today. He was intimidating, acerbic, "known as a hard-ass." He describes Paul's way of criticizing others as incompetent was folksy but damning. You didn't want Paul to think you were a "fuzzy head," Art says. "You really wanted him to respect you. Once you earned his respect, he was fiercely loyal to people he believed in. If you failed early to get his respect, it was over. He didn't have time to trifle with you."

"He was never a cheerleader," Dave observes. "He can be very blunt. And he can be sarcastic. He has treated me with respect since the day I walked in the door. I don't call him Paul. He's 'The Chief.' He's not an average guy." Art agrees: Paul was a model mentor, with the model created by the boss. "I worked with him five or six years before we forged a personal relationship," Art notes. "Paul doesn't get overly personal; he maintains a professional distance. He was very astute; he cared for his employees, but he maintained a professional relationship." As he and Paul got more acquainted, however, the mentor in Paul emerged. He would host what his executives called "Jesus lunches." For Art, that meant driving with Paul back to his Bendel Gardens home for lunch, where Paul would then personally serve Art, the employee. It was a role reversal from how things functioned at the office, and it provided some one-on-one time with the boss. "We'd talk shop, but this was not a structured meeting," Art says. "He was the best mentor you could ask for." If there was an overriding message in much of what Paul said, Art notes, it was "Be your best person at all times."

Art recalls a clipping from the *Wall Street Journal* that Paul saved and posted above the copy machine at Badger Oil. Today, it is on the wall behind his office door. The clipping, reprinted in the *Journal* from a United Technologies advertisement, delivers a message that defines Paul's career. "It's What You Do—Not When You Do It." Ted Williams, at age forty-two, "slammed a home run in his last official time at bat." Mickey Mantle was only twenty when he hit twenty-three homers in his rookie season. Golda Meir was seventy-one when she became Israel's prime minister, and William Pitt II was twenty-four when he became one of Britain's greatest prime ministers. Mozart was seven when his first composition was published, and George Bernard Shaw was ninety-four when one of his plays was first produced.

Paul's message in posting that item is clear: it's your contribution that counts, at any age. For that very reason, Art could assume important roles at Badger in his twenties, while Paul himself was by no means finished contributing to the company in his seventies. The lesson takes on added resonance as Paul continues to learn and to contribute to the world around him, year by year, well into his nineties.

Art says that Paul has given people within the company free rein to succeed. He was especially intentional in giving employees the opportunity to buy into the company's profitable projects. "When we make money, they get to make money," Art says. If the company bought fields, key employees, as many as a dozen, buy in on the deal. "We want you to be in the same business we are in," Paul tells them, and that is not merely oil, but the business of being an entrepreneur.

"He's been very fair with that," Dave says. "He set aside portions of wells so that guys could buy in. That's been in place for thirty years. That's very much based on Hilliard. He's an entrepreneur. That's what he wants: a team of entrepreneurs." Dave adds, in perhaps the highest compliment an employee can pay his boss, "We've made him a lot of money. And he's shared that opportunity with us."

CHAPTER 7
SPOKESMAN FOR AN INDUSTRY

Apples in a Barrel

What we might call the first half of Paul Hilliard's career was consumed with gaining professional traction: supporting his family, launching Badger Oil, and keeping it afloat during tough times. His hard work in all those areas eventually paid off. By the mid-1960s, he had already begun to have some success in the oil business. He earned enough money to buy a summer home in Wisconsin's Lake Country in 1964, which he called "The Louisiana Purchase," an unwinterized cottage on two lakeside acres for $6,500. He also bought a small plane, in which he flew himself and his family to the cabin and home again. He took off what time he could, usually a week, to enjoy the fresh air, fish, and water ski. Sally and the girls stayed much longer, sometimes for the duration of the summer.

Owning a private plane ended up teaching him more than he realized, and as always Paul tells the story with a chuckle. "In the early 1960s, I took flight lessons, obtained a private pilot's license, and as soon as I could afford it (which I really couldn't), I bought a minimum aircraft, a Piper Tri-Pacer. For the next twenty-five years, I went through the throes of periodically upgrading to a superior aircraft, until in 1986, the collapse of oil prices, combined with company debt, led me to the easy conclusion that my own aircraft was no longer a 'necessity.'"

Flying his own plane also taught him to exercise a certain caution, or at least to temper his more aggressive instincts: "The twenty-five years or so that I flew my own plane delivered several incidences of bad judgment and frightening consequences: icing conditions, low fuel, weather misjudgments, descent of darkness ahead of estimate, etc. And so, I learned the lesson that all pilots come to accept: 'There are old pilots and there are bold pilots, but there are no old bold pilots.'"[1]

While Paul enjoyed his material success through the years, as we all do, he also yearned to do more. As part of the immense wave of post-World War II veterans who came home and made a difference, Paul looked beyond home and office to the wider world beyond. How could he contribute to the community? Much of the second half of his career was concerned not so much with success, but with putting that success to work in service of others, with finding new ways to impact his community for the better. "I was raised with the concept that you should put more apples in the barrel than you take out," Paul says. "In other words, you're supposed to make a contribution. We're put on this earth to provide for ourselves and to help others." Paul's search for service would define his life away from work.

Tom Brokaw's 1998 book, *The Greatest Generation*, lionized the men and women of Paul's age and also instantly coined a phrase that soon joined the ranks of cliché.[2] It's easy to pick apart Brokaw's concept or label it a patriotic cliché, and a lot of critics have done just that over the years.[3] After all, what exactly is a "generation"? The Bible says thirty-three years, but that isn't what we're talking about here. Likewise, there have been many great generations of Americans, and there will be many more to come.

Brokaw was on to something, however, and the millions of readers who bought and enjoyed his book recognize it. Americans who were born within a very specific time frame—say, 1911 to 1927—were destined to face down some of the greatest challenges in the nation's history: the Great Depression, World War II, and the Cold War. They aren't a generation so much as an "age cohort." They grew up with Ford Model Ts, pocket watches, and party lines on the telephone. The had "general stores" in their small towns that sold 100-lb sacks of rice for $1.95, coffee at 10¢ a pound, and men's work shirts for 45¢.[4] They endured the pain and fear of living through the 1929 Stock Market Crash and the Great Depression that followed, when fortunes were lost and good men killed themselves rather than face ruin. Many rural youngsters like Paul also suffered through the widespread drought that choked farmland across the country—an experience that would require a great deal of explanation if you were trying to describe it to an urban dweller in New York or Philadelphia.

Tom Brokaw wasn't part of the greatest generation he described. Born in 1940 in South Dakota, the son of two government employees, Brokaw remembered that all the grown-ups he knew seemed to have a sense of purpose, one that was evident even to someone of his tender years. At the time, 12 million men and women were in uniform, war production made up some 44 percent of the gross national product, and the entire nation was "immersed" in a single effort: winning the war. Here is Brokaw at his most stirring: "The young Americans of this time constituted a generation birthmarked for greatness. . . . It may be historically premature to judge the greatness of a whole generation, but indisputably, there are common traits that cannot be denied. It is a generation that, by and large, made no demands of homage from those who followed and prospered economically, politically, and culturally because of its sacrifices."

"It is a generation," he adds, "of towering achievement and modest demeanor, a legacy of their formative years when they were participants in and witness to sacrifices of the highest order."[5]

Even after the war was over and won, the members of this generation returned to their cities, hometowns, and farms imbued with similar sense of purpose, Brokaw argues, with the goal of making a better and fairer America. President Roosevelt had put it best. There wasn't simply a singular concept called "freedom." Freedom came in a four-pack: freedom of speech and worship, freedom from fear and want. Painted in inspiring colors by artist Norman Rockwell, the "Four Freedoms" formed the vision that inspired the World War II generation, and working to put it into practice, even if they did so imperfectly, was their real legacy.[6]

Paul didn't have to look far for examples of young World War II veterans like the ones described in Brokaw's book. He needed only look as far as Acadiana. Here in Cajun country he could meet former soldiers with similar backgrounds, experiences, and ambitions as his own. One such man was Paul's good friend in Lafayette, Louis Joseph Michot Jr. A man who saw his life's purpose in deeper terms than simply work and success, Michot always wanted to do more. He strove to improve his town and community, and in so doing, he managed to open Paul's mind to other possibilities.

Michot was born in 1922 and was a few months older than Paul's brother Bill. Like Bill, he worked in the Civilian Conservation Corps, one of the New Deal programs that aimed to give American youngsters a taste of the outdoors life (and keep them off the unemployment rolls), while doing useful work for the country.[7] His father was a teacher, and he was reared in rural Evangeline Parish and Lafayette. Like Paul, Michot left school (Southwest Louisiana Institute, later the University of Louisiana at Lafayette) to enlist in the Marines and spent much of the war in the Pacific theater. There was even a curious complementarity to their two paths: Michot was an antiaircraft battery gunner aboard the aircraft carrier USS *Enterprise* and served on ten combat cruises. He shot at planes while Paul flew on them.

Like Paul, Michot married soon after the war, and he and his wife eventually had eight children. Like Paul, Michot invested in myriad business and financial ventures: Burger Chef fast-food restaurants (eventually he owned forty-five of them), commercial air and water transportation, offshore and marine construction, oil well drilling, insurance, textiles, and cattle ranching in Central America, to name just a few. Both men were bank founders (Michot at the Bank of Lafayette and Paul at MidSouth) and both were active at the Lafayette Chamber of Commerce and the Louisiana Gulf Coast Oil Exposition (LAGCOE). Both were licensed pilots. Both men were possessed of broad vision and determination.

There were differences, however. Paul had always been determined to earn his law degree. The Hilliards, he said, were always educated. With the GI Bill, the country had given him much-needed financial support for acquiring his degree. Michot followed a different path. He believed in teaching himself enough to get started in his career, and he became a staunch advocate for vocational education. At the young age of twenty-four, he was already starting his own businesses. The years Paul devoted to college and law school delayed his entry into the oil business until he was thirty.

Both men shared a common goal. How could they give back? Both were concerned with putting apples back into the barrel. Both wanted to make lasting contributions in the energy industry and beyond. This became an *idée fixe* for Paul as he moved into his late thirties and early forties—the prime of a man's life, we might say. One way to serve the community, he felt, was through participation in politics. Of course, successful military service has always been a springboard to political career in America, starting with the nation's first president, George Washington, continuing through Andrew Jackson and Ulysses S. Grant, and culminating in the

World War II generation. Every president from Dwight D. Eisenhower through George H. W. Bush was a World War II veteran, and a few— Eisenhower and John F. Kennedy—qualify as legitimate war heroes.[8] The same dynamic applied to lower-level races from school board to statehouse and everything in between. Being a vet was good politics. Here, Michot showed Paul the way, running successfully for state representative from Lafayette Parish in 1959.

As he approached forty, Paul jumped into the ring, as they say, trying his hand at public life and politics. He devoted himself to Republican politics in 1964, working for the campaign of Senator Barry Goldwater, the archconservative Republican from Arizona, who became the party's candidate for president in 1964 against the incumbent Texan Democrat, Lyndon B. Johnson. Goldwater, a US Air Force pilot in World War II, had returned home after the war to help run the family business. He was elected to the Phoenix City Council in 1949 and to the US Senate in 1952. At a time when traditional Rooseveltian liberalism had become something of a national consensus, Goldwater was different, bracing (to his fervent supporters) and abrasive (to his equally fervent detractors). He was an unapologetic voice for a new kind of conservatism: a rollback of the welfare state, free market capitalism, and an emphasis on individual liberties. Some called him an extremist; he actually welcomed the title. "I would remind you," he famously declared in his acceptance speech at the San Francisco Cow Palace, site of the Republic National Convention in 1964, "that extremism in the defense of liberty is no vice!"[9]

Goldwater may have been too far in front of the electorate on that one. President Johnson used Goldwater's own words to paint him into a corner as a dangerous and frightening figure, aided by television advertisements that raised the specter of nuclear war in a Goldwater presidency, the famous "daisy ad."[10] Johnson won the 1964 presidential election by a landslide, taking every state except Goldwater's native state of Arizona and five southern states—Louisiana, Mississippi, Georgia, Alabama, and South Carolina. Although Goldwater lost the presidential election, he had lit a fire under a generation of young Republican operatives who embraced his conservative, even libertarian philosophy.

Paul decided to run as a Republican for the Lafayette Police Jury that spring of 1964, one of six men who formed the first local Republican ticket since the Civil War. The South had been solidly Democratic since the age of Reconstruction, but the times were changing. Atop the Republican ticket was gubernatorial candidate Charlton Havard Lyons Sr., known as "Big Papa," an Abbeville native, Shreveport oilman, and World War I veteran. It was the first serious Republican bid for governor office in a century. Ronald Reagan, former Hollywood actor and now a conservative Republican activist, came to Louisiana by train from California to campaign for him. His presence infuriated the Democratic candidate, John McKeithen, who urged voters to "repel the second invasion by the carpetbaggers." McKeithen was a populist, an effective stratagem in Louisiana politics since the old days of Huey Long, and ran on the slogan, "Won't you he'p me?"[11]

Lyons had been a Democrat since 1960, when he broke with the party rather than support the presidential candidacy of John Kennedy. At the time of his switch, he declared, "I am not leaving the Democratic Party, for it had already deserted me," a sentiment expressed by many former Roosevelt Democrats who felt that the party was moving too far to the Left. He was now the chairman of the state GOP organization and a Goldwater enthusiast, sometimes called "Louisiana's Mr. Republican," the father of the Republican movement in the state. Paul got to know Lyons, an optimistic and charismatic figure, who attracted other young people into the fledgling Republican fold.[12] Paul would cross paths with "Big Papa" again through the years, as Lyons served as president of the Mid-Continent Oil and Gas Association. He was also chairman of the Independent Petroleum Association of America from 1951 to 1953, a position that Paul himself would later hold.

For Paul, politics in the heady atmosphere of the Republican Party in 1964 proved to be fun, but futile. Paul says that he and his Republican colleagues running for police jury conducted an issues-based campaign, but they did so in the classic style of Louisiana politics. Using Paul's plane, the candidates took aerial photographs of what they claimed were dubious projects that the Lafayette Parish Police Jury was doing for private citizens in violation of the law. "We made black and whites, eight-by-tens," Paul says. "We laid them on the DA's desk. One guy never ran again." Paul remembers the whole thing as "kind of a lark." In the end, however, he wound up on the losing end, respected the voice of the electorate, and never again sought public office.

Even after his unsuccessful bid for public office, however, Paul did not wholly vacate the public arena. He knew that his chances of winning an election had been slim at the outset. He was running for office in the Deep South as a Republican during the Civil Rights era, he was a Wisconsin native, and perhaps most injurious to his chances, he was the great-grandson of a Union soldier. He may have been welcomed in Louisiana as an industrious entrepreneur, but not as a serious candidate for political office.

His friend Michot, on the other hand, found greater success as a politician. Michot had local roots and was also a Democrat. Running for the state House of Representatives—former Governor Jimmie Davis led the ticket that year—Michot won his first political office and began serving. In 1963, he resigned as a state representative to seek the governor's seat. Like Paul, Michot was attracted to the Goldwater campaign and although he was seeking the Democratic nomination for governor, he suggested that he might back Goldwater for president. He finished sixth in the Democratic primary, but later sought and won a seat on the state board of education. In 1971, he became state superintendent of education, an office he held for four years. Although Michot and Paul campaigned under different political party banners, both men saw politics as a way not only to fulfill personal ambition, but to serve their community and state. "You can't be interested in civics or community work without considering politics," Paul says.

Paul's oil work and political interests also combined to introduce him to some of the most influential folks in Louisiana over the course of his career. "I remember what that guy told me about Louisiana politics in 1951: it's not about governance. It's about entertainment. We had Earl Long, Jimmie Davis, John McKeithen, Edwin Edwards. We did have some characters." Paul met Edwards, the legendary "charismatic Cajun," and his brother Nolan back in 1951. Paul was a novice landman working for the California Company then and was buying oil and gas leases in Acadiana; Crowley, Edwards's hometown, was part of his territory. "You couldn't help but like Edwin. I took a landowner to him who had a legal problem. Edwin would act on it immediately. He didn't procrastinate; he could act. He was very clever, very intelligent with a great sense of humor," Paul recalls.[13]

Edwards served his final term as governor from 1992 to 1996. Midway through his term, in March 1994, he spoke at the annual meeting of the Louisiana Independent Oil and Gas Association. Paul introduced the governor as a guest speaker in a typically lighthearted manner and recalled their relationship, which by that time extended back more than forty years. "Edwin is a Democrat," he explained to the gathering, because "there's no way on his salary that he could afford to be a Republican": "the parties' scandals are very different: Republican scandals usually concern money. Democratic scandals are more likely to concern women. This is an important distinction; it not only makes the Democrats more interesting than the Republicans, it also accounts for there being more Democrats than Republicans."

Paul also called to mind former governor Earl Long and his peccadilloes. "Earl told reporters they could merely look at him and tell he wouldn't know what to do with one of those go-go girls if he caught her. No one has ever accused Governor Edwards of not knowing what to do if he caught up with a go-go girl."

But Paul also had a serious point to make with that audience. He appreciated Edwards's advocacy on behalf of Louisiana oil and gas, and he says so. "In my forty-three years in Louisiana, we have never had a governor with a better understanding of our industry; of its value to the state and of the difficulties it faces in competing in a global market." Paul's affection for Edwards survived the four-time governor's eccentricities and personal failings, including the convictions for federal racketeering, extortion, and money laundering charges, even the long stint he spent in federal prison (2002–2011).[14] As Paul likes to remind people, however, "in Louisiana, crime isn't illegal," and the aphorism is especially true in Louisiana politics. What mattered most to Paul was not the governor's problems with the law. It was that Edwards always managed to deliver politically for the oil and gas industry.

And that certainly had not been true of every politician Paul met in his career. Very early on, he discovered that not all policymakers knew anything about oil, and some knew positively nothing. And the independent producers were suffering because of it. "In the 1960s, the biggest challenge we had was the stable but unprofitable price level. It was awful. Natural gas was under price controls; consumption was rising. Just surviving the

'60s was the biggest challenge of all." Paul remembers someone sitting him down, literally, and telling him that there was a place on the political landscape for him. It was a slot he had not thought about before: lobbyist.

Voice of an Industry

The voice belonged to a respected New Orleans oil man. In the late 1960s, Paul sold a lease to Johnny Bricker, formerly of Humble Oil. Bricker asked him to lunch at the New Orleans Petroleum Club. He had more than a meal on his mind, however, as the two sat down in the dark leather chairs. "He was a great guy," Paul says of Bricker, and something of a legend in the business. Born in Kansas in 1909, Bricker joined Humble Oil as a landman in 1928. After twenty-five years with Humble, he retired to become an independent, founding Exchange Oil and Gas, and in the course of his career, he drilled more than five hundred wells.

Bricker talked with Paul about legislation pending in Congress that would have adverse results for the energy industry. Paul's interest in politics had cooled since his run for police jury. He quickly told Bricker no, he wasn't interested. He was too busy, had too many other things on his mind. Well, Bricker replied curtly, "Those politicians are interested in you. You better be interested in them." Paul pondered the wisdom in that and could see that Bricker was telling the truth. He made his decision before the crème brûlée was served. There was more at stake here than the wellt being of his own company. There was the industry and its survival in a dangerous US political climate. Some politicians felt that as narrow as the profit margins were for producers, crucial commodities like oil and gas ought to be cheaper still. "It took a jolt from an older and wiser gentleman," Paul recalls. "If you are going to stay in the business and survive, get involved."

Bricker's admonition started Paul down the road toward involvement with the Independent Petroleum Association of America (IPAA), an involvement that has lasted more than thirty years. His work included lobbying Congress, their staffs, and various congressional committees on issues of energy. Even if Paul had decided not to run again for public office, he could still represent his industry's positions to lawmakers and public office holders. His advocacy also involved interacting with the public and educating news agencies about the energy industry.

The IPAA has been around since 1929, when President Herbert Hoover called a national and state conference to draw up a program for the conservation of America's oil resources. The site of the meeting was the Broadmoor Hotel in Colorado Springs, Colorado, and it was here that oil men, royalty holders, and landowners formed their new national association.[15] The independents were most concerned about the limits that Hoover wanted to place on oil producers' access to public lands, but in general, they wanted an organization to represent independent oil producer interests in developing public policy. The IPAA became one of the industry's chief spokesmen, and though much smaller than the American Petroleum Institute, its aims were more directed toward domestic independents and the role of government in pricing, regulation, and taxes.

"We've worked hard, but we haven't achieved enough, primarily because many of those in politics don't understand our industry well enough to understand the relationship of upstream revenues and downstream profits," Paul says. "From the outset, we were lobbyists." The IPAA focused on Washington, DC, representing independent oil interests. Paul also remained involved in LOGA, the Louisiana Oil and Gas Association, and its predecessor organization in Louisiana, the Louisiana Independent Oil and Gas Association, which focused on state issues in Baton Rouge. The primary goal for both trade associations, Paul says, was to "stop bad stuff from happening." Someone has to, he says, since "the generators of stupid ideas run twenty-four hours a day."

By far, the most important issue facing the industry and independent producers in the 1970s, he knew, was shaking off the shackles of the federal government. By restraining oil and gas producers domestically with stable but very low prices, the United States had not only hurt itself economically, it had also ceded world dominance in oil production to the Middle East, with all the mischief that had created (and would continue to create in the future). In short, oil's problem was not merely a narrow economic interest. It had become America's problem, with implications for diplomacy and global strategy.

Hopes for higher oil and gas prices began to emerge during the administration of President Jimmy Carter, when some areas of the country, especially the industrial Northeast, suddenly faced a heating crisis. With their constituents angry—and in some cases shivering—Congress responded.

Politics is politics, however, and once the Congressional horse-trading and back-scratching was over and done, the result was a mess. The Natural Gas Policy Act of 1978 turned the nation's supply into a veritable Baskin-Robbins, with no fewer that "thirty-one flavors" of natural gas, with a complicated price structure based on when, where, and how deep the well was drilled. Older wells ("old gas") was shipped on interstate pipelines at prices as low as eleven cents per million British thermal units (MBtu); "new gas" might sell for as much as eight dollars. Further, price controls on oil under the Carter administration decidedly favored imported oil.

For both oil and gas reasons, then, Paul's participation in the IPAA increased markedly in the mid-1970s, at a time when the industry needed strong direction from within and smart action from Washington. As chairman of the IPAA's Communications Committee, Paul helped to co-ordinate efforts to lobby lawmakers and to make it clear to them the serious challenges facing independents. For ten years, he worked tirelessly to get the energy industry's message out. The problem, he says, was that people in Washington simply did not understand the oil and gas industry. Sometimes, it seemed to him as if they did not even *want* to understand it. They simply wanted cheap oil and gas, period, and they were not above demagoguing the issue, whipping the public into a frenzy, and demonizing the public reputation of oil men.

On one particular trip to Washington, Paul was in the office of an aide to US Senator Gaylord Nelson (D-Wisconsin), one of the strongest environmental voices in the Senate.[16] The senator was not in. He was back home dedicating a new public building. Paul wound up talking with a young member of Nelson's staff who was assigned to energy issues, but who appeared baffled about what an independent oil producer was and what he might want. "The energy guy said, 'Tell me again what you do.' I told him we were independent oil and gas producers. 'Yes, but what do you do?' he asked again. 'We search for gas and oil and try to sell it.' He just couldn't understand. He only understood the seven major oil companies." The befuddled aide was probably not atypical of American public opinion, then or now. Everyone had heard of the "Seven Sisters," the behemoths. But who, nationally, had heard of Badger Oil? Paul explained that independents did not own oil tankers or operate their own gas stations. The energy guy just looked at Paul. "That," Paul says, seemed like "a foreign concept to him." Paul went on to tell him, "If Washington did not change its regulations and laws, the independent oil man is going to disappear." The aide's response was classic: "How can you disappear," he said, "when no one knows you're there?"

"That made me madder than hell," Paul remembers. "But later I got to thinking about it. He was right." Independents were "strange animals" to politicians and staffers on Capitol Hill, who assumed that all oil producers made millions of dollars and were "rich, greedy, and lacked any sense of responsibility to consumers." Paul did not believe that was an accurate depiction of the oil people he knew, but he also knew it was a typical response from the uninformed. The entire industry, independents included, needed to do a better job of getting its message out.

Paul recalled being on a radio program in LaFayette, Georgia, near the Tennessee state line. People were calling in. Logical questions were easy to answer, he says, while "crazy questions were not," and this evening the listeners were bringing the crazy. Consider this example: A consortium of companies had recently drilled a very expensive dry hole at Alaska's North Slope. An angry caller told Paul, caustically, "I'll bet they just wrote it off their taxes." Of course they wrote it off their taxes, Paul responded. When any publicly held company had a disaster on a major project, the company writes it off. If the company did not report it, shareholder lawsuits would almost certainly result. "They are a public company and responsible to shareholders," Paul said, but it was clear his listener did not want to hear any explanations. It was as if the oil companies involved had decided to drill a dry well on purpose, just so they could "write it off." It was clear that many people had a preconceived idea of what the oil industry was and what oilmen were like.

The real problem, Paul realized, was that oil was something everyone took for granted, but only until they didn't have it. At that point, anger set in. And when the public got angry, politicians would never be far behind. Invariably, the hunt for scapegoats began. And what better target than "big oil," "fat cats," and, we might add after 1973, "oil sheikhs."

A year after the price collapse of 1986, for example, the IPAA brought a speaker to the annual meeting. His message was blunt, but it resonated with his audience. The consumer would never love the industry. He told the audience they needed to keep their perspective. They had to consider a fact that most of them ignored even though it was obvious: their industry was the only one in America to post its prices on every street corner of the country. Those numbers almost served as a challenge to consumers to find a cheaper price or to complain about the one they were seeing. "Get your minds around something," he told the audience of more than five hundred independent oilmen. "The consumer will never love you. At best, he'll tolerate you. Energy represents heat, light, and mobility. Mobility represents freedom. You're interfering with his freedom when you raise the price of gasoline or it becomes scarce."

These were sobering words, but all the more reason, Paul felt, to keep pushing hard to get out the message. He knew the work was important. Paul often heard a standard lament from consumers and the news media: the industry did a poor job of explaining itself. Perhaps there is some truth to that complaint, but Paul has had a standard response over the years to that point. "We explain to deaf ears," he says, and that, too, seems like a fair assessment.

By the mid-1980s, dark clouds appeared over the industry. Paul had enjoyed a decade-long run with higher oil and gas prices, a stretch of prosperity that he suspected would not last forever. In 1986, the bubble burst. Looking back on it, Paul is philosophical: "All of us geniuses at the Petroleum Club asked why would the Saudis hurt the price of oil? They wouldn't do that. The hell they wouldn't," he says. Production rose by some 4 percent in 1986, but prices fell by half as the Saudis turned on the spigots, and the world was suddenly awash in oil. No one in the world can produce oil as cheaply as the Saudis, and American producers suffered mightily for several years. Paul admits that he had many sleepless nights worried about his own business.

In 1989, Paul was elected to a two-year term as IPAA chairman. Despite the challenges faced by his own company, he attacked the challenge with gusto. "With IPAA, sometimes I'd get mad about some of the people I dealt with in Washington. IPAA membership was the lowest it had been in years. Everyone was dragging. I was running Badger, and I had a lot of debt," Paul remembers. "The chairmanship distracted me a little bit." More and more, Paul relied on his trusted subordinates to handle Badger. "Art [Price] was a very capable guy and very numbers-oriented. I was dealing with the IPAA in Washington."

It was an eye-opener for him in many respects, and he didn't always like what he was seeing in the nation's capital. Paul was and is a straight shooter whose word is his bond. But like any number of earnest Mr. Smiths have found out when they "go to Washington," not everyone has so much integrity.[17] Harry Truman supposedly once said, "If you want a friend in Washington, buy yourself a dog."[18] Looking back, Paul can only sigh. "Man, did I learn that lesson."

Godzilla versus the Iroquois

If Paul's tenure with the IPAA has a signal moment, one that defined him as the association's chairman, it was his fight over the so-called "Iroquois pipeline project."[19] The intent of the project was to transport Canadian natural gas to the always gas-hungry northeastern United States. The envisioned line would run from Waddington, New York (on the New York-Ontario border), to the Bronx, passing through upstate New York and southwestern Connecticut.[20]

American natural gas producers and pipelines had supplied markets in New York, Connecticut, and New Jersey for generations, investing billions of dollars in transmission and production facilities capable of meeting the region's needs. Now a new player had come to town. TransCanada Pipelines Ltd., working with major international oil and gas companies (including many big US firms) had made large investments in gas fields in western Canada. The thirteen-partner consortium had a plan to seize a commanding position in natural gas markets in the northeastern United States for themselves, leaving American independents, in particular, the scraps.

The difference between Canadian and American regulatory policies gave Iroquois a decisive edge in competing for US natural gas markets. Mark Seifert, the IPAA's vice president for regulatory affairs and a close friend of Paul's, explains that independent US producers were most concerned about the rate structure, not about competing with Canadian gas per se. Price was key factor that gave Canadian gas the advantage. He also points out that major international oil and gas companies were the ones actually producing "Canadian" gas, not necessarily Canadian firms, so this wasn't really about international rivalry. The advantageous rate design favoring the Canadians made American producers little more than "swing suppliers" for the pipeline, and stuck them with a high marginal cost to boot. Effectively, Seifert says, Iroquois shut American producers out of the prosperous New York area market, and "turned us into incremental suppliers"—the kind you use only in an emergency.

Seifert explains it this way. Think about renting a car in Houston to drive to New York. One car costs a lot to rent, say, $100 (its "fixed cost"), plus a penny a mile for gas. The other has a lower fixed cost of $50 but costs a dollar a mile for gas. The answer for the Houston to New York route is obvious; in fact, it's a no-brainer: choose the former. Translated into natural gas terms, Canada was the first scenario (higher fixed cost, cheaper to transport), gas from US suppliers the second (lower fixed cost, more expensive to transport).[21] Put in simplest terms, Canadian gas came with a higher charge to connect, but US firms were selling more expensive molecules. That made Canadian gas the "baseload" for consumers, the one that you use normally, and turned domestically produced gas into a marginal supplier. Advantage: Canada. The IPAA decided that enough was enough. Seeing that US producers could not bear that disadvantage, the independents went to battle against Iroquois.

That was always the rub for Paul and for the IPAA: their own government's policies seemed rigged in favor of foreign interests. As Seifert notes, the fight was never with Canada, nor was it with the big oil companies that were exploring for oil in Canada. The IPAA was not asking for government protection. It simply wanted a fair deal. On a free and competitive playing field, Paul was certain that American independents would more than hold their own.

The Canadian position was even stronger than it looked, however. Northeastern local distribution companies (LDCs) had become part-owners in Iroquois, thus ensuring substantial US political support for the project. While TransCanada held 29 percent, its partners included American and Canadian pipeline and gas distribution companies such as Brooklyn Union Gas, Long Island's chief gas supplier. Why were these LDCs in? Seifert explains: "The LDCs wanted Iroquois built because the difference between pipeline rate design in Canada compared to the U.S. was certain to rig the competition for Northeastern markets in favor of the Canadian natural gas supplies and keep the Iroquois system the LDC's partially owned full of cheap Canadian gas they could use to cram down prices for natural gas provided by their traditional American suppliers."[22]

In other words, Iroquois wasn't only for carrying cheaper gas. It was also to serve as a club to force US suppliers to lower their own prices, whether they could afford to or not. As Paul puts it, "I was just fighting for what was fair."

Looking back at the controversy, Art Price recalls, "We were fearful of that gas coming into the market." And there was going to be a lot of it, sold at a disadvantageous rate for US producers: Iroquois would extend almost four hundred miles at a cost of $582 million and carry 237 billion cubic feet of natural gas per year. Moreover, Iroquois would be yet another problem on the already treacherous landscape for domestic oil and gas companies. "Even after the end of wellhead price controls under Ronald Reagan in the mid-1980s, we were buried in—embedded in—pipeline regulations," Paul notes. "It was very significant in American markets."

Outrage alone wouldn't get it done. Outrage mobilizes people to fight, however, and that's what works in American politics. Paul "got the industry engaged with congressional people," Art says, but doing so took a great deal of hard work. Paul even had to design a sort of pre-digital version of PowerPoint: "Paul did 'road shows,' trying to educate regulators, elected officials, and people in the industry. He would send me tons of data; I would put it into graphic form. I would use a tripod and camera to photograph the charts displayed on a computer screen to make slides. He would have them organized for his presentation. I learned a lot about the business and how to get things done."[23]

"He was an absolute dynamo with IPAA," Art concludes. "He earned a lot of respect through that process."

Paul testified before a Senate committee in May 1990. From the *Washington Post* reportage of the event, one gets the impression that Washington had never quite heard anything like him. "Usually described as colorful," the *Post* reported, "Hilliard did not disappoint senators looking for strong language at a recent hearing about the Iroquois project." Using a blunt phraseology that would make coast-to-coast headlines were it to be uttered today, Paul employed a historical analogy to make his point: "The Iroquois in their early history were cannibalistic," Hilliard said. "After treatment by the Jesuits in the early eighteenth century, they discontinued cannibalism and became merely scalpers on the side of the British, both prior to and during the Revolutionary War. Hopefully,

gentlemen, this hearing will determine if Iroquois has reverted to cannibalism or is merely continuing their propensities to scalp Americans."[24]

The *Post* noted that, "energy-state senators" were sympathetic to Paul's
point of view. It just seemed senseless to transport gas all the way from
Alberta to New England, when US supplies were much closer—half as far
away, in fact. But there wasn't all that much that energy senators could
do about it. Despite a strong coalition against Iroquois—including an
"unlikely bedfellows" group of independent oil producers, homeowners
in the Housatonic Valley, and environmentalists concerned with the permanent alteration of historic wetlands—the Iroquois controversy wasn't
about politics in the end. Rather, it was a matter for federal bureaucrats to
decide, specifically the Federal Energy Regulatory Commission, or FERC,
which regulates the interstate sale of electricity and natural gas, as well as
the transportation of oil by pipeline.

As the *Post* put it, "the fate of Iroquois isn't up to the Senate, it's up
to the FERC," and FERC was expected to approve the project. Granting
"right-of-way" acquisition was a key first step, and that was just a couple of months away. In the end, the formidable political coalition against
Iroquois couldn't budge FERC, and to be fair, FERC had an argument.
Residents of the Northeast wanted it both ways: demanding cheap gas
but unwilling to have a pipeline in the region to deliver it and more concerned with the woodpeckers or beavers on their pristine property than
they were with the economic health of the region and their neighbors. The
IPAA lost the Iroquois battle, and the pipeline was up and operational by
1992—replete with all the built-in advantages that its rate system afforded
the Canadians.

Still, something good came out of Paul's efforts on behalf of the IPAA.
In 1992, the independents won a change to pipeline rate design policy.
Martin Allday, FERC chairman, persuaded the commission to adopt a
new rule, still in use thirty years later. US pipeline rate structure now
mirrored the Canadian model, giving all participants an equal opportunity to compete for natural gas business. "Martin Allday understood that
our point was valid," Seifert says. The new structure change represented a
"gigantic victory for our team."

No one emerges from a fight unscathed, and so it was with the
Iroquois battle. Paul forced the resignation of the IPAA's then-president,

Harold C. "Bud" Scoggins. Scoggins had been too timid in standing up for IPAA members' rights in the Iroquois case. Some believed he was too closely linked to the major oil companies, or at least to their advocates in Washington, rather than to the smaller independents within the trade organization that he was supposed to be leading. Others, like Seifert himself, suggest that Scoggins was simply too easy-going for the bruising political and bureaucratic fight in which the IPAA was involved. Scoggins's dismissal gave Paul a reputation, with one local gas distribution company president supposedly describing him as the "meanest man in America." Hardly. But Paul still keeps a caricature of himself with that moniker hanging in his office.

The new "straight fixed variable rate" policy from FERC not only served the interests of fairness, but it also had a dramatic impact on overall natural gas markets. Because only about 2.2 percent of total costs are variable, largely consisting of the cost of gas needed to operate the pipeline compressors, the collection of all fixed costs in a "demand charge" (referring to the sunk costs of building the pipeline and getting it ready to move gas) relieved the pipelines of having to collect up to half of their fixed costs through their variable charges. The new rate made natural gas instantly more competitive in markets that could easily switch fuels, such as electrical power companies. "Partly as a result of this 1992 competitive enhancement," Seifert notes with satisfaction, "natural gas use in electricity production has skyrocketed, benefiting consumers and energy providers alike, while reducing the nation's carbon output as a side benefit." With pipelines profitable again, natural gas consumption in the United States doubled since 1992, and in 2020 we exported more than 5 trillion cubic feet of gas, in addition to supplying the American consumer.

There is an improbable postscript to this story. In 2001, nearly ten years after the Iroquois pipeline troubles, Paul was attending his University of Texas Law School class's fiftieth reunion. In a coincidence that seems like it was out of a movie, Paul saw a familiar face—that of his old nemesis. "Damned if I didn't run into Martin Allday," Paul recalls of that night in Austin. "I had to work and couldn't participate in social events in college. So, I couldn't recall Allday as a classmate." The two men had a good conversation. Allday proved to be a formidable man, a US Army soldier who had fought in Paul's war in the Pacific theater and who was wounded on

Okinawa. He had a Purple Heart and a Bronze Star to show for his service. After the war, he practiced law in Midland, Texas, befriended George H. W. Bush, and chaired Bush's Senate campaign in 1964. That connection led to his appointment as FERC chairman from 1989–1993.

That night at the reunion, Allday let Paul know where he stood. Allday told him that the spirited fight he had put up on behalf of the IPAA had made a real difference. "Everyone on my staff was against you guys but you were so determined, and convincing, that it was the right thing to do. I prayed about it a lot. You sued me twice, Paul! But I said, 'I believe those independents are right.'" Paul's justified verdict: "Martin Allday was one great gentleman."

If Allday had proven to be a friend during the Iroquois fight, however, few others did. Paul recalls meeting with Senators Fritz Hollings (D-South Carolina) and Bill Bradley (D-New Jersey). They barely listened to his arguments and seemed to assume that the IPAA simply did not want to compete with the Canadians. But Paul had allies, too. The Texas delegation was a solid ally to the IPAA, and he also remembers the support he received from his own state of Louisiana, with Senator John Bennett Johnston Jr., a Democrat and the chairman of the Energy and Commerce Committee being particularly helpful.

In the end, Paul was the difference in getting a fair shake for the independents. Seifert gives him due credit. "Paul had his hands full," he says, in a tone of admiration: "Everyone was against him, from the Canadian embassy to LDCs to US politicians, even some independents. A lesser man would have folded, said 'To heck with it,' and gone off and ordered Canadian bacon with his breakfast. But Paul is like Godzilla—he just won't be stopped."

Seifert goes on: "I came from the oil fields, and I love oilmen. Paul is the paradigm. He's a force for good, in the oil business, in his own community, and on a national level."[25]

Service with the IPAA changed Paul, too. He remembers once, as chairman, joining a small contingent of association members taking a trip to Saudi Arabia. On the flight over, Paul had a chance to think about his life. For a man in constant motion, such contemplative moments are necessarily rare. Paul had some time to look back. "I'm a contemporary of the airplane; my mother was born two years before the Wright brothers' successful flight and I was born in 1925, just two years before Charles Lindbergh flew solo over the Atlantic. Now here I was, sitting in first class on a huge jet, 37,000 feet in the air, 580 miles an hour, staring at a movie screen, eating a nice meal, headed to the Middle East." That trip on Saudia Airlines, he says, made him feel "like I was flying on Aladdin's magic carpet."

From Saudi Arabia, it was on to Iraq. The group arrived just a few months before Saddam Hussein's invasion of Kuwait in August 1990 and the subsequent Iraqi occupation of the emirate. These events would lead to the US-led war against Saddam in early 1991, Operation Desert Storm. Paul's group of a dozen or so had no way of knowing what was in store, but Paul remembers the air being filled with tension and armed guards. "We were meeting with the Iraqi oil ministry officials. Their security force was all around us." Paul remembers one IPAA member taking pictures and talking on his Dictaphone, a bad idea in any sort of repressive dictatorship, when a squad of burly Iraqi bodyguards suddenly took him to a side room for interrogation. A couple of hours later he was free, after the Iraqis had satisfied themselves that the man was not a spy and was merely dictating notes about the trip to his wife. It was, no doubt, the longest two hours of the man's life.

Once he completed his two-year term as chairman, Paul began to limit his IPAA activity. The chairman's job is exhausting, says Mark Miller, owner of Merlin Oil & Gas of Lafayette. Miller served as IPAA chair from 2015–2017, only the third Louisianian of forty-three energy leaders to serve in the chairman's role up to that point. "On matters like energy, the IPAA president, who is permanent, would say 'Let's get Paul Hilliard on board or on TV to meet with committees.' We would focus our lobbying efforts on the hottest topic or the membership's concerns or both," he says. Service to the IPAA could take up to 60 percent of his time during his leadership tenure, Miller figures.

During a crisis, the chairman might meet with committee heads, express the concern of the IPAA, and inform its members and member companies. On Capitol Hill, the IPAA chairman would have lunch with the Speaker of the House of Representatives or spend time with congressional delegations. "There were very few doors we could not get into," Miller said. After rising to chairman, Miller said Paul called him to offer his help.

"He reached out to me when I became chair and said, 'If you need anything, let me know.' That meant the world to me. I wasn't sure I was big enough for the job." Miller said, "It was a big honor to be in his footsteps."

Paul always kept his sense of humor during those days of being a voice in the industry. For example, he often joked about what he thought of Congress. "Watching our Congress in action is educational and tells me we should not object to the use of our tax dollars in the search for intelligent life on other planets. In less than 20 minutes, that group can actually subtract from the total sum of human knowledge."

After more than sixty years in the oil industry, Paul maintains his passion to educate the public on the complex nature of the oil industry. A few days after his ninety-seventh birthday, on June 23, 2022, he authored a guest column in the Baton Rouge *Advocate*, an opinion piece on the Biden administration's oil policies. The heart of the piece was Paul excoriating the administration's "lack of concern for or understanding of the domestic petroleum industry." It is another unstable moment in world history. Putin's invasion of Ukraine, and the resulting western sanctions against Russian energy companies, have already led to shortages in oil and gas that are sure to get much worse before they get better. With the world clamoring for more oil, meanwhile, the leader of the Free World wants to abolish the oil industry altogether. Paul, as always, doesn't bother to mince his words. The Biden administration, Paul wrote, "promised to end the oil and gas industry. Now, this might have been just another foolish lie, a throwaway blandishment tossed to his environmentalist constituents and soon to be forgotten, but no."

Beginning with his first official acts—shutting down the Keystone XL Pipeline and canceling leases in Alaska—Biden began making good on his campaign promise to end the American oil and gas industry, canceling more leases and lease sales and unleashing every government agency to maximize roadblocks to petroleum production, refining, and marketing.

Rather than seek ways to raise domestic production, however, Paul believes that the current administration is courting foreign producers, cajoling them into raising their production, and promising them favorable deals. As always, he believes that finding and producing oil in the United States is the best path forward for the country's economy, but has taken second place to short-term political considerations: "At the same time

Biden's policies were closing doors to domestic producers and driving up the price of fuel, Biden opened the Strategic Petroleum Reserve—designed for real, not political, emergencies—to withdraw about 1 million barrels a day, a drop in the bucket in a world where demand is nearly 100 million barrels per day. Concerned that his policies were causing political damage because of high fuel prices, Biden went hat in hand to Venezuela's dictator, to the Saudis, to anyone and everyone, except American producers for help increasing supply."[26] Meanwhile, Paul notes, there hasn't been a new refinery built in the country in more than fifty years, nor are any currently planned. The administration, he charges, is "impairing the industry that brings forth the lifeblood of the American economy."

Paul's accusation that government does not understand the oil business—whether it is deliberate or simply a product of ignorance—has been a remarkably consistent message over the years. It is one that motivated him during the Iroquois fight, that he has delivered before and will no doubt deliver again. His policy prescriptions may be controversial, but the very fact that he is still in the ring, slugging away, is entirely characteristic. We may also make a reasonable guess that he is the oldest man ever to publish an opinion column in the history of the *Advocate*, and the paper is even older than Paul is, having been around in one form or the other since 1842.

Paul's passion for educating the public about America's oil industry has been a distinguishing feature of his persona for decades and clearly still invigorates him. After he served his term with the IPAA, however, his drive to educate, to give others the benefit of his long years and the dramatic experiences of his life, from the Pacific to the Louisiana oil patch, was soon going to move in entirely new directions. Even as he testified before Congress, jetted to Saudi Arabia, and faced down Saddam's security guards in Iraq, Paul never forgot the wisdom he had learned as a boy. There were a lot more apples lying around, he could see, and he was determined to find new ways to "put them into the basket."

PART IV
THE GIFT

CHAPTER 8
GIVING BACK

The Gift of Reading: The Foundation

Throughout his life, Paul Hilliard's personal goals have constantly expanded in breadth. From that burning barn to Bougainville, from the battlefield to the boardroom, he's always been a man of energy and determination. He's been through good times and bad times—more of the former than the latter, we can say—but he never seems to stop moving forward. He's always seeking new challenges to conquer and new horizons to explore. It's just who he is.

One thing has stayed constant, however, and that is his desire to give back. It has been a feature of his life since he was a boy. He feels gratitude for the things that life has given him. Speak to him for any length of time, and chances are his favorite classical quote will emerge. It is from the great Roman orator and rhetorician Marcus Tullius Cicero, in the *Pro Plancio*: "Gratitude is not only the greatest of virtues, but the parent of all the others."[1] Gratitude is the glue that holds Paul's character together. It enables him to empathize with those who must go without and drives him to make sure that he never misses an opportunity to put more apples back into the basket than he takes out. Ask anyone who knows him, and they will inevitably mention that he is "generous"—of his time, his energy, his money. If, as philosopher Jean-Paul Sartre tells us, our choices and deeds define who we are, then Paul is a philanthropist, a lover of his fellow human beings, in the truest sense of the word.[2]

While Paul was riding the roller coaster of the oil industry, his personal life was changing. He and Sally divorced in 1969, and he and Eula "Lulu" Burton married in 1972. "Lulu and I were married almost thirty-four years," Paul says. "She was three years older and much more mature. She had very accomplished children; they were all good friends of mine."

As he turned sixty, nearing the age when most people retire, he was just getting started. He developed a new passion, studying history, and focused his reading on his own war, World War II. Finally, he began to perceive that broader picture of the conflict that had eluded him and his fellow Marines at the time, to feel the connections between Europe and the Pacific, between the difficult start of the war and its victorious conclusion. He and Lulu began to travel, visiting some of the most interesting and diverse places in the world. Their wanderlust peaked with a trip to India sponsored by the New Orleans Museum of Art. The Hilliards spent three weeks crossing the subcontinent by train and brought home multiple treasures. Lulu was adventurous and open to new experiences, he says. She always lived on "the sunny side of the street," Paul remembers. Closer to home, Paul also turned his attention to community affairs, seeking new ways to improve public education.

His interest in schools began in the 1970s, when he served on an education committee for the Lafayette Chamber of Commerce. He visited schools and determined where businesses leaders could help. Four Lafayette schools were on his visitation list: Vatican School, Scott Middle School, Ossun Elementary School, and J. Wallace James Elementary School. "I was so impressed with the principals and teachers in those schools," he says. He attended one 6 a.m. meeting for parents in the Vatican School and was surprised by the number of parents who were in attendance, concerned folk who were sacrificing precious morning hours to be there.

He began by donating modest items like rugs for the classrooms where children and teachers could sit in a circle and read a book aloud. "For one program, we bought a lot of freezer bags so that kids could carry books without getting them wet," a real issue in rain-drenched Louisiana, as anyone who's lived there can attest. "We tried to teach them to revere their books," he says. Paul also sponsored guest speakers to talk to the kids and provided support for teacher in-service days. Our schools have become the target of so much politicized criticism today, but Paul's only comment on what he has seen is this: "I was fortunate to work with many dedicated people."

Paul sees education not only as an American tradition but as a birthright, something intrinsic to our way of life. He looks back to the Founding Fathers, who believed that "democratic republican success was based on an informed electorate," and argues that "it is even more true today." He is fond of quoting Thomas Jefferson, "An educated citizenry is a vital requisite for our survival as a free people,"[3] and sees the lack of knowledge about our democratic institutions as a real danger to their survival. "People today know so little about their country," he says. "That's not a good thing."

In 1997, Paul decided to get more deeply involved. He created the Badger Excellence in Education Foundation (BEEF).[4] Given his own love of reading, it should come as no surprise that he decided to focus it on helping to develop reading skills in at-risk children. Reading was a passion close to Paul's heart since the day he first picked up a book in that one-room schoolhouse back in Buffalo County, Wisconsin. The foundation's mission is "assisting and improving public and private educational efforts in the state of Louisiana." The means could vary, including student tutors, teacher development programs, direct aid to schools—they could be anything, in fact, that advanced the mission. Art Price says that Paul had been active in supporting schools "as long as I have known him," but he usually made things happen by "working around the edges."[5] Public schools are funded by state dollars, of course, but Art says that Paul has always found "creative ways" to help. "I don't know where he got it, but he said if you didn't reach children by a certain age, it would be too late." Paul, like most educators, thinks that age is third grade: old enough to be aware and to have reached the classical "age of reason," yet still young enough to be shaped for a lifetime.

Nancy Manuel can attest to Paul's impact. She is a reading coach at Alice Boucher Elementary School in Lafayette, where she serves a mostly at-risk student population. Paul, she says, "believes that every person, every child, should be able to read so they can contribute to society." At first, he supported programs to promote reading in the home and funded tutors for Manuel's intensive reading program. The following year, he donated books and materials to her classes. He'd also drop by on occasion, not to interfere but merely to see how things were going and to ask if Manuel had any additional needs for her classroom. "That's how he was. He was willing to give you money. But you had to show him the proof it would work out," she says.[6] Paul has helped out on a number of other fronts, as well. He has lectured to students in grades three to five in the Junior Achievement program, provided staff development programs on how to encourage lifelong reading among their students, and also, perhaps most important in encouraging international understanding, he has purchased globes for each classroom in the building—a throwback to his own love of maps as a child.

Paul has earned accolades not only from the teachers, but from leadership as well. According to the principal at Alice Boucher, Madeleine McNulty, Paul was calling her regularly to say, "I haven't heard from you. What do you need?" At Ossun Elementary School near Cankton, Principal Becky M. LeMaire says something similar: "He has always focused on reading to help our students increase their reading scores."[7] He also knows the ultimate way to create a book-loving child, and he frequently gave away books as gifts, to stock classroom library shelves, or to use as student incentives.

Tina Fremin, Paul's longtime executive assistant, says that Paul took underprivileged local kids more than once on a field trip to a bookstore in the Lafayette's Oil Center. There, he bought each child a book of their own, so they could get to know the excitement of being in a bookstore, choose a book, and solidify their love of reading. "He was hands-on with what he would do," Tina says. "His goal was to improve reading levels, and he granted rewards to students who challenged themselves."[8]

Paul's educational work hasn't stopped. It is a cloudless spring day, May 16, 2022, at Isidore Newman School in New Orleans. Just a month before Paul's ninety-seventh birthday, he is taking center stage. The seventh graders in front of him have been studying World War II for weeks, and now they have a chance to speak to a veteran, someone who was actually there. No one can tell authenticity quite like a child—they have a radar for it. Paul wins over the group instantly with warmth and humor, always his calling cards. He describes his generation in words that can probably apply to the present one, as well: "In those days we weren't educated, but we weren't stupid."

As he speaks, a black-and-white photo of a younger Paul looms up behind him on a huge screen. His eighteen-year-old self is smiling in the rear gunner seat of an SBD dive-bomber. The students are surprised to find that Paul was only a few years older in that photo than they are. He describes his vivid memories of sitting down for Sunday lunch, when his uncle burst through the door and told them the Japanese had just attacked Pearl Harbor. Suddenly, the kids in front of Paul have gone back in time. It is December 7, 1941. "We had no idea," he says, "we were about to be engaged in a global war."

After Paul's remarks, the questions flow fast and furiously from the young crowd. They want to know how often he heard from his family during the war. "Not very often," Paul replies. "The married guys got letters by the dozens, but I was single. I actually felt sorry for them being separated from their wives and children."

Another seventh grader asks, "Did you know about the German concentration camps?"

"No," Paul says, "I had no idea. We were doing our part in the war in the Pacific."

"What's your opinion of the atomic bomb," asks another student.

"President Harry Truman had no recourse," Paul says. "The Japanese would not surrender. It saved a lot of lives by ending the war."

And so it goes—another good day of teaching in Paul's life. Newman teacher Amy Beard was impressed with his approach, especially his insistence on the importance of geography. Paul says it all the time: "In order to understand history, you have to understand geography, and vice versa." Teacher Beard agrees: "That really resonated with me right off the bat," she says. "To understand the way things are now, you have to have a grasp as to why they are the way they are. To do that you have to study history and geography together." Beard says it was an honor to have a real World War II veteran speak to her students, and it was heartbreaking to think that these men and women won't be around to share their personal experiences much longer. "It was such a pleasure to meet him," she says. "It's such a rare experience, and he was so positive and upbeat, he was just a joy to have."[9]

After class, Paul gets a surprise. One of the seventh graders, Emeric Parker Laborde, comes up to introduce himself. He is the great-grandson of Paul's longtime friend John Laborde, who has recently passed away. Laborde was one of the first men Paul had met and befriended in the oil industry in Louisiana, way back when. The elder Laborde talked enough about Paul for young Emeric to make the connection. Both smile as they have their photo taken together, the younger boy and the World War II vet, an emotional example of contact across the generations, and proof once again that age really is nothing but a number.

The Gift of Art: A Museum in Lafayette

Most people look forward to retiring and transitioning to a relative life of ease. Not Paul. As always, there were things to do and goals to reach, still more apples to be put into that basket. He didn't know it at the time, but two big public projects were calling his name. He was still a young man—of seventy-five.

It started with a conversation in their car. Paul and Lulu Hilliard were traveling home from a trip to Houston in late 2000. They had taken a quick side excursion to Jennings, Louisiana, to see the Zigler Art Museum (often called simply "the ZAM"). The museum had its origins in the personal collection of artworks owned by Ruth and Fred B. Zigler, and indeed was originally housed in their former home, which the couple had owned since 1908. When Fred died, Ruth donated the collection and home—along with two additional wings she had built— to the city over the course of several years in the 1960s and 1970. The museum was later relocated to Jennings City Hall in 2015, which is where it stands today.

Paul remembers that drive well. "We looked at the art there, a nice collection," Paul recalls. "It was a nice show in a little museum in Jennings, of all places," he says. Jennings is a historical town, site of the first oil well to produce in the state of Louisiana. It's also the county seat of Jefferson Davis Parish. But it's small, very small, with a population just a bit over 10,000. Driving past it on I-10 between Lake Charles and Lafayette, you could easily miss it. And yet, here was a wonderful little art museum— more proof that the "small town" is the real treasure of American life.

"Why can't we have a museum in Lafayette?" Paul remembers his wife asking him. Lulu had a long-standing and passionate interest in art. He did not. Indeed, he has never been reticent about his dislike of modern art. He likes to describe the time he was in Houston with Lulu attending an exhibition at the Museum of Fine Arts. The show featured the works of Mark Rothko, the renowned abstract painter. Touring the exhibit, curious but admittedly mystified, Paul found himself seated in front of a "huge block on the wall—just black." He was looking at Rothko's famous painting "Untitled (Black on Gray)" from 1969–1970.[10]

The painting, an enormous acrylic on canvas, is precisely as the title describes it, and Paul admits that he was not quite getting it. "A guy was sitting there, looking at it, looking at it, looking at it, and I asked, 'What am I supposed to be looking at?'" There was a pause. Then the other fellow looked at Paul and informed him somberly, "It's about feeling." With perfect comedic timing, Paul says he knew one thing in that moment: he had a "feeling" it was time to move on, that he'd been standing in front of this baffling painting long enough.

"I don't know anything about art," Paul will admit. "Art to me is whether you like it or not." There is always more to Paul than the quip, however. He's also realized over time that it's more than a personal preference. "It's an expression of man's visions, his dreams, his creativity. It is man's imagination at work," he says. Just for the record, Rothko himself has always maintained that his paintings from this period were about death.

Nevertheless, years later, seeing that exhibit in Jennings sparked a desire. Lulu had asked a good question. Lafayette had a population of 110,000 population then (over 125,000 today) and boasted a state university. Certainly, it was important enough to have its own world-class art museum and the infrastructure, facilities, and population to support one. The university already had an art museum of its own, under the direction of university professor Herman Mhire, housed in a home modeled after L'Hermitage plantation, designed by the noted southern architect A. Hays Town. The Hilliards were thinking bigger, however. Like the Ziglers before them, their personal collection of art and sculpture had grown, a product of their world travels.

In March 2001, with her health deteriorating, Lulu called Mhire to her Bendel Gardens home to review their considerable collection of art from India. She wanted to see if he was interested in the paintings as a museum donation. "She made coffee, we talked and waited for Paul to come home from work," Mhire recalls. He was impressed with what he saw: "Just looking at their home, he recalls, it appeared the interest in art had lasted many years. Art came from India, Tahiti, southeastern Asia, Europe. They collected from everywhere they traveled. Their home was their own version of a museum."[11]

As Mhire viewed the collection, however, he started to feel misgivings. The museum's Town building was not suitable for housing or displaying this art. A second building that had been discussed in the 1960s would have been more suitable, but it had never gone beyond the planning stage.

Mhire unveiled plans of his own to the Hilliards that night. He was about to visit Paris to lay the groundwork for an art exhibition in Lafayette, timed to coincide with Louisiana's bicentennial celebration in 2003 (the 200th anniversary of the Louisiana Purchase). He hoped to convince the great French museums—the Louvre, the Musée d'Orsay, the Centre Pompidou, the Musée National Picasso-Paris, the Musée Carnavalet—to lend period pieces to the university's art museum if an appropriate, professional museum facility could be built in time. Intrigued, the Hilliards asked Mhire to call them when he returned from France.

The trip went well, and when Mhire returned, Paul invited him to a May 9 meeting at Badger Oil offices. Paul, his vice presidents, Mhire, and UL Lafayette President Ray P. Authement were in attendance. Art Price recalls that Paul took charge, presenting his idea to build a "world-class art museum" at UL Lafayette. He cited the benefits that Mississippi had gained by opening the Mississippi Museum of Art in Jackson in 1978, and how it had boosted economic development in that city. "World-class exhibitions would make [Lafayette] a destination," Paul told the group. "He saw that vision for Lafayette," Art remembers.

And, as always, Paul was ready to put his money where his vision was. Four days later, Paul pledged $100,000 to assist with architectural fees for a preliminary design for a new museum. Two weeks after that, he pledged $3 million toward the construction of a new university art museum, and a bit later, he added an additional $2 million. "That's how the whole project got off the ground," Art says. From the start, Paul was the driver of the project. No surprise there. If you want someone to stand around, passively accept the opinions of others, and wait to be told what to do, Paul is probably not your man.

Groundbreaking took place in April 2002 and construction started in June. The completion date was a hard deadline: November 2003. The grand opening—a spectacular exhibition of French art to celebrate the state's bicentennial—was scheduled for December. As the building went up, Paul was tireless. He came by the construction site constantly, checking on progress, reaching for his wallet if more money were needed. He did Paul things, in other words. He also brought donuts to the workers on-site. When he was out of town, he had his assistant at Badger, Tina Fremin, do donut service in his stead. "It took dollars and donuts to build it," Paul comments. And, we might add, a lot of both.

Building the Paul and Lulu Hilliard University Art Museum proved less challenging than opening it. Mhire continued to work on his goal of a grand opening that paired with the state bicentennial. Twenty-eight museums had agreed to participate by lending their works, Mhire says. But the planned opening was ill-fated. In October, the university announced that the opening was postponed. Fundraising problems—the bane of so many great ideas in the academic and cultural worlds—had once again risen their ugly head.

The grand opening was rescheduled for April 21, 2004. The exhibition featured *Andrew Wyeth: The Helga Pictures*, *Francis Pavy's Louisiana*, and *Real Peoples: Selections from the Sylvia and Warren Lowe Collection*. Late or not, the opening was an auspicious debut for the museum Paul had championed: the star power of Wyeth and his most controversial series of paintings; the authentic Cajun vision of Lafayette native Pavy, narratives tinged with local folkways; and works from the Lowe Collection of self-taught southern artists (sometimes called "outsider works.")

The Wyeth show, in particular, was the blockbuster that every new museum needs to grab public attention. Wyeth was perhaps the best-known American painter of the twentieth century, a realist in an age of increasing artistic abstraction. His best-known work is arguably *Christina's World* (1948), at once an idyll and a paean to a vanishing small-town and rural America. Wyeth was widely recognized in his lifetime, of course, but he was hardly an artist who stoked the fires of public debate or controversy.

That was until 1986, when the "Helga paintings" first became known to the public. For the previous fifteen years (1971–1985), Wyeth had been painting portraits of Helga Testorf, a German native and neighbor from Chadds Ford, Pennsylvania. He painted her in various seasons, poses, and locations, in various degrees of dress and undress. He painted her 240 times, without the knowledge of his own wife, Betsy, or Helga's husband, John. A painter painting nudes hardly seems surprising, yet Wyeth's work with Helga seemed shocking to many people, given his reputation as a wholesome painter of Americana. Both denied any impropriety, but that didn't stop *Time* magazine's cover story from trumpeting "Andrew Wyeth's Stunning Secret."[12]

For all these reasons, the Wyeth show was a perfect choice for a museum opening. Mhire knew the museum had hit a home run. And if he had any doubts on that score, he found out for certain when the phone rang: "I received a surprise phone call the morning of the opening," he says. "I was ready to go to work when I got the call. It was from Helga, along with Mr. Wyeth. They called to say how pleased they were with the quality of the [exhibition] publications."

While Paul had good reason to feel satisfied by the museum's grand opening, his excitement was overshadowed by personal tragedy. Lulu's health continued to decline. The once-avid tennis player did manage to attend the museum's opening but couldn't walk on her own. "Lulu got to see it in a wheelchair," Paul says. It was to be her sole visit to the museum she had inspired, even though it was barely a mile from her home. The Paul and Lulu Hilliard University Art Museum opened in April 2004; Lulu died on Thanksgiving Day 2005.

Along with its impressive opening, the new museum won praise nationally and internationally. The innovative design, courtesy of the New Orleans architectural firm Eskew Dumez Ripple, is stunning. This "study in contrast," as the firm calls it, pairs the traditionalist ethos of the original Town building with a new, modernist glass and steel enclosure. As the new structure reflects the old Town house, the design achieves a real synthesis of past and present, not so much as opposites to one another but as stops along a seamless continuum of time. No surprise, then, that the design won the American Architecture Award for 2006. The 2009 edition of the authoritative volume *Collection: U.S. Architecture* (Michelle Galindo, ed.), also notes the interaction between the Town building and the new edifice in almost poetic language: "Depending upon position and time of day, the facade oscillates between opaque and transparent and at night is rendered a deep blue using cold cathode tubes, contrasting the new museum with its older neighbor."[13]

The museum was one of Paul's greatest triumphs. It would be nice to add a "happily ever after" postscript here, but troubles were ahead. Mhire's time at the museum was ending. After the Wyeth show opening, differences of opinion had manifested themselves about the museum's future. Mhire wanted the museum to establish a reputation nationally and internationally through big shows. University leadership saw it primarily in terms of serving the university, putting students (and fiscal prudence) first.

Paul wasn't neutral here. He had signed on to the project as presented by Mhire. "Herman got us involved in that thing," he says. "He wasn't just talented and experienced, but a visionary, which I'm not. We had every bit of confidence, total confidence, that he could do something with it if he got a museum facility."[14] Paul remained an admirer of Mhire's, whose retirement became official six days after Lulu's death. After Mhire's departure, Paul says the museum became moribund. It might not have been official, he says, "but it was really dead," an institutional victim of a leadership lacking in vision. "I didn't go back to the place for five years." Things only began to change when Dr. E. Joseph Savoie (nicknamed "T-Joe" in the Cajun vernacular) became the new president of UL Lafayette in 2008, followed by a new museum director, LouAnne Greenwald, in 2014. Paul saw the change. "When LouAnne took over, the place came back to life," Paul recalls.

For Paul, the years after Lulu's death were a very difficult time. He was lucky to have a close group of friends who supported him emotionally. Dr. Charles Boustany and his wife, Madlyn, had been close friends with Paul and Lulu for decades. They shared tennis, family barbecues, holiday parties, birthdays, graduations, and more. Charles was one of the pallbearers at Lulu's funeral. Madlyn was a mother of ten and an active leader in the community. Just as the Boustanys had supported him, Paul was there for Madlyn when Charles passed away in 2009. As longtime friends, Paul and Madlyn understood each other deeply. Their relationship grew into something more, and Madlyn became Paul's third wife—blending their large families.

Madlyn is a force of nature in her own right. Because she saw the museum as being so important to Paul, Madlyn targeted her energies toward reviving the museum and turning it into a major attraction. She contacted Dr. Savoie soon after he became president and the two discussed the "lack of activity and university engagement" at the museum. Paul credits Madlyn for her leadership. "She keeps the museum going, Madlyn and her daughter Kathryn Scurlock," he says. "They are interested in art.

My wife and her daughter have been great in getting that thing going and have helped boost it. I'm grateful to Madlyn and Kathryn for what they've done for the museum. They are both activists—they make things happen." The results of new energized leadership were dramatic. "Paul got reengaged. Kathryn helped to organize the Hilliard Society, the support organization," Savoie says. The hiring of LouAnne Greenwald was crucial. "She had clear eyes and a good background. Things have been moving ever since."[15] Museum hours have expanded, programming is vibrant, and attendance is up dramatically.

Greenwald has a broad vision. The museum, she says, serves as a bridge between the university and the community. A modern museum must be more than a storehouse for artifacts. Rather, it has to be "a center for community engagement," a space "that serves the [UL Lafayette] faculty, staff and students," as well as the local community in Lafayette. From that base, the museum must also reach out to the broader region of Acadiana. Since the Hilliard is the only art museum in the area, its programs also serve K–12 students as far away as Lake Charles, and even engages visitors in Houston and New Orleans.[16]

Museum planner Marcy Goodwin says UL Lafayette ought to appreciate how far the Hilliard Art Museum has advanced from an insufficient space at Fletcher Hall on campus to the 33,000-square-foot facility for which Paul provided lead funding and oversight. "You have to think that the joy and spectacular grounds that is the Hilliard didn't exist at all in 2001," she says. "Now, with the Hilliard Art Museum here, the community has gone from zero to 80 mph."[17]

"Zero to 80" might well describe the entire trajectory of the Hilliard since its founding. On January 30, 2018, the museum hosted a "mortgage-burning ceremony," a celebration that confirmed the institution's long-term fiscal health. A photo taken at the event shows Paul wearing a shirt that reads, "I paid off the mortgage and all I got was this lousy T-shirt." In November 2022, the Hilliard received its highest accolade yet, when the American Alliance of Museums (AAM) granted it accreditation status. Only a tiny percentage of museums in the United States are AAM-accredited, just 1,099 out of the country's estimated 33,000. The process is rigorous, combining self-assessment with peer review, in order to determine which institutions are "appropriate stewards of the collections and resources they hold in the public trust." With AAM accreditation, LouAnne Greenwald says, the Hilliard has received "the industry stamp of approval," which will make it easier to borrow important works of art and to stage bigger and better exhibitions. Even the normally taciturn Paul admits that "it's a big deal," though he typically hastens to add, "Now we have to live up to it."

The Gift of Memory: The National WWII Museum

The key moments of Paul's life—the determining ones—were the World War II years. While involved in the war, as he has stated many times, he was not aware of its full significance or the precise details of his own role. Neither did he obsess on those events in the postwar years. Few of his wartime generation did. The experience of industrial-age global war at such a young age left most of them yearning for a return to something "normal." Going to school, getting a good job, marrying and starting a family, buying a house: these were their typical goals. Even if you had done something heroic in wartime, you typically buried it. You also buried your psychological and emotional scars. You tried to "get over it." Memories of the war grew dim. People forgot.

Only as the veterans aged did that process of "forgetting" begin to change. Retirement is a time to reflect on your journey: your origins, the path, and the meaning of it all. It is no surprise, then, that the 1980s began to see a revival of interest in World War II, and especially in the men and women who had fought it. The decade included a number of fortieth anniversaries: Pearl Harbor (1981), D-Day (1984), and V-E and V-J days (1985). The country had taken a more conservative turn from the 1960s and 1970s. Ronald Reagan held the office of president, proclaiming that it was "morning in America" again, and traditional values were back in, including, perhaps, honoring your parents and trying to understand their life struggles. Above all, the wartime generation was now in its mid-sixties and in the mood for self-reflection. Not only was the country more interested in the veterans, but the veterans were also more interested in themselves and the war they had fought.

A landmark in this new rush of memory was President Reagan's speech at Omaha Beach on the fortieth anniversary of D-Day (June 6, 1984). He spoke in the presence of sixty-two US Army Ranger veterans who had scaled the cliffs of Pointe du Hoc, one of the most daring and dangerous acts of heroism in the annals of military history. "These are the boys of Pointe du Hoc," the President said. "These are the men who took the cliffs. These are the champions who helped free a continent."[18] The "boys" seated directly in front of him were boys no longer, of course, but they were moved to tears, revisiting their younger selves and contemplating the poignancy of young men being sent off to do or die for their country. Reagan himself was choking back tears. And so do most people who watch a video of that speech even today.

For the next fifteen years, discussing World War II and honoring its veterans suddenly became the order of the day. Books and films seemed to pour out. Studs Terkel's *"The Good War": An Oral History of World War II* (1984) relied upon the voices of those who were there to tell the story. Many readers and commentators still seem to miss the ironic quotation marks around "good war," however, and the work as a whole is anything but triumphalist or flag-waving.[19] Stephen E. Ambrose's *Band of Brothers* (1992, made into a film in 2001) was a tribute to the men of "Easy Company" (actually E Company, 506th Regiment, 101st Airborne Division), based on oral interviews Ambrose conducted with veterans and written in his typically brilliant, gripping, prose.[20] The title itself is a reference to Shakespeare's play *Henry V*. The Bard has the king speaking to his outnumbered men before the Battle of Agincourt in 1815, on the eve of St. Crispin's Day:

> From this day to the ending of the world,
> But we in it shall be remember'd;
> We few, we happy few, we band of brothers;
> For he to-day that sheds his blood with me
> Shall be my brother; be he ne'er so vile,
> This day shall gentle his condition.[21]

The peak year for public remembrance of World War II may well have been 1998, which saw the release of a book and a film that still define the entire "memory industry" of World War II: Tom Brokaw's *The Greatest Generation* and Steven Spielberg's film, *Saving Private Ryan*. The former delivered an instantly recognizable (and now omnipresent) sound bite in its title; the second, in the first twenty-two minutes of the film, at least, provided a level of cinema verité in recreating the tough US landing at Omaha Beach that will probably never be exceeded in its intensity. Museums and cultural institutions even found that they crossed veteran opinion at their own peril, as the Smithsonian Institution discovered in 1995 when planning its exhibit of the B-29 Enola Gay, the aircraft that had dropped the atomic bomb on Hiroshima. Veterans found the first draft of the exhibit's script to be tendentious, overly critical of the American decision to drop the bomb, and too focused on Japan's wartime suffering.[22]

Paul Hilliard was not immune to any of these trends of public memory. He had always been an avid reader, and increasingly the subject matter was World War II, not just his own service or theater, but the entire vast conflict. His passion for World War II history grew from spark to flame when he attended an event at the University of New Orleans in 1985. The university's Eisenhower Center was putting on a two-day symposium on Pegasus Bridge, the dramatic British glider landing to seize the crucial bridge over the Caen Canal between Caen and Ouistreham, France. That event, featuring British and German commanders who had actually fought during the battle, Paul later wrote, "was and still is meaningful for me because it was there that I realized I wanted to look more closely at those 'small' battles that comprised an enormous war, and I then also realized how little I knew about the scope of the war."[23] He spent the day there. "I was fascinated," he recalls. "Wars consist of thousands of little battles. The small-unit actions intrigued me."

He began to read more and more, not just small unit accounts, but the big picture as well. His library eventually came to include some four thousand books. He gravitates not just to the best information, but to good writers: Ambrose, of course, Max Hastings, Carlo D'Este, Donald Miller, Rich Frank, Victor Davis Hanson, and the masterful works of Rick Atkinson.[24]

The 1985 conference was not only instrumental in forming Paul's reading habits. He also made the acquaintance of two men who were destined to become the true "dynamic duo" of World War II memory: Ambrose and his best friend, Gordon H. "Nick" Mueller. On the surface they were two ordinary professors in the Department of History at the

University of New Orleans, but each of them had gifts that marked them apart from their colleagues: Ambrose the brilliant writer, a charismatic celebrity, one of the most popular historians in all of America in terms of book sales, and Mueller the visionary, an entrepreneurial genius, a man of enormous energy and who can kick-start a room just by walking into it.[25]

Together, in 1990, the two men hatched an idea for a museum in New Orleans. It would sit on a lakefront property by Lake Pontchartrain and serve as a tribute not only to D-Day veterans, but also to Andrew Higgins, the redoubtable New Orleans shipbuilder and father of the Landing Craft Vehicle and Personnel (LCVP), more popularly known as the "Higgins Boat." An ungainly vessel with a ramp that allowed personnel or small vehicles to exit through the front, it made beach assaults possible and was therefore a crucial contributor to Allied victory in World War II. Indeed, President Eisenhower, looking back, once called Higgins "the man who won the war for us."[26] Ten years of fundraising followed their initial inspiration, with Mueller leading the way.

It wasn't easy; it never is. Money ran short, interest from donors seemed to be lagging, but Mueller was tireless in pursuing the dream. Tom Hanks, actor and good friend of the museum, put it best: "Nick had a vision for the museum, like a prophet in a desert, or a wise man up on a mountain. For years and years, dinner after dinner, meeting after meeting, one phone call at a time, he got the place built."[27] With an eye to future visitors and tourists, he also decided to move the museum to a new location away from the relatively remote lakefront and into the heart of the city, to an old warehouse on Magazine Street near Lee Circle. Finally, on June 6, 2000, the D-Day Museum opened its doors, replete with media and film stars, parades, and hundreds of veterans.

Like a magnet and steel, it seems inevitable that Paul, a World War II veteran with a growing interest in the history of the conflict, would find himself attracted to the new and growing World War II Museum just a few miles away. The museum's programming was already featuring many of the same authors that Paul was reading, and its educational touring program was organizing trips to the battlefields of Normandy. Paul himself made the sixtieth anniversary of D-Day trip in 2004. With a dozen or so veterans along, the group spent five days in Normandy, touring key sites from the battle and listening to lectures by historians. That sense of having put his feet on sacred ground was palpable. "I got really interested in what they were doing," Paul says. A few years later, he raised his involvement to a whole other level.

There's a saying, or at least there ought to be, that "you can buy anything on eBay." One day in spring 2006, Paul got a call from one of the museum's historians. There was a Douglas C-47 for sale on eBay. The C-47 was a transport plane that had done workhorse duty on all fronts in the course of the war. In the postwar era, it would become famous in its civilian incarnation as the DC-3. According to the tail number in the eBay listing, this particular aircraft had actually flown Pathfinders (advanced scouts) for the Eighty-Second Airborne Division the night before D-Day and had also seen action in the Battle of the Bulge. Its final mission took place in Operation Varsity in March 1945, the airborne landing across the Rhine River and into Germany. Later, the C-47 had been used in connection with the movie *A Bridge Too Far*. And now it was sitting on the tarmac of a small airport in Hondo, Texas.

A find, no doubt! The museum's historian-in-residence, Marty Morgan, sent the good news up the chain, and it finally landed on the desk of Mueller, by now museum's president and CEO. Money was tight at the museum at the time, however. This was the post-Katrina era, when the museum's very survival had been in doubt. Morgan had no great hopes: "We all expected a dose of reality from the boss. We all knew that he would be perfectly justified in saying that this was something we could not afford or alternatively that precious resources were needed to be directed toward something other than acquiring a sixty-two-year-old airplane."

Mueller's response, in a tone familiar to anyone who has worked with him, was enthusiastic. "Sounds great! Go for it!"[28]

Paul was already known to the museum. Indeed, he had been a fixture since that 2004 trip to Normandy. Paul was always looking for ways to help the museum and had been talking about finding an aircraft for purchase. A few days later, he, Morgan, and collections manager Tom Czekanski were on their way to Hondo. None of them knew what to expect. The airfield was tiny. The C-47 was the only plane there, and it was leaking oil from one engine. But a few hours of inspection quickly revealed that it was "the real deal," in Czekanski's words. He also wielded the tape measure, to ensure that it would fit in the building.

C-47s had been on the market before, and the museum had been interested. But the price was usually around $500,000. "We didn't have that kind of money," Mueller says. Paul had been encouraging the museum leadership to buy airplanes. Otherwise, he says, the prices for such vintage pieces were going to climb out of reach or even disappear from the market altogether. For Mueller, this was just another freewheeling day at the office in the early days of the museum: "The thing was going up for auction online. We had to put in a bid by noon that day. We had to make a decision to bid on it without having the money. The starting bid had to be $250,000. We put in a bid for $255,000 and won the bid. I knew exactly who I was going to call: Paul Hilliard."[29]

Although the C-47 was purchased at a "bargain price," it needed a great deal of work: an engine replacement, a fresh paint job, new windows. The original floor was put back into the plane. Czekanski says the repairs were doable because there were still plenty of C-47s around; they are the most numerous surviving planes from World War II. It took about six months to repair and restore the aircraft, the cost of which roughly matched the purchase price. Those who were closest to the deal still differ about the final cost, but this much was certain: the C-47 was repaired over the summer, made flight-worthy, and flew to New Orleans, with a weekend stopover in Lafayette, in September 2006. The plane was in Lafayette for a weekend, allowing the locals to see the aircraft and to experience living history by actually flying in it.

From Lafayette, the plane was flown to Lakefront Airport in New Orleans, Czekanski says. There, workers disassembled it. On September 17, with police escort, a flatbed truck took the bulk of the plane, sans wings, down Elysian Fields Avenue and through the streets of the city to the museum. The C-47 hangs in the museum's Louisiana Pavilion today, beautifully restored, seemingly alive, and ready for action. She is a vivid tribute to the World War II generation, to Mueller and Ambrose's original vision, and to Paul's drive, generosity, and spirit of giving.

Paul had another major item on his wanted list: a Douglas SBD Dauntless dive-bomber. Not only had he flown in one personally during World War II, the Dauntless had also played a significant role in the crucial Battle of the Coral Sea, which blunted the Japanese drive toward Australia, and then an even more crucial role in the decisive victory over the Japanese at Midway. Here the Dauntlesses had their greatest success, sinking four Japanese aircraft carriers in quick succession—the *Akagi*, *Kaga*, *Hiryū*, and *Sōryū*—breaking the back of the Imperial Japanese navy and changing the entire course of the war.

Paul also admits a sentimental attachment to the aircraft. In his fifty-plus missions in the SBD, he says, he and his pilot never had to abandon an assignment because of mechanical trouble. Sometimes, the weather was too treacherous to fly, but the Dauntless, true to its name, never failed him. "The SBD served America well, and it served me well." In other words, procuring a Dauntless for the museum fulfilled Paul's need to link his own personal experience with the broader course of the war, something he had been yearning to do since he returned from the Pacific.

With Paul footing the bill, the museum managed to secure a Dauntless on loan from the National Aviation Museum in Pensacola, Florida. This SBD had a career as varied and, we might say, as tragic, as any wartime veteran. She came off the assembly line of the Douglas Aircraft Company in El Segundo, California, and flew combat missions from Henderson Field in the Guadalcanal Campaign. In 1943, she returned to the states to serve as a trainer at Naval Air Station Glenview, Illinois. The next year, the aircraft was lost on a training flight in Lake Michigan. It remained in its watery grave until 1990, when the US Navy recovered and restored it. It was not an uncommon fate, Paul says. There are perhaps fourteen more aircraft still underwater in Lake Michigan. Training accidents—perhaps an inevitable result when you put a young guy who is just learning to fly into the cockpit of a high-performance aircraft—were far more common in wartime than most Americans realize.

Today, the SBD hangs, seemingly ready to pounce on an unsuspecting Japanese warship, from the ceiling of the Boeing Center in the Museum's Freedom Pavilion. Joining it is an impressive cohort of other World War II aircraft: a North American B-25 Mitchell medium bomber, a General Motors TBM Avenger dive-bomber, a Chance Vought F4U Corsair fighter, a North American Aviation P-51 Mustang fighter (painted in the "redtail" colors of the renowned Tuskegee Airmen), and, the biggest and baddest of them all, a Boeing B-17 Flying Fortress four-engine strategic bomber.

Paul didn't just buy airplanes, however. He also provided funds to purchase a collection of World War II artillery. The guns were the property of a family in Houma, Louisiana, whose father had owned a company that produced ammunition during the war. There were twelve pieces in the collection in all. The most recognizable one is a German flak 88 mm antiaircraft gun, a devastating weapon that the Germans often employed in an antitank role. With its barrel length of sixteen feet, it commands visitor attention on the floor of the Louisiana Pavilion to this day.

As Paul was helping buy aircraft and guns, some of the jewels of the museum's collection, he didn't know that the museum had its eye on him, as well. "I was impressed by Paul," says Mueller about the 2004 trip. "He had been at conferences since the late 1980s, had been involved, but never focused. I had more in-depth time with him on this trip. I was trying to build a board beyond New Orleans. He was interested in that, too." At the time the museum was transitioning from a focus on D-Day to the Pacific theater. "He asked about the board, about the master plan, about our vision. How were we going to do it?"[30]

Paul called Mueller after Katrina, when the storm and its horrible aftermath had effectively shut down the museum, to talk. Paul himself recalls driving to New Orleans right after the museum reopened and being struck by the desolation of the city, or what was left of it. "It was like being on the dark side of the moon," he says, thinking perhaps of the devastation he had seen in the wartime Philippines.

Mueller got right to the point. "I asked him if he would consider being nominated for the board. He was all in with what we were doing. That was clear to me. He appreciated the significance and the impact of a World War II Museum in Louisiana." Paul had an ideal profile for a board candidate. He was interested in the work, he had been coming to conferences, he had already traveled to Normandy with the museum. He had a deep and abiding interest in the museum's mission and was well familiar with its recent challenges. The kicker: he was a decorated World War II veteran, with significant wartime experience in the Pacific theater.

Pete Wilson is a longtime trustee and former board chairman. He is also a Marine veteran and a successful politician, serving both as a US Senator (R, 1983–1991) and governor (R, 1991–1999) of the state of California. Wilson notes that being a board member is a demanding task. Board members are "not just wallpaper," he says; they have real tasks: fundraising, committee assignments, travel on behalf of the museum.

Wilson himself chaired the capital campaign committee at a tough time for the museum: between Katrina in 2005 and the financial downturn of 2008. He had been the museum's first "national chairman"—the first from outside the region. Since the museum's charter specifies that 40 percent of the trustees have to come from Louisiana or Mississippi, Paul filled a need for regional leadership.

Wilson and Paul went to lunch a couple of times after Paul joined the board in 2006, and the governor found out what a lot of people already know about Paul. "He was not Mr. Big," Wilson recalls. Paul was humble and good natured, one of the funniest men you will ever meet. But as the conversation took a more serious turn, Wilson says, "the more impressed I was with who he was," a man of accomplishment who was shrewd and sage about both business and politics. "I took to him as a new friend and have great respect for him," Wilson says. Wilson notes that Paul spoke sparingly as a board member. When he spoke, however, people paid attention. "He was worth listening to," Wilson says. "He's not a guy who likes to pop off. But he makes his point, makes it effectively and usually with some comment that has his audience convulsed— but they listened."[31]

Along with his trustee duties, Paul has continued to donate time and money for acquisitions. According to Stephen Watson, the president and CEO of the museum since 2017, Paul and Madlyn have been among "the museum's strongest supporters for the past fifteen years." Watson runs down the impressive list: "Between the C-47, his plane the SBD Dauntless, the P-40E and ME 109 airplanes, the M3A1 Stuart Tank and the PT-305 boat, he more or less owns his own fleet of military vehicles at this point," he says, adding a quip that, "The museum is just his garage."[32] Watson also lists the places where Paul Hilliard has traveled with the museum in support of the program: London, Anzio, Warsaw, Berlin, Iwo Jima, Peleliu, Tunisia, Malta, and more. Indeed, Paul has practically done a heritage tour of US military campaigns in World War II.

Paul's efforts on behalf of the museum have been incredibly broad. In addition to World War II artifacts and support of battlefield tours, the Hilliards underwrote the cost of a 20,000-volume research library in the newly built Hall of Democracy, a state-of-the-art facility to ensure that the museum speaks to the world through fresh research and digital programming; they funded and named the conference center in the newly built Higgins Hotel; they back the museum's educational programs and symposia; they support volunteer programs and fund staff members to collect oral histories. They even pay for the annual staff Christmas party for 300–400 people, a deluxe event in New Orleans's City Park.

In 2018, Paul reached the pinnacle of his museum involvement when he was selected as chairman of the museum's Board of Trustees. He was the first World War II veteran to serve in the post. The moment was one for Paul to reflect upon and savor. He was ninety-two at the time and had received his share of lifetime honors. This one, however, was different—and special. "I was a pissant on a subsistence farm," he puts it in his inimitable way, "born before the Depression, becoming chair of the National WWII Museum in New Orleans," he says. "In what other country would this happen?" He has a real sense of gratitude, he says, for the opportunity to serve and for the benefits he earned through his Marine service. As an airman, he says, he never spent a night in the mud. He was never wounded or shot down. The government sent him to college. He bought his first home with a government loan. All of that, he says, for a guy who spent his war missions flying while facing the rear of the aircraft at 12,000 feet. "We were masters of hindsight," he jokes.

As always with Paul, however, his joke is merely a device to make a deeper point, this one about America: "I tell young people today to pay attention, not only to the external, but the internal. Be thankful for the country we live in. It is the best ever. Have a sense of gratitude for what they have and where they live and what you are trying to teach them about freedom and fragility."

Once, during one of the museum's educational trips to the Pacific in 2007, a guest asked Paul: "How are you going to make this museum mean something in fifty years?"

"It's a good question," he responds. "It's always a huge obstacle. The challenge is to get the story out about the American experience in the war that changed the world but also to make the story meaningful to young people," he says. "It's difficult to make young people see the relationship between the past and now." Outreach is the key. "You can bring up to a million people to New Orleans" annually to visit the museum, Paul says, but what about the other 330 million Americans?

Madlyn Hilliard was thrilled when she heard that Paul had been offered the chairman's role. "I knew he would make a marvelous chairman of the board," she says. "He did not know, at his age, if they would ask him." Paul, characteristically, says that he would accept the post only after he talked with his wife. No problem there. When former board chairman Boysie Bollinger approached her, seeking her approval for the decision, Madlyn remembers being "tearful with joy." When she sees Paul visiting the museum, she says, he's a different person. "He's twenty years younger." She is grateful that the museum has given him "an outlet to tell people about his service." When Paul talks to an eighth grader, she says, "he puts himself in other people's shoes, and empathy is deeper than sympathy."[33]

She too is taken back in time when she visits. She was a child, she recalls, and suddenly there were no candy bars or chewing gum. "I was only ten years old, but the museum brings back plenty of memories: newsreels, family reunions, hearing FDR's voice. Our family members were over there, and I remember the pain in the face of my mother and grandmother." She says that young people who visit the museum are fascinated when they get there, when they see the "price paid for their freedom." Like Paul, Madlyn feels that young Americans need to understand the war, the heroism, the sacrifice. The soldiers, sailors, and airmen who marched, sailed, or flew off to war were the same age as the young people visiting the museum. That is the point of contact, she says. "I've developed the passion, and I recognize the importance and the value of the museum for our children and our grandchildren and all youth. World War II affected every person in this country and other countries. There was so much sadness and yet so much joy."

Madlyn, too, knows her history. She understands that not every generation is the same. Some may be asked to fight, while others may face different challenges. She knows that history doesn't differentiate. Democracy is a gift, she believes, one of the greatest gifts that God has given humanity. For centuries, human beings were told, "Don't act above your station." And suddenly, starting in 1776, a different message resounded. "All men are created equal." In words that echo Paul's, that is the precise reason why Madlyn says we need to remember, and why she and Paul support the museum: "What impresses me about it is the youth that visits it. You

can see them understanding something they previously didn't get. They
seem enthralled. They are learning history that they are not getting anywhere else. It's about training young people, the expression on their faces.
They're hungry to know what happened. The museum is an educational
institution, absolutely. Not just educating youth—it's also about educating teachers."

"Everyone," she says, played a part. "Men, women, children, victory
gardens, rationing, mothers praying for their sons." Americans faced down
the challenge. It is a message, she and Paul believe, that transcends politics
or debate. "World War II affected everybody," Madlyn affirms, "and each
story is important."

Paul turned ninety-five years old just days before his term as chair
formally ended. Museum staff and personnel gathered with his friends to
serenade him in front of his family home in Lafayette. A band played the
"Marine Corps Hymn." Paul stood to salute. Still vigorous, still captivated
by the war, its history, and its ramifications, he plans to continue his affiliation with the museum as long as he can. Paul believes there is still so
much work to accomplish.[34]

He was a man who fought for his country. He founded and nurtured a
company through six difficult decades, raised children and grandchildren,
and traveled the world. An art museum bears his family name. He served
his industry at the highest levels, championing the cause of energy in the
corridors of the nation's capital and in the halls of Congress. He made fortunes and gave fortunes away for the benefit of others. He has fulfilled so
many desires, seized so many opportunities, answered so many questions.

Except one, perhaps: what's next?

Man of Bronze

In the course of his long and storied life, Paul Hilliard has won his
share of awards: the Distinguished Flying Cross (twice) and the Air
Medal with six bronze stars for his wartime service as a radioman and
gunner; the Lafayette Civic Cup in 2003; the prestigious Horatio Alger
Award in 2009. In 2016, he received the Circle of Honor Award from the
Congressional Medal of Honor Foundation, for his "lifetime of placing
others first" and for epitomizing "the principles of courage, sacrifice, self-
less service and patriotism." At the awards ceremony, he shared the stage

with actor and heartthrob Bradley Cooper, who was receiving the Bob Hope Award for Excellence in Entertainment for starring in (and producing) the film *American Sniper* (2014). Paul topped that one in 2023, when the Congressional Medal of Honor Society selected him to receive its Patriot Award. It is the highest honor the society can bestow and puts Paul in the company of luminaries from Will Rogers to George H. W. Bush to Roger Staubach.

While this is an impressive list of accomplishments under any circumstances, the honor that probably lies closest to Paul's heart took place in January 2020, when he was the subject of a gala on the campus of the University of Louisiana at Lafayette. It was a fitting event for him, an almost perfect summation of his career and achievements up to that point. The gala included the opening of a new art exhibition, a scholarly symposium, and the unveiling of a bronze sculpture of Paul, the museum's namesake and chief benefactor.

The theme of the scheduled events was, in a single word, "Winston." The exhibition, *The Art of Sir Winston Churchill*, brought together twelve of the many artworks that the great statesman executed during the course of his long career. It may come as a surprise to many that this man of war and oratory, politics and struggle, who wrote over five thousand speeches and forty-two books in his career and who won the Nobel Prize for Literature in 1953, also managed to find the time to create more than 550 paintings. Art, he believed, was a mental exercise, keeping his memory acute and his powers of observation sharp. The exhibition was stunning, and, with Curator Tim Riley of America's National Churchill Museum in Fulton, Missouri, on hand to offer expert commentary, enlightening as well.

The accompanying symposium, staged by the Institute for the Study of War and Democracy (the research wing of the National WWII Museum), examined the theme "Churchill in Conflict and Culture." Museum historians and faculty from the University of Louisiana at Lafayette presented their scholarship and research on Churchill to a packed hall. The talk was not only of Churchill as a politician, but as an artist, an orator, a very successful journalist, and even as a supreme self-salesman. Paul and Madlyn were front row and center throughout the day, taking it all in.

Elevating the gathering—consecrating it, in a sense—was the presence of the Honorable Emma Soames, the granddaughter of Winston Churchill. She seemed deeply touched at the interest and respect afforded her grandfather. "I had wrongly assumed," she said, "that in popular culture the memory of Churchill and his works would be fading by now, more than fifty years after his death."[35]

Churchill is another of Paul's conversational touchstones, a subject to whom he returns again and again. Churchill resides in Paul's consciousness under many guises: the leader who "carried the free world on his shoulders" in 1940–41, the bulldog who stood up to Hitler, the orator who rallied his people when all seemed lost. The admiration that young Paul developed for Churchill has only sharpened with time. "Our politicians come and go," Paul will say. "Churchill is a permanent figure." "He's sort of like Lincoln or Washington. He grows over time. He gets bigger and bigger. There's a lot of history still being written, lots of facts coming out. A closet opens and more information comes out about him. But Winston Churchill survives it all."[36]

Indeed, celebrating Churchill this evening had been Paul's decision in the first place. The event planners had asked him which artist he wanted to celebrate that night, and for Paul, there was no question. The display of Churchill's artworks even included a lithograph owned by Paul himself.

The sculpture of Paul stands in front of the museum. Executed in bronze by Ivan Schwartz of EIS Studio out of Brooklyn, New York, the piece is anything but stentorian or triumphalist. It is a realistic likeness of Paul that also manages to capture the essence of his personality. He is not declaiming profound slogans or looking heroic. He is wearing his glasses and a sports coat, with one hand in his pocket and the other cradling a book. He looks like he just can't wait to tell you about some new volume he's just read. A low wall behind the sculpture bears a favorite phrase of Paul's, a paraphrase from historian Will Durant: "Education is the interminable process of discovering our own ignorance."[37]

That night had it all. Art and learning, Winston Churchill (and a member of the great man's family to boot). And finally, a man in bronze, wearing a sport coat and glasses, holding a book, keeping an eternal watch, urging us to seize the opportunity to educate ourselves. It was a Paul Hilliard night.

Summing Up

Clayton Paul Hilliard can look back on his life with some satisfaction. In the course of his long life—his paternal grandparents were actually born before the American Civil War—he's done it all. While he's endured Shakespeare's "slings and arrows of outrageous fortune," he's also worked hard, made good choices, and prospered.[38] He came when his country called and did three years of active duty in World War II. To this day, he tells anyone who will listen that America more than paid him back: five years of college education courtesy of the GI Bill, a VA loan to buy his first home, regular medical checkups to this very day. "Has any country on earth ever taken better care of its veterans?" he asks.

He came back from that war, thankfully whole in mind and body, and built a successful business against long odds. He has set aside a great deal of the money he earned, as well as a great deal of his free time and energy, and given them to worthy causes in the realm of education, culture, and public memory. For a self-professed "dead-end kid" born on a struggling farm in northern Wisconsin, it's not a bad record.

And about that farm? For years it remained a blighted memory for Paul, a Depression-era Dust Bowl with too many chores, not enough rain, and nowhere near enough money for his family. But even here, things change. Paul had a chance to visit "Sand Burr Coulee" again in June 2021, just a few days past his ninety-sixth birthday. The withered, dry landscape that was so much a part of his consciousness was now barely recognizable. New owners Jon and Metta Belisle greeted Paul warmly and showed him around the property. The hardscrabble farm of Paul's memory is today a nature conservancy, lush and verdant, highlighted by a tall grove of black walnut trees. Paul reads scripture regularly, and as he looked around, he had to have been thinking of the words of St. Paul, "Behold, all things are become new."[39] In a sense, it is a perfect motto for a man like Paul, who has never rested on his laurels and always sought the next challenge.

Even though she is far too modest to claim the privilege, let us allow Madlyn to have the last word. From the moment she met Paul, she says, "I've been a fan." Speaking on a beautiful fall day in their mountain home in North Carolina in September 2022, Madlyn opens her heart: "From the moment we met, Paul thought the way I thought. His career impressed me. I trusted him. Trusted his judgment. My husband trusted him. There was nothing fake about Paul. He says what he thinks. Doesn't dress it up for different audiences. I knew his intelligence and sincerity, but I didn't know how strong his faith was. That attracted me. I wanted to be with someone who made me a better person."

Unlike a lot of other people, Madlyn says, "he walks the walk."[40]

AFTERWORD
A PERSONAL NOTE

I first met my good friend Paul Hilliard when I spoke at the National WWII Museum some ten years ago, in 2012. Soon thereafter, I became the museum's senior historian, a position I continued to hold while Paul was serving as the chairman of our Board of Trustees. Over the years, we've enjoyed our share of adventures together. We've visited World War II battle sites, stood on the hallowed ground of Omaha Beach and gazed out to sea, wondering just how in the world those young American boys made it through the D-Day landing alive. We've endured storms at sea and dined out in Paris.

And yet, whenever I think about my relationship with Paul, one phrase inevitably trumps all the others:

"You've got mail."

Oh, sure, my email program doesn't actually say that to me anymore, but it doesn't need to. It's a cold day in July—a rare thing, indeed, in New Orleans—that a note from Paul doesn't drop into my inbox. These are almost never jokes or trivial chat. They almost always deal with history, especially military history, and most especially World War II. The topic might be a book Paul has read recently or a book review. Or an article by one of his favorite authors. Or a film review. Or simply a quote he wishes to share with me.

People tell me that Paul is a very successful oilman. If that's true, then he must have negotiated some sort of pact with the Almighty that makes his days longer than twenty-four hours. The man is a voracious reader and thinker. He'd be great in a DC think tank, one of those high-level institutes dealing with the intricacies of foreign policy, global diplomacy, and war. He could brief the president. Sometimes I wish he *would* brief

201

the president. There are even times when I think that he could *be* the president! I'd certainly sleep more soundly at night.

Consider this very partial list of Paul's notes to me over the years.

He loves opinion pieces, and the feistier the writing and argumentation, the more strongly he recommends them. He's sent me pieces on the relationship between Hitler and Stalin at the time of the Nazi-Soviet Pact; on the serious political divisions within reunified Germany after 1991; and on the incredible depth of US Army logistics in World War II's European theater. He likes articles that sting, especially if the target is pompous enough, Charles De Gaulle or Field Marshal Bernard Law Montgomery, let's say. He also likes pieces that praise, such as the stirring paean to the heroic wartime defenders of the island of Malta and their commander, Lieutenant General Sir William G. S. Dobbie, which he sent me in September 2018.

He is an equal fan of book and film reviews, especially when the reviewer writes sharply, and over the years he has sent many dozens of shorter pieces. He's shared George Will's take on *Vietnam: An Epic Tragedy, 1945–1975* (by Max Hastings), which Will called "an unsparing look at the Vietnam War's mountain of lies," as well as Paul Kennedy's review of a new book on the Marshall Plan (the one by Benn Steil from 2018). Dr. Kennedy calls the plan "a great act of American statecraft," a sentiment that Paul shares. He also sent me Antony Beevor's list of favorite and not-so-favorite movies, a hot little article in which Beevor torched, among other films, *Saving Private Ryan*. Paul and I are still shaking our heads over that one.

But that's the thing about Paul. Unlike a lot of people whom I know today, he doesn't just choose reading material that he agrees with. What is the fun of that? Paul wants to be challenged; indeed, he actually seems to thrive on it.

And that brings me to the last major group of Paul's notes to me over the years: the "Thought Provoking Quote." Paul is, quite simply, the Maestro of the TPQ, and I never quite know what I'm going to be reading next. It might be Winston Churchill (in fact, it very often is), or it might be Cicero (another of Paul's favorites). It might be Franklin Roosevelt or Abraham Lincoln. It might be the opening statement by Justice Robert H. Jackson to the International Military Tribunal at Nuremberg in November

1945: "That four great nations, flushed with victory and stung with injury stay the hand of vengeance and voluntarily submit their captive enemies to the judgment of the law is one of the most significant tributes that Power has ever paid to Reason."

Or it might be a quotation from Virgil's *Aeneid*, when Paul and I were discussing how best to word a tribute to the American generation that fought World War II: "As long as rivers shall run down to the sea, or shadows touch the mountain slopes, or stars graze in the vault of heaven, so long shall your honor, your name, your praises endure."

Most recently, writing in the shadow of Russia's February 2022 invasion of Ukraine, Paul reminded me of the profound words of the great German philosopher G. W. F. Hegel: "We learn from history that we do not learn from history."

Paul has an active mind, to put it mildly. He's engaged: historically, intellectually, critically. He doesn't settle for easy slogans or comfortable clichés, and he's constantly challenging himself with new books, concepts, and ideas. If you want to have a good knock-down, drag-out fight over some arcane point of history, Paul is your man.

I hope you enjoyed the biography you've just read, about a great man and a great American. World War II gunner, successful entrepreneur and oilman, generous patron of culture and the arts; he amazes me with his knowledge, his energy, and his warm spirit. It has been an honor to write this book of his life. I am proud to call Paul my friend, and someday, when I grow up, I want to be just like him.

And on that note, I had better run. I think I've got mail.

NOTES

Preface

1. Plutarch, "Alexander," in *The Age of Alexander* (New York: Penguin, 1973), 25. He also notes, "The most brilliants exploits often tell us nothing of the virtues or vices of the men who performed them."

2. The primary source—the key account—of flying a Dauntless in the South Pacific, also told from the same Marine perspective as Paul, is Colonel John Howard McEniry Jr., *A Marine Dive-Bomber Pilot at Guadalcanal* (Tuscaloosa, AL: University of Alabama Press, 1987). See especially Colonel McEniry's descriptions of the typical dive-bomber run on pp. 21–23, including the startling revelation on p. 22 that "everyone pulled between nine and twelve Gs and went into some stage of a blackout."

3. "As early as the end of 1942, American war production was already greater than that of all the Axis nations combined. It was also more efficient, with productivity per capita far greater than German or Japanese workers." Mark A. Stoler, *Allies in War: Britain and America Against the Axis Powers, 1940–1945* (London: Hodder Arnold, 2005), 48.

4. Paul is a voracious reader—of the Bible, historical works, memoirs, opinion pieces, and much more. He took note of an article in *The Spectator US* in May 2022 and (as is his wont), sent a copy to me. Joel Kotkin, "How the Boomers Robbed the Young of All Hope," describes the high rates of anxiety recorded among recent college graduates. "In contrast to baby boomers' massive rise into the property-owning middle classes, millennials inherit a world in which the middle ranks are struggling almost everywhere," Kotkin notes, as they perceive a future in which they will be "propertyless serfs," living a "denatured, wired existence" devoid of normal and healthy human relationships. The article may currently be found online at https://thespectator.com/topic/how-the-boomers-robbed-the-young-of-all-hope/ (accessed on October 14, 2022). Kotkin is a conservative scholar, thinker, and demographer, most recently the author of *The Coming of Neo-Feudalism: A Warning to the Global Middle Class* (New York: Encounter Books, 2020).

5. When I last visited Paul's North Carolina home in September 2022, a copy of Wilfred M. McClay, *Land of Hope: An Invitation to the Great American*

Story (New York: Encounter Books, 2019) was prominent among his formidable stack of recently read (and in some cases re-read) books. The quotation is taken from p. xiv.

Chapter 1

1. The Dust Bowl, an ecological and environment disaster of epic proportions whose psychological wounds still run deep in American memory, has generated an enormous literature. For further inquiry, however, begin not with a history book, but with a novel, a film, and a television program. Start with the novel by John Steinbeck, *The Grapes of Wrath* (New York: The Viking Press, 1939), which immortalized its lead character, Tom Joad, as a kind of American everyman. The movie comes next: *The Grapes of Wrath* (d. John Ford, 1940), a stunning performance by Henry Fonda as Joad. And finally, the PBS documentary series, *The Dust Bowl* (d. Ken Burns, 2012), one of Burns's best (and briefest) docuseries. Among the prodigious number of available books, start with the work by *New York Times* journalist Ken Egan, *The Worst Hard Time: The Untold Story of Those Who Survived the Great American Dust Bowl* (Boston: Houghton Mifflin Harcourt, 2006).

2. Almost all quotes from Paul Hilliard reproduced in this book are taken from oral interviews conducted either by Louisiana journalist Ken Stickney (the *Acadiana Advocate*) or myself. Exact quotations taken from actual published sources, or from interviews conducted by others, will be cited and annotated in the usual fashion in these notes. Paul has told his stories many times, in front of various audiences and in various venues—print, radio, video—and as with any master storyteller, minor variations in his chronology and phrasing will (and do) occur.

3. "The Farmer Is the Man" is a classic American folk song, composed (music and lyrics) by John Carson in 1924. Its power derives from the contrast it draws between the farmer's importance to society to the treatment that society affords him in return. A representative verse runs,

> When the lawyer hangs around,
> While the butcher cuts a pound,
> The farmer is the man who feeds them all.
> And the preacher and the cook
> Go a-strolling down the brook,
> The farmer is the man who feeds them all.
> The farmer is the man,
> The farmer is the man,

Lives on credit till the fall.
With the interest rate so high,
It's a wonder he don't die;
The banker is the man who gets it all.

4. For the tumultuous career of Fr. Coughlin, see Charles J. Tull, *Father Coughlin and the New Deal* (Syracuse: Syracuse University Press, 1965), where he labels Coughlin a "frustrated, disgruntled demagogue," as well as the biography by Donald Warren, *Radio Priest: Charles Coughlin, the Father of Hate Radio* (New York: Free Press, 1996).

5. Duranty won the Pulitzer Prize for journalism reporting in 1931, still a black eye for the Prize Board. For the *New York Times* disclaimer on Duranty, see https://www.nytco.com/company/prizes-awards/new-york-times-statement-about-1932-pulitzer-prize-awarded-to-walter-duranty/ (accessed October 26, 2022). Noting that "Ukrainian-American and other organizations have repeatedly called on the Pulitzer Prize Board to cancel Duranty's prize," it pointed out that "the Pulitzer board has twice declined to withdraw the award," and that, at any rate, "The *Times* does not have the award in its possession."

6. Perhaps the best biography on FDR, the standout in a very crowded field, is H. W. Brands, *Traitor to his Class: The Privileged Life and Radical Presidency of Franklin Delano Roosevelt* (New York: Doubleday, 2008).

7. The text of Roosevelt's first inaugural address, one of the most stirring orations in American history, may be found online on the website of the Gilder-Lehrman institute, at https://www.gilderlehrman.org/sites/default/files/inline-pdfs/00675_FPS_0.pdf (accessed October 26, 2022). Audio recordings of the speech are available on numerous online sites.

8. No book better captures the mood of America in this dangerous era than Lynne Olson, *Those Angry Days: Roosevelt, Lindbergh, and America's Fight Over World War II, 1939–1941* (New York: Random House, 2014), focusing on the battle between the president and his chief rival, isolationist and American hero Charles Lindbergh. As in all her books, Olson brings a sharp eye and an even sharper pen to the matter at hand.

9. A fact attested in various sources. See the series *The Great Depression*, produced by Iowa PBS, especially the segment, "The Great Depression Hits Farms and Cities in the 1930s," located online at https://www.iowapbs.org/iowapathways/mypath/2591/great-depression-hits-farms-and-cities-1930s (accessed October 20, 2022).

10. For details on the depredations wrought by the Dust Bowl on Wisconsin agriculture, which correlate perfectly with the situation that Paul

describes, see the article by Michael J. Goc, "The Wisconsin Dust Bowl," in *Wisconsin Magazine of History* 73, no. 3 (Spring 1990): 163–201.

11. For the full report, see "Summary of the Great Plains Drought Area Committee's Preliminary Report and Conclusions Submitted during Drought Inspection Trip," on *The American Presidency Project* on the website of the University of California, Santa Barbara, available at https://www.presidency.ucsb.edu/documents/summary-the-great-plains-drought-area-committees-preliminary-report-and-conclusions (accessed October 26, 2022).

12. Quoted in Goc, "Wisconsin Dust Bowl," 169.

13. Goc, "Wisconsin Dust Bowl," 163.

14. The phrase is often attributed to Rudyard Kipling, although the precise source and provenance seem obscure at this point. See, for example, the review by Randolph Paul of Walter J. Blum and Harry Kalven Jr., "The Uneasy Case for Progressive Taxation" in *Harvard Law Review* 67, no 4 (February 1954): 725–731.

15. This would have been the older and shorter version of the Pledge, pre-1954, without reference to the Almighty. See Rachel Siegel, "The Gripping Sermon That Got 'Under God' Added to the Pledge of Allegiance on Flag Day," *Washington Post*, June 24, 2018.

16. The phrase is from a sermon by Puritan John Winthrop in 1630, as the first group of colonists departed Southampton to settle Boston. Over centuries, the phrase "city upon a hill" has become an important part of American political discourse, particularly in the development of a sense of "American exceptionalism." Most recently, President Ronald Reagan revived the phrase as a key component in his campaign for a renewed pride in America's democratic ideals and traditions. See, to give just one example out of dozens, Frank W. Fox, *City Upon a Hill: The Legacy of America's Founding* (Provo, UT: BYU Press, 2007).

17. The king's scandalous affair with Mrs. Simpson, as well as his subsequent abdication, were a media sensation at the time and interest in the event has not died down even to the present day. See, for example, Alexander Larman, *The Crown in Crisis: Countdown to the Abdication* (New York: St. Martin's Press, 2021).

18. For both the text of the "Arsenal of Democracy" speech and the audio, see the website *American Rhetoric*, at https://www.americanrhetoric.com/speeches/fdrarsenalofdemocracy.html (accessed October 19, 2022). The strongest moment of this powerful speech may well be, "The experience of the past two years has proven beyond doubt that no nation can appease the Nazis. No man can tame a tiger into a kitten by stroking it. There can be no

appeasement with ruthlessness. There can be no reasoning with an incendiary bomb. We know now that a nation can have peace with the Nazis only at the price of total surrender."

19. The volume titles alone of Winston S. Churchill, *History of the Second World War* (Boston: Houghton Mifflin, 1948–1953), 6 volumes, have become immortal: *The Gathering Storm* (1948); *Their Finest Hour* (1949); *The Grand Alliance* (1950); *The Hinge of Fate* (1950); *Closing the Ring* (1951); *Triumph and Tragedy* (1953).

20. Churchill delivered his "finest hour" speech on June 18, 1940, first to the House of Commons, and then, almost word for word, to the nation via BBC radio.

21. The full text of the "Some chicken, some neck" speech may be found on the website of America's National Churchill Museum at https://www.nationalchurchillmuseum.org/some-chicken-some-neck.html (accessed October 24, 2022).

Chapter 2

1. For the great US industrial effort in World War II, see Arthur Herman, *Freedom's Forge: How American Business Produced Victory in World War II* (New York: Random House, 2012), which locates the real source of US advantage in our corporate leadership and entrepreneurial economy.

2. FDR's speech, delivered in Boston on October 30, 1940, was one in a series designed to reassure the American public, especially "mothers and fathers," that the new draft did not mean that the United States was going to war.

3. US Army recruiting standards were low to start the war and got lower as losses mounted. "A conscript had to stand at least five feet tall and weigh 105 pounds; possess twelve or more of his natural thirty-two teeth; and be free of flat feet, venereal disease, and hernias. More than forty of every hundred men were rejected." Rick Atkinson, *An Army at Dawn; The War in North Africa, 1942–1943* (New York: Henry Holt, 2002), 9. The work is volume one in Atkinson's marvelous *Liberation Trilogy*.

4. There is a copious historical literature on Rosie the Riveter, her actual identity (still a matter for contentious debate), her "construction" as a cultural icon, and her continued meaning for society today. For a brief introduction, see Peggy Colman, *Rosie the Riveter: Women Working on the Home Front in World War II* (New York: Yearling, 1998).

5. Editions of *Ragged Dick* are too numerous to count. Like all of Alger's works, it is viewed today primarily as an artifact of its time and place, rather

than as a literary treasure, and is little read. See Horatio Alger Jr., *Ragged Dick; or, Street Life in New York with the Boot Blacks*. See the 2008 version edited by Hildegard Hoeller (New York: W. W. Norton). For Alger and his rags-to-riches *oeuvre* in general, see the biography by Gary Scharnhorst and Jack Bales, *The Lost Life of Horatio Alger, Jr.* (Bloomington: Indiana University Press, 1992).

6. James Fenimore Cooper, *The Leatherstocking Tales: A Library of America Boxed Set* (New York: Library of America, 2012). Once omnipresent in the school curriculum, Cooper's masterwork is all but unknown today to younger Americans. The five novels are *The Pioneers*, *The Last of the Mohicans*, *The Prairie*, *The Pathfinder*, and *The Deerslayer*.

7. Most likely, Paul's class was reading Shakespeare, *Julius Caesar*. In Act II, scene 1, line 907, Portia speaks to Brutus:

Dwell I but in the suburbs

Of your good pleasure? If it be no more,

Portia is Brutus' harlot, not his wife.

8. "What a Difference a Day Makes," was first written in Spanish by Mexican singer Maria Grever (1934). It entered the "great American songbook" in its English version, penned by Stanley Adams, and has been sung or recorded by everyone from Bing Crosby to Ben E. King. The best-known version is Dinah Washington's Grammy Award-winning recording from 1959.

9. Mastery of the immense number of books on Pearl Harbor would be a lifelong task. The preeminent work, as it has been for decades, is still Gordon W. Prange, *At Dawn We Slept: The Untold Story of Pearl Harbor* (New York: Penguin, 1981). Prange was on the civilian staff of General Douglas MacArthur at General Headquarters, Far East Command, Tokyo. The work was four full volumes in its original manuscript, amounting to three thousand pages, but Prange died before he could finish it. The book eventually appeared as a single volume, edited down considerably by Donald M. Goldstein and Katherine V. Dillon.

10. Despite its size and its significance to the shape of our present-day world, the Japanese War in China (often, the "Second Sino-Japanese War") has been virtually unknown in the West since the end of World War II. While the situation is beginning to change, there is much work still to be done. A good starting point for the Chinese perspective is Rana Mitter, *Forgotten Ally: China's World War II, 1937–1945* (Boston: Houghton Mifflin Harcourt, 2013). For the Japanese view, see Edward J. Drea, *Japan's Imperial Army: Its Rise and Fall, 1853–1945* (Lawrence: University Press of Kansas, 2009). For an overall view, see Richard B. Frank, *Tower of Skulls: A History of the*

Asia-Pacific War: July 1937–May 1942 (New York: W. W. Norton, 2020), the first volume of an intended trilogy.

11. For the American Volunteer Group (better known as the Flying Tigers), the best place to start is Jack Samson's account of their commanding officer, *Flying Tiger: The True Story of General Claire Chennault and the U.S. 14th Air Force in China* (Lanham, MD: Rowman & Littlefield, 2011). Chennault's own memoirs are also fascinating: Claire Lee Chennault, *Way of a Fighter: The Memoirs of Claire Lee Chennault* (New York: G.P. Putnam, 1949).

12. The best introduction to this sprawling war remains the collection of articles found in Daniel Marston, ed., *The Pacific War Companion: From Pearl Harbor to Hiroshima* (Midland House: Osprey, 2005), especially the contributions by Ken Kotani ("Pearl Harbor: Japanese Planning and Command Structure") and Raymond Callahan ("Coping with Disaster: Allied Strategy and Command in the Pacific, 1941–1942").

13. For the battle of Peleliu, see, above all, the eloquent and gritty memoir by E. B. Sledge, *With the Old Breed at Peleliu and Okinawa* (New York: Presidio, 2010), a book that every student of the war—perhaps every American—should read.

14. For a comprehensive history of the corps from its origins to our own day, written with verve by one of the deans of the US historical profession (and a Marine himself), see Allan R. Millett, *Semper Fidelis: The History of the United States Marine Corps, the Revised and Expanded Edition* (New York: Free Press, 1991).

15. The stirring events on Wake early in the war are ably discussed in Greg Urwin, *Facing Fearful Odds: The Siege of Wake Island* (Lincoln: University of Nebraska Press, 1997). Since Urwin bases his narrative on interviews with some seventy surviving American and Japanese participants, it's unlikely to be bettered at any point in the future.

16. *Wake Island* (d. John Farrow, 1942). While the battle was a Japanese victory, it had been dearly bought, and the film ends with a voice-over, "This is not the end."

17. For the long and bloody fight for Guadalcanal, see Richard B. Frank, *Guadalcanal: The Definitive Account of the Landmark Battle* (New York: Penguin, 2002). The memoir by Richard Tregaskis, *Guadalcanal Diary* (New York: Random House, 1943), is also essential. Tregaskis was what we would call today an "embedded journalist," and his book is a marvelous evocation of how the Marines fought, talked, and ate on "the Canal." *Guadalcanal Diary*, too, was turned into a film (d. Lewis Seiler, 1943), with Preston Foster, Lloyd Nolan, and William Bendix. Equally essential is John Hersey, *Into the Valley:*

Marines at Guadalcanal (Lincoln, NE: Bison Books, 2002), which may be the first source to use the phrase "apple pie" to describe what US servicemen were fighting for in World War II. "Make mine apple with a few raisins in it and lots of cinnamon," one Marine says. "You know, Southern style" (43).

18. For the career and tragic end of La Follette Jr., see the biography by Patrick J. Maney, *Young Bob: A Biography of Robert M. La Follette, Jr.* (Madison: Wisconsin Historical Society Press, 2003). In February 1953, La Follette shot himself, perhaps out of fear that he was about to be the next target of a witch hunt by Senator Joseph McCarthy, who had accused him of employing suspected communists on his staff.

19. Victor Davis Hanson, *The Second World Wars: How the First Global Conflict Was Fought and Won* (New York: Basic Books, 2017). Historians increasingly find themselves wrestling with a basic problem: World War II is too large to be dealt with in one volume (hence, Hanson's use of the plural in his title). Many historians have turned to writing trilogies. Others simply choose a specific lens and use it to refract the war as a whole, even if some distortion might creep in. See Richard Overy, *Blood and Ruins: The Last Imperial War, 1931–1945* (New York: Viking, 2022), who emphasizes the downfall of the Western colonial empires in Asia and Africa as the war's most important outcome, or Sean McMeekin, *Stalin's War: A New History of World War II* (New York: Basic Books, 2021), who focuses on the role of the Soviet generalissimo in determining the shape of the conflict.

20. As one Fred Harvey advertisement put it, "K.P.? Not for Private Pringle! Private Pringle is our guest. For him and all the other men and women in uniform, we'll peel the potatoes and make the coffee and set the table. We'll serve the finest meals our chefs can prepare . . . and then we'll wash the dishes and tidy up the kitchen." For more on the wartime history of this iconic firm, see the company website, https://fredharvey.info/ (accessed October 23, 2022).

21. Napoleon famously referred to the soldiers of his Old Guard, some of the finest infantry in Europe, as his *grognards*, or "grumblers." See also Stanley Peebles, *Welcome to the Suck: Narrating the American Soldier's Experience in Iraq* (Ithaca, NY: Cornell University Press, 2011) discusses the myriad ways that US service personnel today use the vulgar word "suck" to describe military life—a more generalized and profane version of Napoleon's old *grognards*.

22. From the memoirs of Marine recruit Weston D. Eastman, *Strictly Scuttlebutt: From Ivy Halls to Duty Calls* (CreateSpace Independent Publishing Platform, 2017). Eastman also describes the Marine haircut in unforgettable prose: "Prior to entering he had long Victor Mature style wavy hair that he

always kept well groomed. The next time we saw him, he looked like a cue ball going into the side pocket" (31).

23. The great Allied victory at Tunis, which also represented a coming-out party for the newly formed US Army, is the centerpiece of Atkinson, *An Army at Dawn*. For the German perspective on fighting the Americans in 1943, see Robert M. Citino, *The Wehrmacht Retreats: Fighting a Lost War, 1943* (Lawrence: University Press of Kansas, 2012).

24. The best book on Cartwheel—highly informative and readable—is still the official history of the campaign by John Miller Jr., *Cartwheel: The Reduction of Rabaul* (Washington, DC: Office of the Chief of Military History, 1959), part of the series *The United States Army in World War II*, better known, for their appearance, as the "Green Books." See also the short piece by Robert M. Citino, see "Mac Does a Cartwheel," found online at https://www.historynet.com/fire-effect-mac-cartwheel/ (accessed November 30, 2022).

25. A good starting point to investigate the bloody battle for Tarawa is, once again, the entry into the Green Books series, this time Philip A. Crowl and Edmund G. Love, *Seizure of the Gilberts and Marshalls* (Washington, DC: Office of the Chief of Military History, 1955). For a discussion of the grisly visual record of the battle's aftermath, see Robert M. Citino, "Photo Finish: The Battle of Tarawa," found online at https://www.nationalww2museum. org/war/articles/photo-finish-battle-tarawa (accessed December 6, 2022).

Chapter 3

1. Everyone agrees that logistics is a paramount factor in modern war (as in the phrase, "Amateurs discuss maneuver, but professionals discuss logistics"), but despite the respect accorded to the subject, very few people go on to write books about it. By its very definition, logistical analysis is technical and devoid of drama. No one builds heroic statues of clerks, and no one is ever going to make a film entitled *Supplying Private Ryan*. For that very reason, we should celebrate the rare works that do deal with wartime logistics in any detail. For the topic of the Pacific War, see the highly informative article by Patrick H. Donovan, "Oil Logistics in the Pacific War," *Air Force Journal of Logistics* 28, no. 1 (2001), 29–44. Steve R. Waddell, a faculty member at the US Military Academy at West Point, has written two books that are required reading: *United States Army Logistics: The Normandy Campaign* (Westport, CT: Greenwood Press, 1994), and *United States Army Logistics: From the American Revolution to 9/11* (Westport, CT: Greenwood, 2009). For the daunting challenges in another logistics-heavy theater, North Africa, Sicily, and Italy, see the recent

work by David D. Dworak, *War of Supply: World War II Allied Logistics in the Mediterranean* (Lexington: University Press of Kentucky, 2022).

2. Indeed, Allied leaders themselves believed that Germany was a far more serious enemy than Japan. At the Arcadia Conference, Roosevelt and Churchill even codified the allocation of resources: 75 percent to 25 percent in favor of the European theater (i.e., the war against Germany). General George Marshall, Chief of Staff of the US Army, was on record repeatedly arguing, that "the defeat of Germany means defeat of Japan, probably without firing a shot or losing a life." Quoted in Rick Atkinson, *An Army at Dawn: The War in North Africa, 1942–1943* (New York: Henry Holt, 2002), 17.

3. In the great mass of books on D-Day, two works by Stephen E. Ambrose are a good place to start: *D-Day, June 6, 1944: The Climactic Battle of World War II* (New York: Simon & Schuster, 1994), and *Citizen Soldiers: The U.S. Army from the Normandy Beaches to the Bulge to the Surrender of Germany, June 7, 1944–May 7, 1945* (New York: Simon & Schuster, 1997). Carlo D'Este is an unfailing guide the intricacies of the landing and the difficult and bloody campaign that followed. See his *Decision in Normandy* (New York: Harper Perennial, 1994). Finally, never forget the entry in the "Green Books" series, Gordon A. Harrison, *Cross-Channel Attack* (Washington, DC: Center of Military History, 1993), which remains highly useful on the details.

4. *Saving Private Ryan* (d. Steven Spielberg, 1998).

5. The logistical build-up, size, and scope of Operation Forager are ably recounted in Philip A. Crowl, *Campaign in the Marianas* (Washington, DC: Center of Military History, 1993), yet another addition to the redoubtable "Green Books" series.

6. For a perceptive and even-handed comparison between Operations Overlord and Forager, see Vincent P. O'Hara, "A Tale of Two Invasions," *Naval History Magazine* 33, no. 3 (June 2019).

7. For the gritty fighting on Saipan and the almost apocalyptic end of the battle, as frightened Japanese civilians committed suicide to avoid capture by US troops, see James H. Hallas, *Saipan: The Battle That Doomed Japan in World War II* (Mechanicsburg, PA: Stackpole, 2019).

8. For an easily accessible discussion of the entire strategic bombing campaign, including problems in the Pacific, see Malcolm Gladwell, *The Bomber Mafia: A Dream, a Temptation, and the Longest Night of the Second World War* (Boston: Little, Brown, 2021), a book that Gladwell based on his original podcast.

9. Keith Wheeler, *The Pacific Is My Beat* (New York: E. P. Dutton, 1943). Wheeler was badly wounded—shot through the neck—on Iwo Jima.

10. Wheeler's angry comments, which spoke for many of the US servicemen stationed in the Pacific, appeared in *Time* magazine under the heading, "I Accuse" (Monday, August 7, 1944).

11. The Green Books, as so often, are still the place to start in any inquiry into the Philippines campaign, the largest in the long history of the US Army. Appropriately, three full volumes concern themselves with this big fight. In order, they are Robert Ross Smith, *The Approach to the Philippines* (Washington, DC: Center of Military History, 1996); M. Hamlin Cannon, *Leyte: The Return to the Philippines* (Washington, DC: Center of Military History, 1993); and Robert Ross Smith, *Triumph in the Philippines* (Washington, DC: Center of Military History, 1993).

12. For a well-researched biography of General Krueger, a relative unknown even to many aficionados of the war, see Kevin C. Holzimmer, *General Walter Krueger: Unsung Hero of the Pacific War* (Lawrence: University Press of Kansas, 2007).

13. Colonel John Howard McEniry Jr., *A Marine Dive-Bomber Pilot at Guadalcanal* (Tuscaloosa: The University of Alabama Press, 1987), 18–19.

14. McEniry, *Marine Dive-Bomber*, 18.

15. McEniry, *Marine Dive-Bomber*, 22.

16. For Pomasl's story, See John C. Chapin, ". . . And a Few Marines: Marines in the Liberation of the Philippines," *Marines in World War II Commemorative Series* (Washington, DC: Marine Corps Historical Center, 1995), 10–11.

17. For the operational details of the raid on Santo Tomas, see Robert Sherrod, *History of Marine Corps Aviation in World War II* (San Rafael, CA: Presidio, 1952), 300–303, as well as Chapin, ". . . And a Few Marines," 12–15.

18. Jeff Dacus, "The Diving Devil Dogs of Luzon," *Leatherneck*, March 2022, 24–31.

19. Sherrod, *Marine Corps Aviation*, 295.

20. Dacus, "Diving Devil Dogs of Luzon," 29. For a good overview of the raid from the perspective of the American captives, see Joseph C. Huber Jr., *Rescue Raids of Luzon!* (Bloomington, IN: Author House, 2021). The author was at the time a ten-year-old boy, whose father worked on Goodyear's Philippine rubber plantation.

21. Quoted in Chapin, ". . . And a Few Marines," 14, and in Sherrod, *Marine Corps Aviation*, with minor variations in the wording, 303.

22. For these horrific days in Manila, which resulted in the virtual destruction of the city, see James M. Scott, *Rampage: MacArthur, Yamashita,*

and the Battle of Manila (New York: Norton, 2018). Scott is one of the finest scholars and authors working today, and his meticulous recreation of what happened in Manila is one of the most stomach-turning accounts you will ever read. While the crimes are undisputed, the subsequent war crimes trials are not, and many analysts accuse MacArthur of targeting the Japanese commander in the Philippines, General Tomoyuki Yamashita, solely because he had defeated MacArthur in the original campaign in the Philippines in 1941–42. Indeed, at least one of the justices, Radhabinod Pal of India, voted for the acquittal of all the Japanese defendants on all counts, solely on the basis that the Western powers had no right to try the Japanese for crimes against the peoples of Asia when they had been the brutal imperial masters of the region for centuries. For a highly critical analysis of the legal proceedings that condemned Yamashita, which also accuses the US prosecution of disregarding the Army's own rules, and delivering the verdict MacArthur wanted, see Allen A. Ryan, *Yamashita's Ghost: War Crimes, MacArthur's Justice, and Command Accountability* (Lawrence: University Press of Kansas, 2014). The "Tokyo Trials," which have a very different historical reputation today than the Nuremberg proceedings, are also the subject of Richard H. Minear, *Victor's Justice: The Tokyo War Crimes Trial* (Princeton, NJ: Princeton University Press, 1971) and B. V. A. Röling and Antonio Cassese, *The Tokyo Trial and Beyond* (Cambridge: Polity Press, 1994).

23. Quoted in Chapin, ". . . And a Few Marines," 25.

24. There are so many editions of *Leaves of Grass* that even choosing which version to read can be difficult. Whitman himself added a great deal of material throughout his lifetime, which can add to the confusion. A good place to start is Walt Whitman, *Leaves of Grass: The First (1855) Edition* (New York: Penguin, 1961).

Chapter 4

1. The Dauntless was a ten-year-old design by 1945 and was widely regarded as "obsolete" or "obsolescent." To provide just one example, see one of the very few references to Marine aviation in the Philippines in the pertinent Green Book, Robert Ross Smith, *Triumph in the Philippines* (Washington, DC: Center of Military History, 1993), 133. "Fifth Air Force fighters and A-20's, together with Marine Air Groups 24 and 32, equipped with the obsolescent Douglas Dauntless dive-bomber, moved up to Mangaldan by the end of the month, all passing to the control of the 308th Bombardment Wing."

2. The internet is filled with data, information, and photographs of World War II aircraft, and comparisons between the Dauntless and the Helldiver abound. In fact, for all the advantages of the newer plane, it had a busload

of problems: instability, range, high approach speeds which made landing on a carrier a real adventure, and more. Crews took to calling it "the Beast," or "Son of a Bitch 2nd Class" (riffing off its SB2C designation). See Bill Walton, "The Helldiver: Haste Made a Waste of This World War II Dive Bomber," at https://avgeekery.com/the-helldiver-haste-made-a-waste-of-this-world-war-ii-dive-bomber/ (accessed October 22, 2022).

3. John C. Chapin, ". . . And a Few Marines: Marines in the Liberation of the Philippines," *Marines in World War II Commemorative Series* (Washington, DC: Marine Corps Historical Center, 1995), 27.

4. Robert Sherrod, *History of Marine Corps Aviation in World War II* (San Rafael, CA: Presidio, 1952), 323, as well as Chapin, ". . . And a Few Marines," 27.

5. The text of President Harry Truman's speech to the American people announcing the destruction of Hiroshima may be found on website of the Miller Center at the University of Virginia, at https://millercenter.org/the-presidency/presidential-speeches/august-6-1945-statement-president-announcing-use-bomb#:~:text=We%20are%20now%20prepared%20to, Japan's%20power%20to%20make%20war (accessed October 21, 2022). In it, the president declared,

> It is an atomic bomb. It is a harnessing of the basic power of the universe. The force from which the sun draws its power has been loosed against those who brought war to the Far East. . . . If they [the Japanese] do not now accept our terms they may expect a rain of ruin from the air, the like of which has never been seen on this earth. Behind this air attack will follow sea and land forces in such numbers and power as they have not yet seen and with the fighting skill of which they are already well aware.

6. The text of Hirohito's radio address (sometimes called the "Jewel Voice Broadcast"), including the emperor's amazing understatement that, "the war situation has developed not necessarily to Japan's advantage," may be found online on the website of the Atomic Heritage Foundation, at https://www.atomicheritage.org/key-documents/jewel-voice-broadcast (accessed October 24, 2022).

7. The details for Operations Olympic and Coronet are ably reconstructed in Richard B. Frank, *Downfall: The End of the Imperial Japanese Empire* (New York: Penguin, 2001). In the background was the sure knowledge on the part of all the planners that the American public was going to demand at least "a partial demobilization" after the fall of Germany (123).

8. See the article by Richard B. Frank on the website of the National WWII Museum, "There Are No Civilians in Japan," at https://www.national-ww2museum.org/war/articles/there-are-no-civilians-japan (accessed October 29, 2022).

9. For the "glorious death" (or sometimes, "the glorious death of 100 million"), see Samuel J. Cox, "H-057-1: Operations Downfall and Ketsugo— November 1945," on the website of the Naval History and Heritage Command, at https://www.history.navy.mil/about-us/leadership/director/directors-corner/h-grams/h-gram-057/h-057-1.html (accessed on October 28, 2022).

10. The father of the "revisionist" view of the bomb is Gar Alperovitz, *Atomic Diplomacy: Hiroshima and Potsdam* (New York: Simon and Schuster, 1965). Alperovitz argued that there was no need to drop the bomb at all, since Japan was clearly beaten by 1945, and that the only reason the bomb was dropped was to intimidate the Soviets in the postwar era. In Alperovitz's view, then, the bomb wasn't the final, awful blast of World War II, but was instead the opening salvo of the Cold War.

11. This is the argument presented by Richard B. Frank in *Downfall*. The bomb was horrible, but averted an even worse human catastrophe:

> The timing of the assault on Japan's railways came at precisely the moment when it could do by far the most damage. Postwar information has made it clear that Japan reached November 1, 1945 with only enough rich in government hands for four days of consumption (133,000 tons). Japan depended on the distribution of the fall crop to food-deficient areas to see her on to 1946 without a disaster. Had the war continued for even only a few more weeks, the destruction of Japan's rail network would have quickly caused a food-supply crisis in late 1945.

12. Joe McCarthy is one of the most famous (or infamous) figures of twentieth-century American history, and books and films on his career abound. For the consensus view, evident in the title, see Larry Tye, *Demagogue: The Life and Long Shadow of Senator Joe McCarthy* (Boston: Mariner Books, 2020). For a more conservative view and at least a partial defense, look to Arthur Herman, *Joseph McCarthy: Reexamining the Life and Legacy of America's Most Hated Senator* (New York: Free Press, 1999). For films, see *Citizen Cohn* (d. Frank Pierson, 1992), starring James Woods as McCarthy's bulldog lawyer, Roy Cohn, as well as the made-for-television film *Tail Gunner Joe* (d. Jud Taylor, 1977).

13. "Baby boom" and "baby boomer" (or simply "boomer") are ubiquitous terms in American political discourse, whether the term is used with approval and satisfaction (usually from the Left) or opprobrium (mainly from the Right), and even presenting a partial list of books would try the patience of any reader. For the origins of the term, see Landon Y. Jones, "How 'Baby Boomers' Took Over the World," *Washington Post*, November 6, 2015. For a very funny deconstruction of the entire phenomenon from a conservative perspective, see P. J. O'Rourke, *The Baby Boom: How It Got That Way and It Wasn't My Fault and I'll Never Do It Again* (New York: Grove Atlantic, 2014).

14. For Hollywood's role in the war—demonizing the enemy, lionizing our servicemen, and rallying home front workers to do their utmost—see the sumptuously illustrated book by Christian Blauvelt, *Hollywood Victory: The Movies, Stars, and Stories of World War II* (New York: Running Press, 2021).

15. For "Golden Gate in '48," see the stunning documentary *Apocalypse '45* (d. Eric Nelson, 2020). Nelson bases the work on an immense amount of never-before-seen footage, a rare thing indeed in World War II films.

16. The GI Bill is one of the most fundamental laws in the history of the United States in terms of its impact on society, and it remains on the books today, adjusted for changing times and different circumstances. Among the hundreds of books on the legislation, see Milton Greenberg, *The G.I. Bill: The Law That Changed America* (West Palm Beach, FL: Lickle, 1997); Suzanne Mettler, *Soldiers to Citizens: The G.I. Bill and the Making of the Greatest Generation* (Oxford: Oxford University Press, 2007); Glenn Altschuler, *The G.I. Bill: The New Deal for Veterans* (Oxford: Oxford University Press, 2009); and Mark D. Van Ells, *To Hear Only Thunder Again: America's World War II Veterans Come Home* (Lanham, MD: Lexington Books, 2001).

17. The great poet Goethe was the touchstone for many German intellectuals in the post-1945 era, a way of reminding the world that Hitler and the Third Reich did not define the entirety of German history. In his great lament over the "German catastrophe," historian Friedrich Meinecke went so far as to suggest the formation of "Goethe communities" in Germany, where "likeminded friends of culture" would gather on Sunday afternoons throughout the land to celebrate "the most noble German music and poetry." See Meinecke, *Die deutsche Katastrophe: Betrachtungen und Erinnerungen* (Wiesbaden: Eberhard Brockhaus, 1949). Paul's professor, Dr. Friedländer, must certainly have been familiar with Meinecke's book.

18. For this classic evocation of the "Whig theory of history," emphasizing progress over time, see Thomas Babington Macaulay, *The History of England from the Accession of James II: Five Volume Complete Set* (Philadelphia:

Porter and Coates, 1886). While the volumes deal with a fairly narrow time period, 1685 to 1702, they include the Glorious Revolution (1688), seen by Macaulay as a great leap forward for England, out of the realm of autocracy and superstition into the light of rational thought and liberty.

19. See Michele McFee, *A History of Harpur College* (Binghamton, NY: Harpur College of Arts and Sciences, 2000), 26–27.

20. The best one-volume history of Texas is Randolph B. Campbell, *Gone to Texas: A History of the Lone Star State* (Oxford: Oxford University Press, 2017).

21. See Fred Glueckstein, "Churchill as Bricklayer," on the website of the International Churchill Society, at https://winstonchurchill.org/publications/finest-hour/finest-hour-157/churchill-as-bricklayer/ (accessed October 28, 2022), as well as Adam Edwards, "The Other Lives of Winston Churchill," *Express* (UK), March 14, 2011.

22. Charles Tilford McCormick, *Handbook on the Law of Damages* (Eagan, MN: West Publishing Company, 1935).

Chapter 5

1. Socal was one of the thirty-four separate companies created in 1911 when the Supreme Court split up Standard Oil, accusing its owner, J. D. Rockefeller, of running a monopoly. Legend has it that Rockefeller was on the golf course when the news came though, and that he turned to his playing partner, Father J. P. Lennon, and asked, "Have you some money?" When Father Lennon shook his head and asked why, Rockefeller gave him some wise advice: "Buy Standard Oil." The shares of the thirty-four successor companies soon doubled, and then tripled in value compared to the old mother company. Rainer Zitelman, *Forbes*, December 9, 2019. The best biography on Rockefeller remains Ron Chernow, *Titan: The Life of John D. Rockefeller* (New York: Random House, 1998).

2. See "What is a Landman?" on the American Association of Professional Landmen (AAPL) website, at https://www.landman.org/about/who-we-are/what-is-a-landman (accessed on October 29, 2022).

3. See J. W. Beavers III, "What Does a Landman Do?" on the AAPL website, at https://www.landman.org/news-and-blog/what-does-a-landman-do (accessed on October 28, 2022). He also notes that Thomas Jefferson, James Madison, James Monroe, and Robert Livingston were extremely successful landmen. In 1803, "they negotiated the purchase of approximately 530 million (approximately 3 cents per acre) while Jefferson was president of the United States. This famous transaction is known as the Louisiana Purchase. As president, Jefferson wore many hats. I don't believe that being president of the United States is a prerequisite for being a landman, but it sure helped Thomas Jefferson."

4. Ponchatoula, Louisiana, still considers itself the "Strawberry Capital of the World," and hosts an annual Strawberry Festival each spring. See https://www.lastrawberryfestival.com/ (accessed October 20, 2022).

5. The "Greater New Orleans Bridge" opened in 1958 and was the longest cantilever highway bridge in the world at the time. A companion span was completed in 1988. In 1989, after a public contest to name the pair, a fourth-grade class at St. Clement of Rome School in Metairie came up with the winning name: "Crescent City Connection." See the website of the bridge engineering firm Modjeski and Masters, at https://www.modjeski.com/about/history-timeline/1950-1959/crescent-city-connection/ (accessed October 27, 2022).

6. For the Louisiana Maneuvers, including the simulated "battle of Shreveport," see Robert M. Citino, "A Fearsome Attack on Shreveport, 76 years ago: The *Shreveport Times* Revisits its Own Coverage of the Louisiana Maneuvers," at https://www.nationalww2museum.org/about-us/notes-museum/fearsome-attack-shreveport-76-years-ago (accessed October 23, 2022).

7. Camp Claiborne, originally Camp Evangeline, was later renamed for William C. C. Claiborne, the first governor of the state of Louisiana. For details and history, see the Camp's Historical Research Center website, at http://www.campclaiborne.com/about/camp-history.php/ (accessed October 24, 2022).

8. H. L. Hunt, the founder and owner of Hunt Oil Company, has been the subject of several biographies. The most readable is Harry Hurt III, *Texas Rich: The Hunt Dynasty, From the Early Oil Days Through the Silver Crash* (New York: W. W. Norton, 1981). See also the profile by Tom Buckley, "Just Plain H. L. Hunt," *Esquire*, January 1967, with its tagline, "The richest American would like to be no different from you and me. He wears shiny blue suits, cuts his own hair and carries his lunch in a brown paper bag."

9. For Hunt senior's right-wing activities, see David R. Jones, "Magnate with a Mission, *New York Times*, August 17, 1964, which appeared with the tag line, "One of Richest Men in Nation, Oilman Aids Right Wing." In the article, Hunt posed himself as a centrist: "Fascism is socialism and as far left of center as communism, and both constitute a form of tyranny. I have always opposed tyranny." Jones noted, however, that Hunt's office was "overflowing with right-wing literature."

10. Bunker Hunt, and his younger brother W. Herbert Hunt, began buying up large amounts of silver in the late 1970s, convinced that the current oil crisis was about to usher in a global economic collapse. Bunker may well have been influenced by his evangelical Christian faith to see an apocalypse in the offing. Silver prices boomed, then crashed, and Hunt lost virtually all his

fortune. He died in 2014. See the *New York Times* obituary by Matt Schudel, "Nelson Bunker Hunt, Texas Oil Baron Who Lost Much of his Fortune, Dies at 88," October 22, 2014.

11. For America's hopeless love affair with the car in the 1950s, see the article by Karal Ann Marling, "America's Love Affair with the Automobile in the Television Age," *Design Quarterly* no. 146 (1989): 5–20. For a more skeptical view, see Emily Badger, "The Myth of the American Love Affair with Cars," *Washington Post*, January 27, 2015.

12. Sidney Latham to Paul Hilliard (March 23, 1955), in Hilliard's possession (viewed September 2022).

13. For the life of Wallace Pratt, see his obituary on the Geological Society of America website by Amos Salvador, "Memorial to Wallace Everette Pratt, 1885–1981," found at https://www.geosociety.org/documents/gsa/memorials/v14/Pratt-WE.pdf (accessed on October 24, 2022). As a geologist in the Philippines in 1911, Pratt witnessed the eruption of the Taal volcano near Manila. "Pratt, on his own initiative, rushed to the volcano before any other scientific observer and was the first to report the devastation and the frightful loss of life caused by the eruption." Pratt claimed, "The eruption made me. It took a cataclysm to do it."

14. For the troubled history of this film production, see Wendell Jamieson, "Was the Making of 'Tora! Tora! Tora!' Cursed?" *MHQ* (December 28, 2021), located online at https://www.historynet.com/the-making-of-tora-tora-tora/ (accessed October 24, 2022).

15. For the difference between 2D and 3D (very much in favor of the latter), see the article, "What is the Difference Between 2D and 3D Seismic" on the website of the Lundin Group, at https://thelundingroup.com/lundin-group-of-companies/reports-from-the-field/what-is-the-difference-between-2d-and-3d-seismic/ (accessed on October 24, 2022), as well as "Upstream Oil and Gas Exploration Types of Seismic" on the website EKT Interactive, an oil company in Houston, found online at https://ektinteractive.com/exploration/oil-gas-exploration-types-seismic/ (accessed on February 28, 2023).

16. For the history of the LAGCOE, with wonderfully evocative period photographs, see the organization's website at https://lagcoe.com/Organization/history (accessed on October 23, 2022).

17. Heymann's Oil Center deserves a deeper study than it has had up to now. See the very fine master's thesis by Andrew Michael Garber, "The Miracle Mile: The Heymann Oil Center and the Oil Economy of Lafayette, Louisiana 1953–1998 (Appalachian State University, 1998).

18. The iconic site was eventually destroyed by fire. See Ian Auzenne, "Iconic Opelousas Venue Destroyed by Fire," on https://kpel965.com/iconic-opelousas-venue-destroyed-by-fire/ (accessed on October 23, 2022).

19. For the full text of the Supreme Court decision, see the page on the Library of Congress website, "Phillips Petroleum Co. v. Wisconsin, 347 U.S. 672 (1954)," at https://www.loc.gov/item/usrep347672/ (accessed on October 12, 2022).

20. Numerous websites offer lucid histories of the discovery and eventual use of natural gas. See, to give just one example, "A Short History of Natural Gas," available online at https://www.gassouth.com/blog/short-history-natural-gas (accessed on October 24, 2022). See also the Library of Congress website, "History of the Industry," at https://guides.loc.gov/oil-and-gas-industry/history (accessed on October 29, 2022).

21. The passage is from *Cymbeline,* Act III, Scene 6, lines 22–23.

Chapter 6

1. David Glasner is one of the sharpest free market advocates discussing the intersection of energy production and government regulation, and the negative consequences of the latter. See his collection of articles, David Glasner, *Politics, Prices, and Petroleum: The Political Economy of Energy* (San Francisco: Pacific Institute for Public Policy Research, 1985), especially "Natural Gas: Will We Learn from our Mistakes or Repeat Them?," 215–48, wherein he concludes that, "Controls on natural gas prices were a misguided enterprise from the beginning," as well as his feisty argument in "Windfall Profits and What to Do About Them" (193–214).

2. For one of out of thousands of possible references to the "do something" phenomenon, see Charles W. Cooke, "John Cornyn and the Limits of 'Do Something' Politics," *National Review* (June 3, 2022). See also Glasner, "Price Controls on Gasoline and Other Refined Products before the Embargo," in *Politics, Prices, and Petroleum,* 89–110.

3. For the backlog of statistics and the deleterious effects of the *Phillips* decision in general, see David Raley, "The *Philips* [sic] *vs. Wisconsin* Decision and the Decline of Regulatory Effectiveness," on the *Business and Economic History On-Line* website (volume 15, 2017), 6–7, located at https://thebhc.org/philips-vs-wisconsin-decision-and-decline-regulatory-effectiveness (accessed October 29, 2022). The backlog, he notes, left "more than a thousand cases undecided and in limbo. By the following year, the FPC backlog was more than 3,300 rate cases, with more cases coming in."

4. Through must of his long career, Justice Douglas was a lightning rod for criticism from the Right. Two good biographies serve as excellent entry points for the interested reader: Bruce Allen Murphy, *Wild Bill: The Legend and Life of William O. Douglas* (New York: Random House, 2003), and M. Margaret McKeown, *Citizen Justice: The Environmental Legacy of William O. Douglas—Public Advocate and Conservation Champion* (Washington, DC: Potomac, 2022).

5. Quoted in Raley, "*Philips* [sic] *vs. Wisconsin* Decision," 4–5: "In his dissent against the majority in *Phillips*, Justice William O. Douglas argued that there was nothing in the legislative history or the wording of the Natural Gas Act to demonstrate that Congress had any intention of regulating well-head pricing."

6. For the global view of oil, its history, its evolution, and its importance on today's world stage, see the master work by Daniel Yergin, *The Prize: The Epic Quest for Oil, Money & Power* (New York: Free Press, 1991), winner of the Pulitzer Prize for General Nonfiction in 1992. The book was the basis for an eight-hour documentary television series (PBS/BBC, 1992), narrated by Donald Sutherland.

7. The platform was built by Brown & Root out of Houston. For founder Herman Brown, see "Herman Brown Founder of Brown and Root and Father of the Kermac 16," found online at http://www.energyglobalnews.com/herman-brown-founder-of-brown-and-root-and-father-of-the-kermac-16/ (accessed October 28, 2022). Patricia Keefe, "The History of Offshore Energy," *Marine Technology News*, April 30, 2014, offers the broader view.

8. The term *Sette Sorelle* ("seven sisters") was coined by the Italian oil baron Enrico Mattei, founder of the energy conglomerate known as ENI (*Ente Nazionale Idrocarburi*). The sense of the coinage is pejorative, as in seven intimate (and Anglo-Saxon) sisters who connive with one another tirelessly to keep interlopers out of the family business. See Yergin, *The Price*, 485. "His real complaint against this exclusive club of major companies was not its existence, but rather that he was not in it," almost certainly a fair assessment of Mattei's view. See also Anthony Sampson, *The Seven Sisters: The Great Oil Companies and the World They Made* (London: Hodder and Stoughton, 1975), a book written under the shadow of 1973's oil crisis.

9. For the origins and characteristics of "Mr. Charlie," replete with photographs, see B. A. Wells and K. L. Wells, "Mr. Charlie, First Mobile Offshore Drilling Rig," on the website of the American Oil & Gas Historical Society, found at https://aoghs.org/offshore-history/mr-charlie-first-mobile-offshore-drilling-rig/ (accessed October 28, 2022).

10. The other country accused of aiding Israel and thus specified in the embargo proclamation was the Netherlands. See Albert L. Danielsen, *The Evolution of OPEC* (New York: Harcourt Brace Jovanovich, 1982), 269. For the formation and history of OPEC, see "Brief History," on the organization's own website, found at https://www.opec.org/opec_web/en/about_us/24.htm (accessed October 23, 2022). "OPEC's objective," it reads, "is to co-ordinate and unify petroleum policies among Member Countries, in order to secure fair and stable prices for petroleum producers; an efficient, economic and regular supply of petroleum to consuming nations; and a fair return on capital to those investing in the industry." A still useful account, despite its age, is Dankwart A. Rustow, *Oil and Turmoil: America Faces OPEC and the Middle East* (New York: Norton, 1982). Rustow's words seem as appropriate today as when he wrote them: "What we must guard against most in our Middle East diplomacy as in our energy policy, are lingering delusions of omnipotent grandeur and sudden fits of dejection and despair" (268). "Live and let live," Rustow argued, ought to be our approach to OPEC. Four years later, a very different take appeared, one that was already speaking of serious internal tensions within the cartel and suggesting ways to deal with the "potential collapse of OPEC." See Mohammed E. Ahrari, *OPEC: The Failing Giant* (Lexington: University Press of Kentucky, 1986), 199. For an overview, see Yergin, *The Prize*, 501–522.

11. The October 1973 War (the "Yom Kippur War" to the Israelis and the "Ramadan War" to the Arab states) was one of the most important events of the twentieth century, realigning power, both within the Middle East and globally, bringing oil to the forefront of world politics and strategy, and heralding a technological revolution on the battlefield. For the very difficult fighting, see the pertinent chapter in Robert M. Citino, *Blitzkrieg to Desert Storm: The Evolution of Operational Warfare* (Lawrence: University Press of Kansas, 2002), 153–186.

12. Quoted in Yergin, *The Prize*, 586.

13. Golda Meir (born Goldie Mabovitch) was born in Kiev, Ukraine, and emigrated with her family to Milwaukee in 1906 (her married name was Goldie Meyerson). An active Zionist, she moved to Palestine in 1921 and lived on a *kibbutz*, eventually rising through the ranks of the Labor Party. She became prime minister in 1969. For biographies, see Francine Klagsbrun, *Lioness: Golda Meir and the Nation of Israel* (New York: Schocken, 2019) and Pnina Lahav, *The Only Woman in the Room: Golda Meir and Her Path to Power* (Princeton: Princeton University Press, 2022).

14. For a detailed examination of the life of the wildcatter, the triumphs and tribulations alike, see the documentary "Wildcatter: A Story of Texas Oil" (Dallas Historical Society, 1985), focusing on the development of three major oil fields: Spindletop, Big Lake, and East Texas, available on the Texas Archive of the Moving Image website, at *https://texasarchive.org/2015_01012* (accessed on October 30, 2022). See also the introduction by Gregg Davis to Michael Economides and Ronald Oligney, *The Color of Oil: The History, the Money, and the Politics of the World's Biggest Business* (Katy, TX: Round Oak Publishing, 2000). Davis's father was a wildcatter and the founder of Davis Oil, one of America's largest independents. He dug 11,000 wells in his lifetime.

15. For the phrase "eight-eighths," see *The Book of Jargon: Oil & Gas: Latham & Watkins Glossary of Oil & Gas Terminology* (Los Angeles: Latham & Watkins, 2016), 1.

16. Glasner, "Natural Gas: Will We Learn for Our Mistakes?" 231. He continues, "Despite these signs of shortage, FPC made no effort to raise the ceilings on interstate gas prices until as late as 1974. Its belated efforts then were far from sufficient to solve the problem that had been developing for two decades."

17. David Boren (D-Oklahoma) was one of a breed that has all but died out today in US politics, a "conservative Democrat" (along with "liberal Republican"). He served in the US Senate from 1979–94. See Allan Cromley, "Boren's Career Unique for State," *Oklahoman*, April 28, 1994.

18. For the Carter blizzard, as many took to calling it, see David Oestreicher, "N.Y Declared a Disaster Area," *Daily News* (New York), January 30, 1977. Byrne "also ordered all commercial establishments, including restaurants, bars and movie theaters, to go on a 40-hour work week."

19. Glasner, "Natural Gas: Will We Learn for Our Mistakes?" 248.

20. Ernest "Fritz" Hollings (D-South Carolina), like Boren, is another of that vanished breed, the conservative Democrat. He served as an artillery officer in World War II and represented his state in the US Senate from 1966 to 2005.

21. Quoted in Yergin, *The Prize*, 646.

22. William K. Stevens, "Lafayette, LA: Home of a Thousand Millionaires," *New York Times*, March 8, 1981.

23. Stevens, "Thousand Millionaires," also notes that, "Lafayette has joined the Oil Patch's select group of big-money oases that includes Houston, Dallas, and Midland, Texas. The wealth isn't based on headliners—history-making fields like Alaska's Prudhoe Bay. Rather, its source is development in known oil-producing areas. The amounts are modest in world terms, but quite enough to change the face of a local economy."

24. Stevens, "Thousand Millionaires." He goes on to say, "As many as one Lafayette family in 15 may have a net worth of $1 million or more, and the super elite, what one of the millionaire class calls the Big Rich, are the present-day counterparts of the steel, auto and rail millionaires of a half a century ago."

25. The conclusion, then, was "to strike while the iron is hot, protect the results as best one can, and enjoy." Stevens, "Thousand Millionaires."

26. In fact, the letter had been written by the Oil Minister himself. Ahmed Zaki Yamani (the appellation "sheikh" is purely honorary) has been a figure of enormous importance to twentieth-century world history, yet the American public knows him mainly as a caricature; paradoxically, being called "sheikh" has only added to the stereotypes. For the biography of this "supreme negotiator" and "ultimate politician," including the terrifying moment when he and other OPEC ministers were kidnapped by terrorist Carlos the Jackal during a Vienna meeting in 1975, see Jeffrey Robinson, *Yamani: The Inside Story* (New York: Atlantic Monthly Press, 1988). As Yamani tells it, "I suddenly realized that I was going to be murdered. That I was going to die" (154). It appears today that Libyan strongman Colonel Moammar Gadhafi was the mastermind behind the OPEC raid. See the ABC News report from October 17, 2000, Sue Masterman, "Another Member of the Jackal's Pack on Trial," located at https://abcnews.go.com/International/story?id=82352&page=1 (accessed October 29, 2022).

27. Quoted in Yergin, *The Prize*, 729. For contemporary reportage, see Stanley Meisler, "OPEC Faces Crucial Bid for Survival: Saudis Threaten to Open Oil Spigot If Others Flout Rules," *Los Angeles Times*, June 30, 1985. The entire affair is ably explained in Ramon Knauerhase, "Saudi Arabia Faces the Future," *Current History* 85, no. 508 (February 1986), 75–78, 87–88, as well as Rachel Bronson, *Thicker than Oil: America's Uneasy Relationship with Saudi Arabia* (Oxford: Oxford University Press, 2006), 185–88.

28. Rockefeller's formulation about a "good sweating" has become a commonly used term in the language of the international oil business. For a just one example of its usage out of potential dozens, see "Old Money: 'A Good Sweating'—Turning Up the Heat on Oil" on the website *GlobalCapital* (February 18, 2016), found at https://www.globalcapital.com/article/28my28cqtgkytryjq28zk/derivatives/old-money-a-good-sweating-turning-up-the-heat-in-oil (accessed on October 28, 2022).

29. Ken Stickney, "Price Plunge Aside, Oil People Look to Next Opportunity," *Daily Advertiser* (Lafayette, LA), January 24, 2015.

30. Stickney, "Price Plunge Aside."

31. All quotations from Rusty Cloutier are taken from an interview Mr. Cloutier did with Ken Stickney, September 8, 2021.

32. All quotations from Dave Etienne are taken from an interview Mr. Etienne did with Ken Stickney, June 15, 2021.

33. All quotations from Art Price are taken from an interview Mr. Price did with Ken Stickney, May 17, 2020.

34. For definitions of 2D, 3D, and 4D seismic data, see *The Book of Jargon: Oil & Gas: Latham & Watkins Glossary of Oil & Gas Terminology*, 3. Essentially, 2D seismic results in a cross section or square of data; 3D seismic results in a cube, and 4D seismic results in a cube that additionally plots the movement of fluid through the formation—crucial for the detection of petroleum.

35. The disastrous (in political terms as well as environmental ones) Deepwater Horizon spill unleashed a torrent of articles and books, and as is usually the case with politically controversial topics, some are more enlightening than others. The most readable description is found in Tom Shroder and John Konrad, *Fire on the Horizon: The Untold Story of the Gulf Oil Disaster* (New York: Harper, 2011), and it's no wonder: Shroder is a *Washington Post* writer and Konrad is an oil rig captain. The pair eschew issues of culpability and blame in favor of an almost minute-by-minute account of the disaster as it unfolded. Taking a very different approach is Bob Cavnar, *Disaster on the Horizon: High Stakes, High Risks, and the Story Behind the Deepwater Well Blowout* (Hartford, VT: Chelsea Green, 2014), which argues that the disaster was a clear signal to America to "move beyond our comfortable yet dangerous dependence on a fossil-fuel-based economy" (182), as does William Freudenburg and Robert Gramling, *Blowout in the Gulf: The BP Oil Spill Disaster and the Future of Energy in America* (Boston: MIT Press, 2012). The event was also accorded the peculiar American dignity of having a film made about it, *Deepwater Horizon* (d. Peter Berg, 2016), starring Mark Wahlberg and Kurt Russell. It is widely regarded as one of the biggest box office flops of all time. In a more serious vein, the National Oceanic and Atmospheric Administration (NOAA) claims that the penalty imposed on BP and its partners (Anadarko, TransOcean, and Halliburton) was "the largest environmental damage settlement in United States history—$20.8 billion." See "Deepwater Horizon Oil Spill Settlements: Where the Money Went," on the NOAA's website, found at https://www.noaa.gov/explainers/deepwater-horizon-oil-spill-settlements-where-money-went (accessed on October 30, 2022).

Chapter 7

1. The lack of "old, bold pilots" is a piece of twentieth-century folk wisdom that is still in common usage. Its origins are in dispute. See "There Are Old Pilots, and There Are Bold Pilots, But There Are No Old, Bold Pilots: Dorothy Verrill? Charles L. Wright? Harry D. Copland? Harry Copewell? Anonymous?" on the *Quote Investigator* website, at https://quoteinvestigator.com/ 2022/ 06/06/old-bold/ (accessed October 31, 2022), as well as the website for the aviation enthusiast group, Old Bold Pilots, at https://oldbold pilots.com/ (accessed October 31, 2022).

2. Tom Brokaw, *The Greatest Generation* (New York: Random House, 2001). The book would no doubt have been notable on its own, but it also seemed to catch the hem of the *zeitgeist*. Portraying World War II as "the good war," it came out in the same year as the patriotic film *Saving Private Ryan* (d. Steven Spielberg, 1998). Works by Stephen E. Ambrose bracketed these two, publishing *Band of Brothers: E Company, 506th Regiment, 101st Airborne: From Normandy to Hitler's Eagle's Nest* (New York: Simon & Schuster, 1992) in 1992, before Brokaw, which was turned into a very successful television miniseries in 2001, after the appearance of *Greatest Generation*.

3. To give just three examples, Michael C. C. Adams, *The Best War Ever: America and World War II* (Baltimore: Johns Hopkins University Press, 1993); Kenneth G. Rose, *Myth and the Greatest Generation: A Social History of Americans in World War II* (London: Routledge, 2008), and most recently Elizabeth Samet, *Looking for the Good War: American Amnesia and the Violent Pursuit of Happiness* (New York: Farrar, Straus and Giroux, 2021). All three point out the "bad" side of the good war, not only the dead and wounded, but the continued existence of racial inequality even in wartime, the serious psychological problems suffered by many veterans, the high incidence of alcoholism, ruined marriages, and broken homes. The "good war," then, is simply a myth concocted by the government and media to make Americans feel better about themselves. Of all these works—and there are many others—Samet's book may well be the most significant, given her status as a full-time faculty member at the US Military Academy at West Point.

4. All prices taken from an advertisement for Geo. Ackal's General Store in Lafayette, Louisiana, from the 1920s, in Paul Hilliard's possession.

5. Brokaw, *Greatest Generation*, 11.

6. FDR first enunciated his "Four Freedoms" in his 1941 State of the Union Address to Congress. The transcript of the speech is available on the National Archives website, at https://www.archives.gov/milestone-documents/president-franklin-roosevelts-annual-message-to-congress#transcript

(accessed October 23, 2022). For the historical impact of Roosevelt's concept, see Harvey J. Kaye, *The Fight for the Four Freedoms: What Made FDR and the Greatest Generation Truly Great* (New York: Simon & Schuster, 2015). For Norman Rockwell's expression of the four freedoms in his famous series of paintings, some of the best-known images in American cultural history, see Stephanie Haboush Plunkett and James J. Kimble, *Enduring Ideals: Rockwell, Roosevelt & the Four Freedoms* (New York: Abbeville Press, 2018). Plunkett is the deputy director and chief curator of the Norman Rockwell Museum in Stockbridge, Massachusetts.

7. For the Civilian Conservation Corps, see Neil M. Maher, *Nature's New Deal: The Civilian Conservation Corps and the Roots of the American Environmental Movement* (Oxford, UK: Oxford University Press, 2009). Enrollees in the Corps received a wage of $30.00 a month and were required to send $25.00 of it home to their families. For photos of the CCC at work, see Stan Cohen, *The Tree Army: A Pictorial History of the Civilian Conservation Corps, 1933–1942* (Missoula, MT: Pictorial Histories Publishing, 1993).

8. The career of John F. Kennedy, for example, is inconceivable without his wartime service in the US Navy. See the classic account by Robert Donovan, *PT 109: John F. Kennedy in World War II* (New York: Marine International, 2002), as well as the very popular film *PT-109* (dd. Leslie H. Martinson and Lewis Milestone, 1963), starring Cliff Robertson as the skipper and future president. If only for partisan balance, consult the account of George H. W. Bush's military career in Joe Hyams, *Flight of the Avenger* (Boston: Harcourt, 1991).

9. For a statement of his fundamental conservative principles, an important document in the development of right-wing politics in modern America, see Barry M. Goldwater, *Conscience of a Conservative* (Brattleboro, VT: Echo Point Books, 2021). The book appeared originally in 1960.

10. The "daisy ad" may still be viewed on a number of video platforms online, including YouTube. It continues to reverberate in US culture, even as our electoral campaigns feature ever more bizarre mutual accusations between the candidates. See, for example, the discussion in Robert Mann, "How the 'Daisy' Ad Changed Everything About Political Advertising," *Smithsonian Magazine*, April 13, 2016: "On September 7, 1964, a 60-second TV ad changed American politics forever. A 3-year-old girl in a simple dress counted as she plucked daisy petals in a sun-dappled field. Her words were supplanted by a mission-control countdown followed by a massive nuclear blast in a classic mushroom shape. The message was clear if only implicit: Presidential candidate Barry Goldwater was a genocidal maniac who threatened the

world's future. Two months later, President Lyndon Johnson won easily, and the emotional political attack ad—visceral, terrifying, and risky—was made."

11. For the McKeithen-Lyons gubernatorial race in 1964 and how it appeared to the state and the nation, see Claude Sitton, "Democrat Is Victor in Louisiana, But Party Margin Is Cut Sharply: McKeithen Elected Governor Over a Goldwater Backer by Less Than 2 to 1," *New York Times*, March 4, 1964.

12. For the impact of Lyons on state politics, see "State GOP Growth Began in 1964" on the American Press website, at https://www.american-press.com/2014/12/28/state-gop-growth-began-in-1964/ (accessed on October 31, 2022).

13. For the authorized biography of Edwin Edwards, see Leo Honeycutt, *Edwin Edwards Governor of Louisiana* (Baton Rouge: Lisburn Press, 2009).

14. The best book on Edwin Edwards's legal troubles, and a work that captures the sometime zany nature of Louisiana state politics, is Tyler Bridges, *Bad Bet on the Bayou: The Rise and Fall of Gambling in Louisiana and the Fate of Governor Edwin Edwards* (New York: Farrar, Straus and Giroux, 2001). Bridges is a writer for the New Orleans/Baton Rouge *Advocate* and a keen observer of the Louisiana statehouse.

15. For the Broadmoor Conference, see "Conservation: No Oil Contrivance," *Time* magazine, June 24, 1929. The meeting "disbanded without definite accomplishment," *Time* complained, partly because of "the refusal of independent oil producers to enter any limitation agreement until a duty is placed upon petroleum imports. They contend that the major oil companies will reduce their domestic production only to increase their imports from Mexico and South America, thus nullifying the effect of any conservation agreement. In this position the independents were joined by Louisiana, to which most U.S. oil imports come."

16. Gaylord Nelson (D-Washington) was a senator from 1963–1981. He was a World War II veteran who fought on Okinawa, a well-known environmentalist during his political career, and one of the founders of Earth Day. See Bill Christofferson, *Man from Clear Lake: Earth Day Founder Senator Gaylord Nelson* (Madison: University of Wisconsin Press, 2004).

17. Jimmy Stewart plays the earnest lead role in the classic *Mr. Smith Goes to Washington* (d. Frank Capra, 1939).

18. Sadly, as with so many of our favorite quotations, it does not appear as if President Truman ever actually uttered this line, as true as it has proven to be. See Nadia Pflaum, "You know what Truman said, 'You want a friend in Washington, buy a dog.'" on the website of the Poynter Institute, *Politifact*, at https://www.politifact.com/factchecks/2016/mar/17/

john-kasich/john-kasich-misquotes-truman-wins-ohio-anyway/ (accessed on October 30, 2022).

19. The Iroquois pipeline was the subject of an immense controversy at the time, with detailed reportage to match. See Thomas Lippman, "Passions Flow Over Proposed Iroquois Gas Pipeline," *Washington Post*, May 27, 1990; "F.B.I. Investigating Iroquois Gas Pipeline," *Associated Press*, June 13, 1992; and, for the environmental implications as well as the NIMBY ("not in my backyard") opposition of many local residents, see Arvind Dilawar, "Iroquois Pipeline Expansion Opposition Gets More Time" on the *Scenic Hudson* website, at https://www.scenichudson.org/viewfinder/iroquois-pipeline-expansion-opposition-gets-more-time/ (accessed October 29, 2022).

20. For a very useful map, including compressor stations, main line valves, meter stations, and interstate pipelines, see the Iroquois pipeline website, at https://www.iroquois.com/pipeline-services/pipeline-map/ (accessed October 28, 2022).

21. The "rental car" analogy was suggested by Mark Seifert of IPAA in a conversation with the author, October 27, 2002.

22. Mark Seifert, in conversation with Ken Stickney, September 5, 2021.

23. Art Price, in conversation with Ken Stickney, May 14, 2020.

24. For Paul's testimony, see Lippman, "Passions Flow Over Proposed Iroquois Gas Pipeline," *Washington Post*.

25. Mark Seifert in conversation with the author, October 27, 2022.

26. For the full article, see C. Paul Hilliard, "Biden Policies Have Impaired Energy Industry," Guest column, *Advocate* (Baton Rouge, LA), June 23, 2022.

Chapter 8

1. Marcus Tullius Cicero, *Pro Plancio* ("The Speech on Behalf of Gnaeus Plancius"), XXXIII, 80, Loeb Classical Library (Boston: Harvard University Press, 1989). In Latin, "Gratus animus est una virtus non solum maxima, sed etiam mater virtutum onmium reliquarum." (Perhaps best rendered, "A thankful heart is not only the greatest virtue, but the parent of all the other virtues.") Gratitude is the theme of another of Paul's favorite quotes, this one from Stephen Ambrose: "At the core, the American citizen soldiers knew the difference between right and wrong, and they didn't want to live in a world in which wrong prevailed. So they fought, and won, and we all of us, living and yet to be born, must be forever profoundly grateful." *Citizen Soldiers: The U.S. Army from the Normandy Beaches to the Bulge to the Surrender of Germany* (New York: Simon and Schuster, 1997), 473.

2. Sartre's famous proclamation that "existence precedes essence" appeared first in his lecture *Existentialism Is a Humanism*, or *L'existentialisme est un humanisme* in the original French (Paris: Nagel, 1946). The meaning is that a person does not (indeed, he or she cannot) live one's life according to some preexisting pattern of what it means to be good. You may proclaim your goodness, Sartre says, but only after you have chosen to do the right things: "I may say that I love a certain friend enough to sacrifice such or such a sum of money for him, but I cannot prove that unless I have done it."

3. Like so many inspirational quotes by our Founding Fathers, it has not been easy to track down the exact provenance of this alleged piece of Jeffersonian rhetoric. According to the website for Monticello, Jefferson's former home and now a museum, it may not be possible at all. See "An Educated Citizenry is a Vital Requisite for our Survival as a Free People (Spurious Quotation)," at https://www.monticello.org/research-education/thomas-jefferson-encyclopedia/educated-citizenry-vital-requisite-our-survival-free-people-spurious/ (accessed October 31, 2022). In this case, however, the quotation is so close to Jefferson's views (stated at multiple times and in various ways) that the point seems moot.

4. All quotations from Art Price are taken from an interview Mr. Price did with Ken Stickney, May 17, 2020.

5. For a comprehensive report on the activities of the foundation, including details on how it has spent its moneys, see the listing on the website for Grantmakers Project, at https://www.grantmakers.io/profiles/v0/721370346-badger-excellence-in-education-foundation/ (accessed October 31, 2022).

6. Nancy Manuel, Alice Boucher Elementary School, in conversation with Ken Stickney, September 20, 2021.

7. Marsha Sills, "Leaders Gather to Honor Hilliard," *Daily Advertiser* (Lafayette, LA), October 12, 2003.

8. Tina Fremin, Badger Oil, in conversation with Ken Stickney, October 1, 2021.

9. Amy Beard, Isidore Newman School, in conversation with Lori Ochsner, May 16, 2022.

10. For Rothko's life and work, see Diane Waldman, *Mark Rothko, 1903–1970: A Retrospective* (New York: Harry N. Abrams, 1978). Another great "study in black" by Rothko is the chapel he built on the grounds of the Menil Collection in Houston, an enormous structure whose stark interior is meant to stimulate the visitor's own inner reflection. See Susan J. Barnes, *The Rothko Chapel: An Act of Faith* (Houston: Menil Foundation, 1989).

11. Herman Mhire, "From Conception to Realization, the Paul and Lulu Hilliard University Art Museum." Throughout the period in question, Professor Mhire kept and arranged his notes on the founding and evolution of the museum. Copy sent to Ken Stickney, April 3, 2020.

12. "Andrew Wyeth's Stunning Secret: The Helga Collection, a Hidden Treasure Trove," *Time* magazine, August 18, 1986. For the collection itself, see John Wilmerding, *Wyeth: The Helga Pictures* (New York: Harry N. Abrams, 1987).

13. See Michelle Galindo, ed., *Collection: U.S. Architecture* (Berlin: UNKNO, 2009), 208.

14. For the details of the dispute that led to Mhire's resignation, see R. Reese Fuller, "Museum Meltdown," *Independent* (Lafayette, LA), November 23, 2005.

15. E. Joseph Savoie, in conversation with Ken Stickney, April 30, 2020.

16. LouAnne Greenwald, interview with Jan Swift, Discover Lafayette. Found online at https://discoverlafayette.net/podcast/hilliard-art-museum-director-louanne-greenwald, March 2, 2018 (accessed March 2, 2023). Under Greenwald's leadership, the Paul and Lulu Hilliard University Art Museum became the Hilliard Art Museum – University of Louisiana at Lafayette in 2019.

17. Marcy Goodwin, conversation with Ken Stickney, June 3, 2021.

18. The "Boys of Pointe du Hoc" speech is widely recognized as one of the most iconic moments of the Reagan presidency, comparable, perhaps, to what the Gettysburg Address represents for the Lincoln presidency. Like Gettysburg, the Pointe du Hoc address has had entire books written about it. See Douglas Brinkley, *The Boys of Pointe Du Hoc: Ronald Reagan, D-Day, and the U.S. Army 2nd Ranger Battalion* (New York: HarperCollins, 2005). "For sheer oratorical elegance," Brinkley writes, the speech would become "one of the most inspirational presidential speeches ever delivered." For the origins of Reagan's speech, including a profile on the gifted speechwriter who penned it, Peggy Noonan, see Michael E. Ruane, "'The Boys of Pointe du Hoc': The Reagan D-Day Speech that Moved a Nation," *Washington Post*, June 5, 2019.

19. Studs Terkel, *"The Good War": An Oral History of World War II* (New York: Pantheon, 1984). Terkel is an unapologetic man of the Left, and his entire book—from his choice of interviewees to his own brief interjections—is suffused with a strong leftist sensibility, which might surprise the many people who refer to the book but who obviously have never read it. Perhaps the work's characteristic passage comes from Admiral Gene Larocque, founder

and head of the Center for Defense Information, a military reform think tank: "World War II has warped our view of how we look at things today. We see things in terms of that war, which in a sense was a good war. But the twisted memory of it encourages the men of my generation to be willing, almost eager, to use military force anywhere in the world" (193). Indeed, it might be said that, while the book is ostensibly about World War II, much of *The Good War* is actually responding to the American war in Vietnam and to problems of postwar US foreign policy in general.

20. Stephen E. Ambrose, *Band of Brothers: E Company, 506th Regiment, 101st Airborne: From Normandy to Hitler's Eagle's Nest* (New York: Simon & Schuster, 1992), followed by the television miniseries *Band of Brothers* (d. various, 2001).

21. For the king's speech on Saint Crispin's Day speech, the opening act of the battle of Agincourt against the French, see Shakespeare, *Henry V* (Act IV, Scene iii, 18–67). The outnumbered British force would win a decisive victory the next day.

22. The "Enola Gay controversy," as it's come to be called, rocked the museum world to its foundations at the time, and continues to reverberate to the present day, as anyone working in a museum will attest. Generally viewed as the opening salvo in what we refer to today as the "culture wars" in the United States, it has generated an enormous literature from all sides in the conflict. In general, veterans accused the Smithsonian of a biased account that foregrounded Japanese suffering without much in the way of context or explanation about exactly why the bomb was dropped; the Smithsonian argued that it was only trying to present both sides of the issue. See the account by the exhibit's curator, Martin Harwit, *An Exhibit Denied: Lobbying the History of Enola Gay* (New York: Copernicus, 1996); Edward T. Linenthal and Tom Engelhardt, eds., *History Wars: The Enola Gay and Other Battles for the American Past* (New York: Holt Paperbacks, 1996); Arthur Hirsch, "Smithsonian Cancels Exhibit on Atomic Bomb," *Baltimore Sun*, January 31, 1995; and Richard H. Kohn, "History and the Culture Wars: The Case of the Smithsonian Institution's Enola Gay Exhibition," Smithsonian Institution Archives (December 1995).

23. Ambrose turned that symposium into a wonderful book about the battle, based on primary source testimony from the men who were there. He also dug deep into the research, spending a month in the United Kingdom interviewing the survivors of the unit involved, D Company, 2nd (Airborne) Battalion, Oxfordshire and Buckinghamshire Light Infantry, and then another two weeks with the company commander, Major John Howard. It was the first example of what would go on to become his record-shattering literary

oeuvre. Stephen E. Ambrose, *Pegasus Bridge: June 6, 1944* (New York: Simon & Schuster, 1984).

24. No field of historical inquiry (with the possible exception of the American Civil War) exceeds World War II for the sheer number of books devoted to it. Some of these works (those by Ambrose, Frank, and Hanson, for example) have already been cited in these notes. For the rest, which constitute a comprehensive reading list for anyone wishing to know more about World War II, see Max Hastings, *Overlord: D-Day and the Battle for Normandy* (New York: Simon & Schuster, 1985); Carlo D'Este, *Bitter Victory: The Battle for Sicily, 1943* (New York: Harper, 1988); Antony Beevor, *The Battle of Arnhem: The Deadliest Airborne Operation of World War II* (New York: Viking, 2018); and Donald Miller, *Masters of the Air: America's Bomber Boys Who Fought the Air War Against Nazi Germany* (New York: Simon & Schuster, 2007). See also The Liberation Trilogy by Pulitzer Prize winner Rick Atkinson, including *An Army at Dawn: The War in North Africa, 1942–1943* (New York: Henry Holt, 2002), *The Day of Battle: The War in Sicily and Italy, 1943–1944* (New York: Henry Holt, 2007), and *The Guns at Last Light: The War in Western Europe, 1944–1945* (New York: Henry Holt, 2013). All three books in the Atkinson trilogy are definitive, and it is difficult to imagine them being surpassed anytime soon.

25. For a deeper insight into the character of the amazing Nick Mueller, who left the world of academe and built one of the world's most successful museums at a point in his life when most other people are already retiring and who is still a force of nature well into his eighties, see the compilation by Günter Bischof, ed., *Museum Man: Essays in Honor of Gordon H. "Nick" Mueller* (New Orleans: UNO Press, 2014). The editor of the volume, Bischof, is a renowned historian and scholar in his own right, a former student of Stephen Ambrose, and a close friend and colleague of Mueller.

26. The only comprehensive work on Higgins, a figure of enormous importance to the American war effort, is Jerry E. Strahan, *Andrew Jackson Higgins and the Boats That Won World War II* (Baton Rouge: Louisiana State University Press, 1988). Virtually all the most famous Higgins anecdotes (e.g., Eisenhower calling him the "man who won the war for us" or Hitler referring to him as "the new Noah") come from Strahan's book.

27. Chad Calder, "Nick Mueller to Retire as Head of National WWII Museum," *Advocate* (New Orleans, LA), May 27, 2017.

28. Marty Morgan, museum historian, in conversation with Ken Stickney, November 27, 2020.

29. Nick Mueller, museum president and CEO emeritus, in conversation with Ken Stickney, November 27, 2020.

30. Mueller, in conversation with Stickney.

31. Former California Governor Pete Wilson, in conversation with Ken Stickney, December 10, 2020.

32. Stephen Watson, Mueller's successor as president and CEO of the museum, made these remarks at "A Night to Honor Paul Hilliard," the Hilliard Museum, University of Louisiana Lafayette, January 16, 2020.

33. Madlyn Hilliard in conversation with the author, September 24, 2022.

34. Ken Stickney, "Lafayette's Paul Hilliard Will Likely Be the Last WWII Veteran to Lead the New Orleans Museum," *Acadiana Advocate* (Lafayette, LA) June 12, 2020.

35. "Churchill Canvasses at UL's Hilliard University Art Museum Paint More Complete Picture of Complex Man," on the KATC website, Channel 3, the ABC affiliate in Lafayette, January 23, 2020.

36. Ken Stickney, "Churchill Exhibit Honors Paul Hilliard's Contributions at Art Museum that Bears his Name," *Acadiana Advocate* (Lafayette, LA) January 16, 2020.

37. Quoted in hundreds of sources, especially online, as "Education is a progressive discovery of our own ignorance." The location of Durant's original usage, like so much of today's common wisdom, is obscure.

38. William Shakespeare, *Hamlet*, Act III, Scene I, part of the famous "To be or not to be" soliloquy.

39. From Paul's Second Letter to the Corinthians (2 Corinthians 5:17), in the King James Version of the New Testament.

40. Madlyn Hilliard in conversation with the author, September 24, 2022.

ABOUT THE AUTHORS

ROBERT M. CITINO is the Samuel Zemurray Stone Senior Historian at the National WWII Museum and one of America's most distinguished military historians. His award-winning books include *Blitzkrieg to Desert Storm, The German Way of War,* and a trilogy on the German army in World War II. He holds the Samuel Eliot Morison Prize from the Society for Military History, a lifetime achievement award and the highest recognition bestowed by the society.

LORI K. OCHSNER was born in El Centro, California, and grew up in Tennessee. She was a Ford Foundation scholar and received a Masters in Law from Yale Law School. A former award-winning broadcast journalist, Lori has written and produced several documentaries for New Orleans affiliate WVUE, A&E, and PBS. For several years she was the medical reporter for WVUE. She is married to Dr. Lockwood Ochsner. They have two daughters. Ms. Ochsner divides her time between her homes in Louisiana and Montana.

Massachusetts native **KEN STICKNEY**, career news and editorial writer and editor, has worked for southern newspapers for more than forty years, most recently for Georges Media Group in Louisiana. He holds master's degrees in history from the University of Louisiana at Monroe and in journalism at Alabama, where he was a Graduate Council Fellow. The American Society of Newspaper Editors has honored him with the top national editorial writing award. He and his wife, Carey, live in Lafayette. They have four adult children and two grandchildren.